Sam Houston

SAM HOUSTON

AND

THE WAR OF INDEPENDENCE IN TEXAS

BY

ALFRED M. WILLIAMS

WITH PORTRAIT AND MAPS

BOSTON AND NEW YORK
HOUGHTON, MIFFLIN AND COMPANY
The Riverside Press, Cambridge
1893

The Riverside Press, Cambridge Mass., U. S. A.
Electrotyped and Printed by H. O. Houghton & Co.

PREFACE

My purpose in writing the life of Sam Houston and a history of the War of Independence in Texas has been to give as accurate a picture as was in my power of a very remarkable and interesting personality, and a period of great importance in the growth and character of the nation. Houston possessed very strong and original qualities as well as very apparent weaknesses and limitations, and his character and conduct often deserved censure as well as discriminating approval. He had many devoted partisans, attracted by his achievements and personal magnetism, as well as bitter enemies, created by his sharp tongue and masterful temperament, and the written records and estimates of him vary from extravagant and often fulsome eulogy to the harshest depreciation and the most envenomed attack. In later years the detraction and animosity are dying away, and he is becoming a somewhat mythical hero, who represents the traditional pride of a community, and embodies the reverence of a heroic history. But the remembrance of his impressive and original personality is still strong among the contemporaries of his later years, and the anecdotes and reminiscences which are orally current give the illustrative characteristics of the man, in spite of the exaggeration and invention which grow up about them. I believe that I have read all the books which relate to Houston's career, beside consulting a large number of the files of contemporary newspapers, letters, speeches, and pamphlets by himself and his associates. I have also conversed with many who knew him personally, and who have given me facts and anecdotes which have never been published. I have examined the archives of the Republic and State of Texas in the Capitol at Austin, and the records of the national Congress, while he was a member. The facts in regard to his life among the Cherokees in the Indian Territory were obtained from the lips of aged Indians who remembered him, and particularly from the late Judge Riley Keys, an intelligent Cherokee, who was familiar with him during his residence with the tribe. I have endeavored to be impartial as well as accurate, and to present the man as he was, with his faults as well as his virtues, and his failures and errors as well as his successes and achievements. I have used those anecdotes and incidents which, however apparently trifling, reveal the man as an individual and in his daily life as well as in his public career, and have not suppressed or modified those which would show the weaknesses which contrasted with his strong and admirable qualities. It is needless to say that there is no other course to be taken for the truth of history or for intelligent biography. Houston is strong enough to endure an unflattering portrait, and the interest in his individuality, and as the type and product of his time and circumstances, depends upon the absolute accuracy of the resemblance.

The history of the War of Independence in Texas has been several times written. The most elaborate and valuable account is that of Henderson Yoakum, who had access to the original documents, and was familiar with many of the actors in the military and legislative history of the Republic of Texas. He is honest and accurate, and although later researches have corrected some errors, his volumes will remain the principal storehouse of information in regard to the events of the period. William Kennedy, a Scotchman and British consul at Galveston, preceded Yoakum, and his History of the Republic of Texas contains many original documents and much valuable information. Senator Henry G. Foote, of Mississippi, wrote his volumes on " Texas and the Texans " rather in the style of a controversial and oratorical pamphlet to favor annexation than a sober history, although they possess some value in the journals and accounts of participants in the events. Mr. H. H. Bancroft, with his customary industry and accuracy, has investigated the history of Texas in American and Mexican sources, and published the results in his " History of the North Mexican States and Texas." Rev. H. G. Thrall has given some useful statistical and other information in his " Pictorial History of Texas." There are a considerable number of personal memoirs

and sketches which give accounts of individual actions during the time, and the reminiscences of those
who took part in the events. The series of the
" Texas Almanac," published at Galveston, is especially valuable as giving the accounts of personal survivors of the war, although they are often colored by
prejudice and sometimes contradictory in statement.
The period was a heroic one in the achievement
of personal vigor and daring. The defense of the
Alamo will always be reckoned as one of the most
striking examples of desperate and determined valor
in all history, and the fight at San Jacinto conclu-
sively demonstrated the superiority of the Anglo-
American race over the Hispano-Mexican. There
was much turbulence and lawlessness among the adventurers from the United States and the original
settlers, and schemes for conquest which had no patriotic motive, and there was the uncertainty and
irregularity of action inevitable to a people carrying
on the war by volunteer levies rather than by disciplined armies. But the war for the independence of
Texas was not in its governing character a filibuster
enterprise, whatever may have been the motives and
purposes of some of its leaders, but was the result of
the oppression and jealousy of the Mexican authorities compelling resistance, and the conditions which
inevitably brought the American colonists into conflict with those of an inferior calibre and alien institutions and habits. It was fought with courage and
determination and on the whole with practical wis-

dom, and was creditable to the race as well as to the community.

I am indebted to ex-Senator John H. Reagan, to ex-Governors F. A Lubbock and O. M. Roberts, of Austin, to Hon. Hamilton Stuart, of Galveston, to Hon. E. W. Cave and Judge Alexander McGowan, of Houston, and to many others in Texas, for anecdotes and reminiscences of Houston. I am much indebted to Judge C. W. Raines of the Agricultural and Statistical Department at Austin for assistance in examining the archives and newspaper files at the Capitol. I owe my earnest thanks to my friends James A. Hervey, of Medford, Mass., and James Jeffrey Roche, of Boston, for advice and assistance in the details of the book. A list of the books relating to Houston and the history of Texas will be found at the end of the volume.

PROVIDENCE, R. I., June 23, 1893.

CONTENTS

CHAPTER   PAGE

I. BOYHOOD AND YOUTH 1

II. THE YOUNG SOLDIER 11

III. MEMBER OF CONGRESS AND GOVERNOR OF TENNESSEE 22

IV. INDIAN LIFE — THE STANBERRY AFFAIR . . . 37

V. TEXAS AT THE BEGINNING OF THE STRUGGLE FOR INDEPENDENCE 53

VI. HOUSTON'S ARRIVAL IN TEXAS — THE OUTBREAK OF THE WAR 74

VII. BATTLE OF CONCEPCION — CAPTURE OF SAN ANTONIO 97

VIII. ORGANIZATION OF THE PROVISIONAL GOVERNMENT — HOUSTON ELECTED COMMANDER-IN-CHIEF . . 117

IX. FALL OF THE ALAMO — CREATION OF THE REPUBLIC 137

X. THE MASSACRE OF GOLIAD 161

XI. SAN JACINTO 184

XII. FIRST TERM AS PRESIDENT 218

XIII. SECOND TERM AS PRESIDENT — ANNEXATION . 240

XIV. SENATOR OF THE UNITED STATES 296

XV. GOVERNOR OF TEXAS — SECESSION 333

XVI. LAST YEARS — DEATH 363

XVII. CHARACTERISTICS 378

BIBLIOGRAPHY 397

INDEX 401

SAM HOUSTON

AND

THE WAR OF INDEPENDENCE IN TEXAS

CHAPTER I

BOYHOOD AND YOUTH

SAMUEL, or as he called and signed himself, and as
he is known in the familiar language of history, Sam
Houston, was born on the 2d of March, 1793, at a place
called Timber Ridge Church, about seven miles east of
Lexington, in Rockbridge County, Virginia. He came
from that strong and sturdy Scotch-Irish stock which
has given so many notable names to American history
and exercised so powerful an influence in the forma-
tive period of the nation. There was a good deal in
Sam Houston's character and temperament to indicate
a Celtic admixture in the somewhat dour and sober
strain of the Presbyterian Scotch-Irish, but there is no
name in the records of the family genealogy to indicate
it, and it must have been from very remote atavism
or the accident of individual constitution. The Houston family was of Lowland-Scotch origin, of sufficient
rank to have a coat of arms, and representatives of
its branches have occupied positions of provincial im-

portance. There is a family tradition that its representative took part in the defense of Londonderry, but as there is also one that John Houston, the founder of the American branch of the family, came to this country in 1689, the year of the siege, this may be considered as doubtful so far as the immediate ancestor of Houston is concerned. The name of James Huston is, however, to be found attached to the loyal address to King William by the defenders of Londonderry signed the 29th of July, 1689. John Houston, who was possessed of considerable means and was apparently the leader of an emigrant colony of his compatriots, settled in Philadelphia, and left a numerous family of children. His grandson Robert Houston removed to Virginia, purchased a considerable tract of land in Rockbridge County, and married a lady of the Scotch families of Davidson and Dunlop. He also left a numerous family, who became connected with the representatives of the gentry of the neighborhood. His son Samuel inherited the estate and married a Miss Elisabeth Paxton, whose family had been associated with his own in the emigration from Ireland and its subsequent life in America. The position of the family in Virginia was evidently not that of the manorial gentry of the seaboard and eastern river valleys, but that of the wealthier farmers of the interior, who lived in rude plenty mainly by their own labor, and formed a class of substantial and independent yeomen. Samuel Houston served with credit, if not with great distinction, in General Daniel

Morgan's brigade of riflemen during the Revolutionary War, and at its close was appointed Major and
Assistant Inspector - General of the frontier troops.
He died while on a tour of duty in the Alleghany
Mountains in 1806, leaving his widow with a family
of six sons and three daughters. Tradition describes
Major Houston as a man of large frame, commanding presence, indomitable courage and a passion for
military life. Mrs. Houston was also remarkable for
her magnificent physique, and was a woman of great
force of character, respected and beloved in the
neighborhood for her benevolence and helpfulness,
and impressing her individuality and influence deeply
upon the mind and memory of the most distinguished
of her children, who always spoke of her with reverence and affection. After the death of her husband, with the vigor and energy characteristic of that
pioneer age, she determined to remove to the new
settlements in Tennessee; and with her young family,
Sam being then thirteen years of age, she crossed the
Alleghany Mountains, and settled in Blount County at
a point eight miles east of the Tennessee River, then
the boundary between the tribe of Cherokee Indians
and their white neighbors. Here a cabin was built, a
clearing was opened, and the family lived in the rude
and toilsome frontier fashion, while wresting a living
from the wilderness.

Houston's reminiscences of his boyhood included a
few months of schooling in what was called the "Old
Field School," kept in a dilapidated building in the

neighborhood, once occupied by Washington University, which had been removed to Lexington; and that he used to run from his work in the fields to take his place in the spelling class. Only the simplest rudiments of an education could have been given in a country school in a thinly peopled agricultural neighborhood like that of Rockbridge County, and in a pioneer settlement like that in East Tennessee the opportunities must have been even less. Whatever education Houston acquired in his early youth must have been due to his active mind and fervid imagination, eagerly feeding upon what books came in his way and possessing them with a fullness and reality unknown to those whose minds are satiated and dulled with an abundance and variety of reading. Among the few books which had come to the frontier settlement in the pack-saddles and in the corners of chests among the homespun garments and household implements, and which were read by the light of the fat pine fire, was Pope's translation of the Iliad, and this was devoured by the boy with all the fervid appetite of vigorous youthful imagination, until he knew it nearly by heart. The artificiality of Pope's style, which is an offense and an obstruction to the refined literary taste that requires the purest flavor for its fastidious palate, was no drawback in the eager appetite of the boy to the appreciation of the reality of the heroic figures and the fresh and immortal drama of human life behind it; and the battles on the windy plains of the Scamander, the camp-fires,

the ships, and the walls of Troy were as visible and
real to him as the woods and fields of the Tennessee
valleys. Such a book was an education in itself in
all that relates to human life, in the elevation of the
spirit and the kindling of the imagination. Through- ×
out his life Houston was a man of few books. When
commander of the Texas army he deeply studied
Cæsar's Commentaries for their simple and sagacious
lessons of war, which he assimilated with a native
intuition, as well as for the severe fascination of the
narrative. He read and appreciated Shakespeare and
had some familiarity with the standards of English
classical literature ; in his later years, after he became
" converted," he read the Bible thoroughly and constantly, so that its phraseology tinged his oratory.
But his reading was always limited. His wisdom
and knowledge came from contact with men ; and his
literary gifts, his power of vigorous and impressive
writing on great subjects, and his persuasive and figurative eloquence were due to native faculties, to the
power of his mind compelling appropriate words, and
the kindling force of his genius elevating and illumi-
nating common speech, and not to any training in the
arts of rhetoric or the study of masters of language
and expression.

It was during his early residence in East Tennessee
that occurred the first of his recorded escapades, that
breaking out of the wild blood, the longing for
adventure and the free life of the wilderness in the
companionship of its children, which characterized his

whole career and was a part of his nature. He had been placed by his elder brothers as a clerk in a trader's store, but his restless spirit revolted at the tame life behind the counter and the drudgery of the boxes and barrels, and one day he absconded across the Tennessee River to take up his abode with the Cherokees. He was received into their cabins as a friend and a brother, whose natural tastes and instincts were their own, and acquired that knowledge of and sympathy with the Indian character which he manifested through life. It is in a great measure an instinct, a kindred element in the blood, the inheritance of primitive nature, which enables men like Houston and many other pioneer adventurers and soldiers to be thoroughly at home in the Indian camps, to share the emotions and thoughts of their savage friends, and to govern and be trusted by them through the community as well as the superiority of their powers. The records of history and of travel are full of the examples of men of civilized training and scholarly culture who were never so much at home as when in the company of the children of the desert and the forest, whose simple natures they appreciated, and whose wild and free life had an irresistible touch of sympathy with their own instincts ; and the rule of inveterate hostility and antagonism between the white settlers of America and the aborigines has often been broken by cases of natural attraction and the adoption of savage life and companionship by the members of the civilized race. Houston had many of the characteristics of the Indian in his nature: his hot blood, his strong passions and appetites, his fondness for adventure and the untrammeled freedom of the wilderness, his solemnly childish vanity and turn for histrionic effect; as well as the higher qualities of the native chief, a commanding personal power and impressiveness, a shrewdness like that of Ulysses in managing men and affairs, an eloquence of original power and impressiveness, a loftiness of spirit and the dominant quality of determination and courage. All these qualities were doubtless visible in the youth as in the man, and Houston was made welcome to the Cherokee villages and adopted into the family of one of the sub-chiefs of the tribe. He thoroughly acquired the Cherokee language, which is so difficult that it is said never to have been learned by an adult, wore the native dress, and was to all intents and purposes an Indian. It is to be said that the Cherokees were among the most intelligent and civilized of the North American Indians, lived in cabins instead of wigwams, cultivated fields, and in some instances at this time owned negro slaves, had a written language of their own invention, and were not greatly different in their habits and manners of life from their pioneer neighbors. But they were Indians, and the flavor of wildness was as distinct among them as among the gypsies, and this was what attracted Houston and made him at home among them. When the place of his retreat was discovered he was visited by his brothers, who endeavored to persuade him to return home; but he replied, with that touch of grandiloquence which always distinguished him, that he preferred measuring deer-tracks to measuring tape, and that they might leave him in the woods. He remained with the Cherokees until his eighteenth year, occasionally returning to the white settlements for the supplies wanted for himself and his friends.

At this time, finding himself in debt for the ammunition and trinkets which he had purchased, he resolved to return to civilization, and wipe off the debt by opening a country school. The standard of qualification could not have been beyond the most rudimentary elements, or, with all his courage and self-confidence, Houston would not have attempted to fill it. It is recorded through his reminiscences that he raised the price of tuition from six to eight dollars per annum, one third payable in corn at thirty-three and one half cents per bushel, one third in cash, and one third in variegated cotton goods, such as made the teacher's hunting shirt. Houston's popular attributes were illustrated in the success of his school, which soon included most of the children of the neighborhood, and enabled him to pay off his not very formidable debt.

A glimpse of Houston at this time was given by himself in conversation with Colonel Peter Burke, an old comrade of the Indian wars, who had emigrated to Texas after the annexation. He met Houston, then a senator of the United States, on the steamboat going up the Buffalo Bayou from Galveston to the town of Houston. There was a warm greeting between the old comrades, and they sat long on the deck exchanging reminiscences. Finally, the conversation turned upon Houston's successful career, and Colonel Burke said, "Now, Houston, you have been Commander-in-chief of the Texan army, President of the Republic, and Senator of the United States. In which of these offices, or at what period in your career, have you felt the greatest pride and satisfaction?" "Well, Burke," said Houston, "when a young man in Tennessee I kept a country school, being then about eighteen years of age, and a tall, strapping fellow. At noon after the luncheon, which I and my pupils ate together out of our baskets, I would go out into the woods, and cut me a 'sour wood' stick, trim it carefully in circular spirals, and thrust one half of it into the fire, which would turn it blue, leaving the other half white. With this emblem of ornament and authority in my hand, dressed in a hunting-shirt of flowered calico, a long queue down my back, and the sense of authority over my pupils, I experienced a higher feeling of dignity and self-satisfaction than from any office or honor which I have since held."

After teaching for a time Houston attended a session or two of the Academy at Maryville, which completed all the education that he was ever to receive from the schools. The war between the United States and Great Britain had broken out, and the drum was beaten on the frontier for recruits. In 1813 a recruiting party visited Maryville, and

Houston enlisted as a private soldier, being then in his twentieth year. He replied to the remonstrances of his friends at the supposed degradation of his enlistment with his customary grandiloquence and self-confidence, that he would sooner honor the ranks than disgrace an appointment, and that they should hear of him. According to his reminiscences in later life his mother admonished him in the spirit and almost in the language of a Roman matron of the melodramatic stage, handing him his musket at the cabin door, and saying, " There, my son, take this musket, and never disgrace it ; for remember, I had rather all my sons should fill one honorable grave than that one of them should turn his back to save his life. Go ; and remember, too, that while the door of my cabin is open to brave men, it is eternally shut to all cowards ! " These words show that Mrs. Houston was remarkably like her son in the use of inflated language, or that he supplied what he considered the proper expression to a more plain-spoken but vigorous and spirited admonition.

CHAPTER II

THE YOUNG SOLDIER

HAVING taken the silver dollar from the head of
the drum, which was the recognized token of enlistment in those days, and put on a uniform, Houston
was made a sergeant the same day, and marched with
his detachment to join the Thirty-ninth Regiment,
Tennessee Volunteers. He was stationed with his regiment at various cantonments in Alabama and Tennessee, and by his active zeal and devotion to duty
acquired the reputation of being the best drill officer
in the command. He was, however, not left long in
the ranks. His friends made application to President Madison for an appointment, and he received a
commission as ensign, which reached him while the
regiment was stationed at Knoxville.

It was the period of the Creek war. That powerful
tribe had been aroused by the eloquence of Tecumseh
and his brother, the Prophet, as well as by the sense
of the constant aggression of the whites, and the
knowledge that only a desperate struggle could save
them from being crowded out of their lands and
home. They broke out into a sudden attack upon
the white settlements, and perpetrated the massacre
at Fort Mims in Alabama, August 10, 1813. They

were defeated by the troops under General Jackson
and General Coffee at Talladega and Taluschatchee,
their country ravaged, and their villages burned. But
the spirit of the tribe was yet unbroken, and the war
smouldered and spluttered along the border in the
burning of cabins and raids upon the outlying settlers.
It was determined to put an end to it by a decisive
and exterminating campaign, and the volunteer troops
were again called out under Jackson and Coffee.
Houston's regiment joined this army, and marched to
the scene of hostilities. The fighting remnant of the
tribe had rallied for a last stand at To-ho-pe-ka, or the
Horseshoe, a bend on the Tallapoosa River in Alabama, which they had fortified by breastworks across
the neck of the peninsula. Here were gathered some
seven hundred warriors, the flower of the fighting men
of the nation, and three hundred women and children.
At this place Jackson's army, numbering about two
thousand men, arrived on the 27th of August, 1814.

The battle of To-ho-pe-ka was one of the most
hotly contested and desperate which has ever been
fought by the Indian race against civilized arms and
discipline. The Indians had been wrought up to a
high pitch of enthusiasm and desperation by the fervent appeals and predictions of their prophets and
chiefs, and the natural strength of their position gave
them additional confidence. The inclosure, about a
hundred acres in extent, was trenched with ravines,
and thickly wooded with trees and bush. Across the
opening, which was about three hundred and fifty

yards in width, was built a breastwork of three rows of heavy pine logs, set upright in the ground, and arranged with some military skill in zigzags for a raking as well as a front fire. The rest of the peninsula was protected by the steep banks of the unfordable river.

Jackson drew up his main body in a line fronting the breastworks, and the battle was begun at half past ten o'clock in the forenoon by the fire of his small cannon, a four and a six pounder, which had been planted on an eminence about eighty yards from the breastworks. These balls had no effect on the solid pine logs, and were saluted with whoops of derision by the Indians, as they replied through the port-holes to the rifle fire of the besiegers. In the mean time General Coffee with the mounted troops and the bands of Cherokees who had joined the whites against their neighbors, the Creeks, had invested the peninsula on the opposite side of the river. Some of the Cherokees swam across the stream, and brought away the canoes, which the Creeks had hidden under the bushes of the bank. By these canoes General Coffee's troops were taken across, and the crack of their rifles and the smoke from the burning cabins at the head of the peninsula announced to Jackson's army that the Creeks had been taken in the rear. It was then half past twelve. The long roll was beaten and the order given to charge the breastworks. The onset was made with all the vigor and fury of the fiery frontiersmen.

Houston at the extreme right of his regiment dashed forward in front of the line as it charged upon the breastworks, which were spitting fire at every crevice. With a spring and a scramble he gained the top of the palisade from which Major Montgomery of his regiment had just fallen dead with a rifle ball in his head. As he did so a barbed arrow struck deep in his thigh. He sprang down, and at the head of the rush of men who had followed drove the Indians back from the palisade to take refuge among the trees and brush. As the space was cleared and the battle paused for a moment Houston called upon the lieutenant of the company to pull out the arrow. Twice he made the attempt and failed, it was so deeply embedded in the flesh. Drawing back his sword over his head Houston roared to him to try again, and that he would cut him down if he failed. This time, exerting all his strength, the lieutenant pulled out the arrow, leaving a gaping and jagged wound from which the blood gushed in a stream. Houston recrossed the breastworks to have it stanched. While under the surgeon's hands he was seen by Jackson, who was watching the fight on horseback. Jackson ordered him to the rear. Houston made light of his wound, and begged to be allowed to rejoin the fight, but was peremptorily refused. He disobeyed after Jackson had moved off, recrossed the breastworks, and again engaged in the conflict. It was fought with all the fury of savage desperation. The Indians, driven from the palisade, took refuge in the ravines and behind

the trees and bushes. From these they fired, and
were shot by the quick rifles of the frontiersmen, or
killed in hand-to-hand conflicts in which clubbed rifle
crashed against clubbed rifle, and hunting-knife struck
against tomahawk. Not a warrior asked for or received quarter. The fight raged over the hundred-
acre space all the afternoon, until the larger number
of the Indians had been killed in their tracks, or shot
while endeavoring to swim the turbid waters of the
river.

A small band of the warriors had, meanwhile, taken
refuge in a deep ravine close to the river on one side
of the breastworks. It was roofed with heavy pine
logs, and almost as impregnable to assault as a cave.
The only way in which it could be taken was by a
direct charge upon the narrow entrance. An interpreter was sent forward to summon them to surrender,
but they replied with a shot, which wounded him, and
with yells of rage and defiance. Jackson called for
volunteers to storm the ravine, but the task was so
evidently desperate that no body of men gathered to
respond to the call. Houston dashed forward, calling
upon his men to follow him, but without looking back
to see if they did so. When within a few yards of
the entrance he received two bullets in his shoulder,
and his upper right arm was shattered. His musket
fell from his hand, and he was helpless. No one had
supported his charge, and he drew back out of the
range of the fire. It was not until the logs covering
the ravine had been set on fire by blazing arrows, and

the desperate warriors had been shot as they burst out of the smoke and flame, that the last refuge crumbled in ashes and blood. It was sunset when the battle was over, and the last hope of the Creek nation was crushed. In his report of the battle to his superior officer, General Pinckney, Jackson does not mention the exploit of Houston's, although it took place under his eye, but his name is contained in the list of the wounded of his regiment afterward forwarded to Governor Blount of Tennessee. It, however, gained for Houston Jackson's friendship and confidence, which he retained throughout his life.

Houston was borne from the field and put in charge of the surgeons. They considered his wounds necessarily fatal, although it does not appear why they should, unless they believed his lungs to be touched. They extracted one bullet, but made no attempt to probe for the other in an unnecessary torture. He lay all night on the damp ground, receiving none of the attention which was given to those whose wounds were not considered mortal. In the morning he was found to be alive, placed on a rude litter, and conveyed to Fort Williams, some sixty or seventy miles distant. Here he received only some rude surgery, the regular hospital for the wounded officers being at a place called the Hickory Ground. He was kindly cared for, however, a part of the time by Colonel Johnson and a part of the time by Colonel Cheatham, two volunteer officers from his State. At length he was removed to the Ten Islands, where there was a military post and hospital. General Dougherty, who commanded the East Tennessee brigade, had him conveyed by horse litter several hundred miles through the Cherokee country to his mother's cabin. The journey was intensely painful from the rough method of conveyance, and he could only be supplied with the coarsest food. It was nearly two months after the battle of To-ho-pe-ka when he reached his mother's house. He was emaciated to a skeleton by his wounds and privations, and so changed that his mother said that she would not have recognized him, except for his eyes.

He did not recover at home under his mother's care, nor at Marysville, where he was taken for medical treatment. Finally he was removed to Knoxville, which he reached in so low a condition of vitality that the doctor said that he could live but a few days, and declined to take charge of his case. Finding at the end of that time that Houston was not only not dead, but actually somewhat better, he consented to treat him. He slowly recovered strength, and after a time was able to make the journey on horseback to Washington, which he reached shortly after the burning of the Capitol in the raid of the British troops. Being still unfit for active duty, he returned to Lexington, Va., where he spent a portion of the winter with his relatives and friends. He continued to gain in strength, and returned to Knoxville, where he received the news of the battle of New Orleans, and was placed on duty at the cantonment of his regiment.

On the reduction of the army after the declaration of peace, Houston was assigned to the First Regiment of infantry in the regular army, having received his promotion to a lieutenancy for his gallantry at To-ho-pe-ka, and ordered to report for duty at New Orleans.

He made the journey down the Cumberland and the Mississippi in a skiff with only two companions, one of whom was E. D. White, afterward Governor of Louisiana. He has recorded that while voyaging down the vast and lonely stream of the Mississippi they saw, on turning a bend, a vessel pouring out a stream of smoke, which they supposed to be on fire; but it proved to be the first steamboat which had navigated its waters. They left their skiff at Natchez and took the steamer, which conveyed them to New Orleans. In New Orleans, Houston's wounds were again operated upon, and, in his weakened condition, the operation nearly cost him his life. After shattering his right arm at nearly the junction with his shoulder, the bullet had passed around and lodged under the shoulder-blade. The wound never entirely healed, and constantly discharged until the day of his death. After a winter of weakness and suffering in New Orleans, he went to New York for medical treatment, and then reported for duty at the Adjutant-General's office in Nashville, where he was employed until November, 1817. At that time he was appointed a sub-agent of the Cherokees under General Return J. Meigs, at the request of General Jackson, and accepted the duty, although yet hardly fit for active service. General Jackson wrote to Assistant Secretary of War Graham, " He is a young man of sound integrity, who has my entire confidence, and in every way he is capacitated to fill the appointment. Moreover he has some claims upon the government for a severe wound received in the service, which may be considered a disability."   Jackson also wrote to General Meigs, " In him I have full confidence, and in him you will have a friend clear of design and deceit, on whom you can rely under all and every circumstance, as capable to aid you in every respect."   In the previous year the chiefs of the Cherokees had signed a treaty by which they agreed to surrender 1,385,200 acres of their best land in East Tennessee. A portion of the tribe were naturally indignant, and refused to remove from their homes. There were apprehensions of serious trouble when Houston was appointed, and his knowledge of the Cherokee language and acquaintance and friendship in the tribe doubtless made his influence very useful in subduing the hostility and ill-feeling. He received the thanks of Governor McMunn, who had succeeded General Meigs as agent, for the efficiency of his services.

He conducted a delegation of the Cherokees to Washington to receive the funds for the sale of their lands and fix the bounds of their reservation, and while there had trouble with John C. Calhoun, then Secretary of War, which resulted in the termination of his service in the army, and doubtless intensified the antagonism to that wing of the Democratic party represented by Calhoun, which he manifested in later

life. His first offense was in appearing before the
punctilious Secretary dressed in the garments of an
Indian, which he habitually assumed when living with
them. He received a rebuke for this which he did
not relish. But a more serious charge followed. The
Indian country was full of outlaws and desperate adventurers, who were engaged in all sorts of schemes of
plunder and offense against the laws. One of these
was the smuggling of slaves from Florida, then a
province of Spain, who were taken through the Indian
reservation to the border settlements. Houston inter-
fered to break up this nefarious traffic, and naturally
excited the enmity of those engaged in it. Some of
them or their agents in Washington made charges
against Houston affecting his official integrity and
personal conduct. He appeared before President
Madison and Secretary Calhoun, and successfully defended himself, and having concluded his agency
business in Washington, conducted the Cherokee delegation back to the Hilli-bee towns. But his hasty
temper had taken umbrage at the unwarranted attacks
upon him, and the spirit in which the inquiry into
his conduct had been instituted by the Secretary of
War, and he resigned, May 18, 1818. He was then
a first lieutenant, and had served for five years.

Houston's service in the army of the United States
was useful and creditable, although he did not rise
above a subordinate, or take part in any important
military operation. He earned the respect and com-
mendation of his superior officers, and was noted for
his zeal and capacity as a soldier. It was Houston's

bravery under his own eyes which attracted the friendship and confidence of Jackson, which he retained through all the vicissitudes of his career. On the other hand Houston conceived a respect and admiration for Jackson, which made him a devoted follower, personally and politically, and the only person, it was said, to whose judgment he deferred, and who could influence his actions. In many respects alike in passion and temperament, and both characteristic products of the untamed and vigorous life of the frontier, they had essential elements of difference in habits and character, and the stronger, more self-contained and sterner nature of Jackson dominated the more impassioned and enthusiastic temperament of Houston.

Senator Benton in his speech in the Senate, May 16, 1836, in favor of acknowledging the independence of Texas as a consequence of the battle of San Jacinto, bore testimony, in his somewhat highflown and stilted way, to the good qualities of Houston as a young soldier. He said, "Houston was appointed an ensign in the army of the United States during the late war with Great Britain, and served in the Creek campaign under the banner of Jackson. I was the lieutenant-colonel of the regiment to which he belonged, and the first field-officer to whom he reported. I then marked in him the same soldierly and gentlemanly qualities, which have since distinguished his eventful career; frank, generous and brave, ready to do or to suffer whatever the obligations of civil or military duty imposed; and always prompt to answer the call of honor, patriotism or friendship."

CHAPTER III

AFTER leaving the army Houston determined to become a lawyer, which in those days in the South-west was synonymous with politician. (For this career he doubtless felt his remarkable fitness and vocation as a popular orator and manager of men.| He had contracted some debts while in the service, on account of extra expenses caused by his wounds, and he sold his only piece of property, some land, to pay them; it failed to do so entirely, and he began his new life some hundreds of dollars in debt. He entered the law office of Hon. James Trimble in Nashville, and was admitted to the bar after six months' study. It may be supposed that the examination was not very strict, and the requirements of technical knowledge not very exhaustive. Andrew Jackson had been made a district attorney without knowing how to spell, and a knowledge of the intricacies of the law and the pre-cedents of the courts was of much less consequence for a successful practitioner than a flow of popular oratory for the jury, and a courage to hold one's own with the fighting attorneys, who occasionally supple-mented the heated debate in the court room by a per-sonal encounter outside. At any rate Houston never was and never pretended to be a lawyer in the professional sense of the term. He was the political attorney in Tennessee, using the opportunities of the court room to show his powers of rough and ready eloquence, and to obtain professional and political office ; and in Texas, during the rare intervals when he was not holding some public position, he sometimes went on circuit and made effective stump speeches to juries in criminal cases. But he never studied and never knew anything of the law beyond those general principles which are readily appreciated by a strong and capacious mind, and the easy and slipshod requirements of frontier practice. In this he was probably not inferior to most of his associates, and was able to hold his own with credit and success among the attorneys who traveled the circuits of Tennessee, with their libraries in their saddle-bags and a ready tongue and pistol as their chief requirements for successful practice.

After being admitted to the bar Houston settled in Lebanon, Tennessee, bought his books on credit, and hired an office at a dollar a month. He was received with much kindness by Isaac Golladay, a merchant and postmaster of Lebanon, who sold him a suit of clothes, let him have his letters on credit, and introduced him to his friends. One of the pleasant glimpses of Houston's personal life is given in a letter of a son of Isaac Golladay, to whom Houston manifested his gratitude for his father's kindness, while sick and a stranger in Texas : —

" I was traveling in Texas in 1853. Arrived at
the town of Huntsville, Walker County, on Sunday
at about eleven o'clock. The good people of the town
and the vicinity were passing on to the church as I
rode up to the hotel. I was very sick; had a high
fever on me when I dismounted. I told the landlord
I was very sick and wanted a room; he assigned me
a room and was very kind in his attentions. I took a
bed immediately, and while talking to him asked him
in what part of the State General Houston lived. He
replied, ' He lives about one and a half miles from
town, and his family and he have just passed, going
to church in their carriage.' To this I said, ' Please
keep on the lookout, and when he returns from
church let him know that a Golladay of Tennessee is
lying sick here!' After the church hour was over,
say twelve or one o'clock, a large, portly, elegant-
looking man came walking into my room and to my
bedside. I knew from the description which I had
had of him that it was General Houston, although I
had never seen him. I called him by name. He
asked me if I was the son of his old friend, Isaac
Golladay, of Lebanon, Tennessee. I replied I was.
He then asked me which one. I told him I was
Frederick. He said he knew my elder brothers, but
he had left Lebanon before I was born, but added,
' If you are the son of Isaac Golladay I recognize you
as the child of an old and true friend. I went to
Lebanon, where your father resided, a poor young
man; your father furnished me an office for the prac-

tice of law; credited me in his store for clothes; let me have the letters, which then cost twenty-five cents postage, from the office of which he was postmaster; invited me to his house, and recommended me to all the good people of his large general acquaintance.' He then said, ' You must go out to my house. I will come in my carriage for you in the evening.' I replied with thanks that I was too sick to go, but he insisted on coming for me the next morning, to which I consented. Early the next morning he came for me; being better, I went out to his house with him. He placed me in a room in his yard, saying that Mrs. H. was confined to her room with an infant at that time. My fever rose and kept me confined. He sent for a physician. I was sick there for about ten days or two weeks. He made a servant-man stay and sleep in the office with me, to wait on me all the while, but would often come and see me, and spend much of his time with me. One night, especially, while I was sick, the doctor had left orders for my medicine to be given me during the night, and my feet bathed with warm water. He stayed all night with me. He had the vessel of warm water brought, pulled off his coat, rolled up his sleeves, to wash my feet. I objected, the servant being present. He replied, ' My Master washed His disciples' feet, and I would follow His glorious example,' and insisted that he should do so. During the time which he spent with me in my sick room, he gave me much of his early history."

Houston soon began to be a figure in public life.

His remarkable gifts for popularity, the impressiveness and friendliness of his manners, his natural powers of adaptability to all societies, which made him as much at home while telling stories on a store-box or a wagon tongue as in a parlor, and his cultivated dignity of port and gesture gave him the essentials of political success. He was, besides, the friend and devoted follower of Andrew Jackson, who exercised a sort of political kingship in Tennessee in those days. While practicing law in Lebanon he was, in 1819, appointed Adjutant-General of the State with the rank of colonel, and in October of the same year he was elected prosecuting attorney for the Davidson District, which necessitated his removal to Nashville. After his curious egotistical and sentimental fashion he addressed a farewell to the citizens of Lebanon from the court-house steps, in which he said, " I was naked and ye clothed me ; I was hungry and ye fed me ; I was athirst and ye gave me drink," and moved the hearts of his hearers to such a degree that, according to the contemporary account, " there was not a dry eye in the whole assembly." Houston performed his duties as prosecuting attorney with success and éclat, but resigned the office on account of the insufficiency of the fees. He continued the practice of law in Nashville, and in 1821 was elected major-general of the Tennessee militia, a wholly political and mainly honorary office.

In 1823, when thirty years of age, Houston was elected a Representative to Congress from the ninth

district of Tennessee under the new apportionment.
Houston served in Congress for four years without
special distinction, occasionally taking part in the debates, and acting as a member of the Jackson wing
of the Democratic party. Jackson had been elected
a Senator by the Tennessee legislature shortly after
Houston's election as Representative, and both were
members of the Committee on Military Affairs.
Houston in common with the other Jacksonian members opposed the resolution offered by Henry Clay,
then Speaker of the House, for an inquiry into his
political conduct, made personal by the charges of
George Kremer, a Representative from Pennsylvania,
in the newspapers, of a corrupt bargain by which
John Quincy Adams was to be elected President and
Clay made Secretary of State. Houston issued an
address to his constituents giving as reasons for this
opposition that it would be simply a political investigation and that the proper remedy for the personal
grievance would be found in the courts. The main
purpose of the circular, however, was to intensify the
popular indignation at the defeat of Jackson, who had
obtained a plurality of the electoral votes, and to
strengthen the feeling which carried Jackson into the
presidential chair at the next election by an overwhelming majority. Houston's address was written in
that forcible and dignified language, which he always
had at his command when dealing with questions of
state, and indicated that he had received a valuable
education in the comprehension and treatment of pub-

lic affairs by his experience in the halls of Congress. Congress at that time contained a number of notable men, including Daniel Webster, Henry Clay, John Randolph, the veteran of the House, the venerable Nathaniel Macon, and others, and the debates and the consideration of public affairs were on a plane which could not but have afforded a man of Houston's quickness of mind and enlarging capacity very important lessons of comprehension and dignity. Houston's eccentricities were generally kept for an appropriate audience, and there is no reason to doubt that as a Representative in Congress he conducted himself as a sober-minded and practical legislator, if he did not distinguish himself beyond the lines of a political follower of Andrew Jackson, or make a special mark as a debater.

It was during Houston's second term as a member of Congress that his first and only serious duel took place. The appointments of postmasters under the new Federal Administration were naturally not of the Jackson-Houston party. One Colonel Irwin had been appointed postmaster at Nashville, and Houston had expressed his opinion about him with that vigor which always characterized his animadversions upon his political opponents. Houston's words were carried to Colonel Irwin, and it was understood that he would hold him personally responsible for them on his return to Tennessee. Colonel Irwin selected as the bearer of his challenge one Colonel John T. Smith, a noted desperado of Missouri; Houston's friend, Colonel McGregor, refused to accept the challenge from Smith's hands. The challenge was offered and refused in front of the Nashville Inn, McGregor dropping the paper to the ground as it was handed to him. No encounter followed between Smith and McGregor, as was expected, and the news of the action was taken to Houston, who was in a room of the inn with some of his friends. General William White, who was present, expressed himself to the effect that Smith had not been treated with proper courtesy. Houston overheard the remark, and said to White, " If you, sir, have any grievance, I will give you any satisfaction you may demand." White replied, " I have nothing to do with your difficulty, but I presume you know what is due from one gentleman to another." Nothing farther followed at the time, and it was soon spread about the streets of Nashville that Houston had " backed down " General White. This attack upon his courage reached the ears of General White, and he sent a challenge to Houston, which was promptly accepted. An attempt was made by the sheriff to arrest them both for the preservation of the peace, but Houston escaped to the house of a friend in an adjoining county, and sent word to White, who had also evaded arrest, that he was ready to meet him across the state line in Kentucky. The duel was fought at sunrise, September 23, 1826, at a noted dueling-ground in Simpson County known by the name of Linkumpinch, just across the Tennessee line, and on the road from Nashville to Bowling Green. White was severely, and it was supposed at first mortally, wounded, having been shot through the body at the hip. Houston escaped untouched. As they took their places to fire Houston was observed to slip something into his mouth which he afterward explained was a bullet, which he had placed between his teeth on the advice of Jackson, who said that it was good to have something in the mouth to bite on, — "It will make you aim better." On the evening of the day of the fight a large crowd was gathered at the Nashville Inn to hear the news, and among them General Jackson. Presently one John G. Anderson, "a noted character" and a friend of Houston's, who had witnessed the duel, came dashing over the bridge on horseback with the news that Houston was unharmed and White mortally wounded. The grand jury of Simpson County in June, 1827, brought in an indictment against Houston for felony in shooting at William White with intent to kill, and the Governor of Kentucky issued a requisition on the Governor of Tennessee for his surrender. It was not complied with on the ground that the facts showed that Houston had "acted in self-defense." In fact a prosecution for such an offense in those dueling days must have been understood as a farce, and the fight undoubtedly increased Houston's popularity as an evidence of his "game."

Houston's bitter and abusive tongue frequently got him into personal difficulties in which the "satisfac-

tion of a gentleman " was demanded by his antago-
nists ; but he never fought again, while sober, and was
equally ready with a lofty assumption of dignity or a
joke to avoid the necessity. To a challenge from a
political inferior in Texas he replied that he " never
fought down hill." On another occasion, when called
to account by a gentleman whom he had been denouncing, he said, " Why, H., I thought you were a
friend of mine." " So I was, but I do not propose to
be abused by you or anybody else." " Well, I should
like to know," said Houston, " if a man can't abuse
his friends, who in h— he can abuse," and the affair
ended in a laugh. Mr. John J. Linn in his " Reminiscences of Fifty Years in Texas " tells the story
that Houston and ex-President Burnet had an acri-
monious newspaper controversy in which they bandied
abusive epithets until finally Houston accused Burnet
of being a " hog-thief." There was no retort in Texan
phraseology capable of over-matching this, and Burnet
sent a challenge to Houston by Dr. Branch T. Archer.
" What does he predicate the demand upon ? " said
Houston in his loftiest manner. Archer replied that
it was for his abuse of Mr. Burnet. " Has n't he
abused me to an equal degree? He has done so publicly and privately until I am compelled to believe
that the people are equally disgusted with both of us."
Houston's dignity of manner overpowered Archer,
and he took back the challenge. Houston received
challenges from President Lamar, General Albert
Sidney Johnston and Commodore E. W. Moore of

the Texas navy, and a good many others, which he did not accept. On one occasion being visited by a gentleman with a warlike message, he took the challenge and handed it to his private secretary with instructions to indorse it " number fourteen," and file it away. He then informed the expectant gentleman that his affair must wait its turn until the previous thirteen had been disposed of. It is perhaps a wonder that he preserved his reputation for courage in such a community as that of Texas, while persistently declining to fight, but it does not seem to have been seriously doubted. In a speech to his constituents at Tellico, after his duel with White, Houston said that he was opposed to dueling, but had been compelled to fight in defense of his honor. "Thank God," he said, "that my antagonist was injured no worse." There is no record of how his affair with the Nashville postmaster terminated, but it certainly led to no more fighting.

This same year, 1827, Houston was elected governor of Tennessee by a majority of 12,000 over Newton Cannon, and Willie Blount, the old "war governor." Houston doubtless owed much to his personal popularity, but his nomination and election were due to the fact that he was the representative of the personal party of Andrew Jackson, which his competitors opposed. Of his appearance at the time of his election there is a vivid and minute portrait in the reminiscences of Colonel D. D. Claiborne of Goliad, Texas, who saw him with the eager and impressionable eyes of a boy. It shows Houston in that theatrical and sensational manner of dress which was a characteristic of him as long as he lived, and which only his magnificent physique and lofty manner could have prevented from seeming ridiculous and puerile. Says Colonel Claiborne : —

" He wore on that day (August 2, 1827) a tall, bell-crowned, medium-brimmed, shining black beaver hat, shining black patent - leather military stock or cravat, incased by a standing collar, ruffled shirt, black satin vest, shining black silk pants gathered to the waistband with legs full, same size from seat to ankle, and a gorgeous, red-ground, many-colored gown or Indian hunting-shirt, fastened at the waist by a huge red sash covered with fancy bead-work, with an immense silver buckle, embroidered silk stockings, and pumps with large silver buckles. Mounted on a superb dapple-gray horse he appeared at the election unannounced, and was the observed of all observers."

But however bizarre and fantastic was Houston's appearance on election day, his practical good sense and statesmanship were manifested in the office; and his executive administration was successful, and his legislative recommendations conservative.

Houston was a candidate for reëlection for a second term against the formidable opposition of General William Carroll, who had commanded the left wing of Jackson's army at New Orleans, and had been Governor of Tennessee for three terms previous to Houston's election; he was ineligible for the fourth

term in succession owing to the prohibitive provision
of the State Constitution. The canvass was proceed-
ing, apparently in Houston's favor, when the event
occurred which put an end to his successful career as
a politician in Tennessee, and apparently ruined him
forever. On the 16th of April, 1829, he sent in his
resignation to the Secretary of State. In January of
that year Houston had been married to a Miss Eliza
Allen, daughter of a wealthy and influential family of
Sumner County, which was numbered among his political friends and adherents. After three months of
marriage his wife left him and returned to her father's
house. Houston wrote to her father, asking him to
persuade his wife to return, but she refused, and he
threw up his hold on fortune and life. The cause of
the trouble between Houston and his wife has never
been definitely revealed. The only words which he
ever wrote on the matter were contained in a letter
in which he said: "Eliza stands acquitted by me.
I have received her as a virtuous, chaste wife, and as
such I pray God I may ever regard her, and I trust I
ever shall. She was cold to me, and I thought did
not love me." The most probable explanation is that
the young lady had been induced to marry Houston to
gratify the desires of her parents, who were attracted
by his brilliant political position and prospects, while
her affections had been given to another. The inti-
macy of married life revealed her coldness or repug-
nance to her husband, and in a moment of quarrel
she avowed the truth, and left him. Houston's " high-

strung" spirit and personal vanity were deeply wounded, and he acted with all the dramatic intensity of his nature.

There was the wildest excitement in the frontier community over such an explosion of scandal. Houston's enemies circulated the most outrageous reports concerning his conduct, and the mystery, as it generally is, was interpreted at its worst. For a time there was the prospect that he would be subject to personal violence and that there would be bloody affrays in the streets of Nashville over the affair. His friends rallied around him, but he left Nashville in secret, some say in disguise, and went to bury himself among his old friends, the Cherokees, a portion of whom had removed from their homes in Tennessee to the Indian Territory.

Nothing could ever be extracted from Houston as to the cause of the separation between himself and his wife, even when he had lost his self-control from drink, and whenever he spoke of her it was in the most respectful terms. Sometimes he took the inquiries good-humoredly, as when he replied to Hon. J. H. Reagan, afterward Postmaster-General of the Confederacy and United States Senator, who, while traveling with him in Texas on the way to a conference with the Indians at Grapevine Springs, had called his attention to a long, pretended account of the affair in a newspaper. Houston merely said, " There has been a great deal written on that subject by men who know nothing about it. It is an absolute secret and will always remain so." At other times he resented an inquiry as an unwarranted obtrusion into his private affairs. During his early residence in Texas, and when he had no home of his own, Houston spent a good deal of his time at the house of Colonel Phil Sublett at San Augustine. One night he came home so intoxicated that he was unable to mount to his chamber, and was accommodated with a pallet on the floor. Colonel Sublett thought this a good opportunity to obtain a knowledge of the mystery, and began to question him on the subject. This sobered as well as angered Houston, and he called for his horse, declaring that he would not remain longer in a house where an attempt was made to take advantage of his condition to extract his secret, and he was with difficulty pacified by an apology.

Mrs. Houston secured a divorce from Houston on the ground of abandonment, and afterward married a Dr. Douglass. She lived for many years in the town of Gallatin, Tennessee, and enjoyed the entire respect and esteem of the community. She was equally silent as to the cause of the separation of herself and her first husband.

CHAPTER IV

INDIAN LIFE — THE STANBERRY AFFAIR

HOUSTON went by steamboat to the mouth of the Arkansas, not being recognized on the way except at Napoleon, where he was seen by a friend from whom he exacted a promise not to betray his identity; from thence he traveled by way of Little Rock, where he addressed a farewell letter to General Jackson, to the mouth of the Illinois Bayou, which flows into the Arkansas about thirty miles below Fort Gibson. Here was a settlement of the Cherokees, who had preceded the forced emigration of the tribe in 1838, and settled in Arkansas and the Indian Territory. A treaty had been made on their behalf with the Osages in order to secure them a location, and, after some quarrels and skirmishes with that tribe, they had settled into permanent and peaceful residence.

At the mouth of the Illinois was Tah-lon-tees-kee, the principal town and council house of the tribe, and the residence of Oo-loo-tee-kah, or, as he was better known by his English name, John Jolly, the sub-chief, who had received Houston into his family when a boy in Tennessee, and had now become the principal chief of the western fragment of the tribe. He gave a hearty welcome to his adopted son in his second flight for refuge among the tribe, and Houston took up his residence with him, resuming his Indian name of Co-lon-neh, or the Raven, and the dress and habits of the savage. The chief, John Jolly, is described as a man of great intelligence and force of character, and was at that time about sixty years of age, of massive frame, although not tall, with a rotund but commanding countenance, and his long locks plentifully sprinkled with gray. He spoke no English, and had none of the civilized education which some of the members of the tribe at that time possessed. His cabin was under a magnificent grove of cotton-woods and sycamores at the confluence of the streams, and he cultivated a clearing and kept a large herd of cattle, his wealth also comprising twelve negro slaves, whom he had brought with him from Tennessee. He lived in the patriarchal Indian fashion, and he and Houston have been seen seated on the floor together, feeding with their spoons from the trough of ka-nau-hee-na, or hominy boiled to the consistency of paste, which was always kept replenished in the centre of the cabin.

Houston lived with John Jolly for upward of a year, was formally adopted as a member of the tribe, and took part in its counsels and deliberations. At this time the eastern Cherokees had adopted a system of government with a constitution and laws after the model of those of their white neighbors; but the western Cherokees still managed their affairs after the aboriginal fashion. They had a principal chief and sub-chiefs, who were the natural leaders in war and council, but their authority was very limited, and the actual government was by a republic in which the tribe decided all matters of importance by discussion and vote in a general council. The chief matters decided at the sessions of the council, which were held in an open shed, roofed with branches, were the relations of the tribe with the United States, as represented by its agents and contractors, and with neighboring Indian tribes, propositions for grants of land to missionary stations and schools, the maintenance of formal intercourse with the eastern Cherokees, and such matters; and it also administered a rude justice for murder and theft by the bullet and the lash.

It is said that Houston did not take a very prominent part in the deliberations of the council, and this was probably due to that feeling of jealousy toward the members of an alien race which would be natural among the native Indians. He preserved the fondness for dress and display among the Indians which he had shown among the whites. The Cherokees did not paint their faces and wear scalp-locks like their neighbors, the Osages, but they wore the blankets, buckskin hunting - shirts, leggings and moccasins, and adorned their hair with the feathers of the eagle and wild turkey. On state occasions Houston appeared in all the glory of an Indian brave. He has been described as wearing in full dress a white hunting-shirt brilliantly embroidered, yellow leggings,

and moccasins elaborately worked with beads, a huge
red blanket, and a circlet of turkey feathers around
his head.   He let his hair grow, and wore it in a long
queue which hung down his back, and wore his beard
on his chin, shaving the rest of his face.   The Indians
are very quick to ridicule any tricks of ways and manners, and Houston's theatrical dignity and splendor
did not escape their satire.   On one occasion at a
council meeting they arrayed a negro in a caricature
of his attire, and stationed him behind his seat, where
he imitated his pose and manner to the great glee of
the assembly.   Houston bore the presence of his imi-
tator with shrewd indifference, and the joke was not
repeated.

Houston did not sink out of sight, or at least out of
the public attention, after he had buried himself in
the forests of the Indian Territory.   His reputation,
and the dramatic manner of his disappearance from
public life, made his name the subject of wild conjecture and rumor, and he was credited with being
the centre of all sorts of enterprises and conspiracies.
Among them was a scheme for the invasion of a
province of Mexico by a force of Cherokee Indians,
and this took such definite form as to be regarded
with some uneasiness by President Jackson, who instructed a government agent in Arkansas to report
to him on the subject, and wrote to Houston a letter
alluding to it, which also shows Jackson's unfaltering
confidence in his friend and his sympathy with his
misfortunes.   Jackson wrote : —

"It has been communicated to me that you had the illegal enterprise in view of conquering Texas; that you had declared that you would, in less than two years, be *emperor* of that country by conquest. 1 must really have thought you deranged to have believed you had so wild a scheme in contemplation; and, particularly, when it was communicated that the physical force to be employed was the Cherokee Indians! Indeed, my dear sir, I cannot believe you have any such chimerical, visionary scheme in view. Your pledge of honor to the contrary is a sufficient guarantee that you will never engage in any enterprise injurious to your country, or that would tarnish your fame. . . . My affliction was great and as much as I could well bear, when I parted from you on the 18th of January last. I then viewed you as on the brink of happiness and rejoiced. About to be united in marriage to a beautiful young lady, of accomplished manners and of respectable connections, and of your own selection, — you, the Governor of the State and holding the affections of the people; these were your prospects, when I shook you by the hand and *bade you farewell !* You can well judge my astonishment and grief in receiving a letter from you, dated at Little Rock, A. T. conveying the sad intelligence that you were then a private citizen, *an exile from your country.* What reverse of fortune! How unstable are human affairs ! "

Houston himself occasionally reappeared in public life to take a part in affairs. He found that the

Indians were being outrageously swindled, as they have generally been, by the agents and contractors. The Cherokees, who had been induced to give up some lands on the Lower Arkansas, were to receive twenty-eight dollars per head for the exchange. The agents who were to pay them issued certificates, which they redeemed themselves for trifling sums, or, in Houston's words, " for a Mackinaw blanket, a flask of powder, or a bottle of whiskey." These frauds and others aroused Houston's indignation, and in 1830 he accompanied a delegation of the Cherokees to Washington, where his representations and evidence resulted in the removal of five agents, and caused the bitter hostility of the Indian ring. Houston himself became a bidder for the contract to supply the Indians with rations. The price which he bid was eighteen cents, and he secured a wealthy partner in New York to carry out the contract. A clamor was raised by the representatives of the Indian ring, including Thomas L. McKinney, the head clerk of the Indian Bureau, whose connection with the discredited Indian "factory system" had not been above suspicion. General Duff Green, as a self-constituted adviser and factotum of President Jackson, took it upon himself to remonstrate, stating that the rations could be furnished for ten or twelve cents, and the contract was not given to Houston. Houston's whole career is unstained by any charge of pecuniary dishonesty or greed, and he put aside many temptations to accumulate a fortune which were thrust upon him, while at the head of affairs in Texas, and he was also a sincere friend of the Indians. It is fair to assume that his intentions in regard to the contract were honest, and that it was his purpose to furnish rations of a good quality and at a fair price, and not, as so many of the contractors did, of damaged flour and rotten meat, recouping themselves for their nominally low prices in the many ways familiar to the Indian ring. The scandal of the rejected contract followed Houston, and was exploited in the partisan newspapers to the discredit of himself and his assumed patron, President Jackson. Houston issued a silly and bombastic " proclamation," dated Nashville, July 13, 1831, in which he promised immunity to all his slanderers, and "a gilt copy (bound in sheep) of the ' Kentucky Register,' or a snug, plain copy (bound in dog) of the ' United States Telegraph,'" to the most successful. But the attacks did not cease, and finally led to an event which gave him renewed, if doubtful, notoriety, and evinced his fiery, if calculating, passion.

In 1832 Houston was again in Washington. On March 31, Hon. William Stanberry, Representative in Congress from Ohio, in the course of a debate, which lasted several days, on charges of misconduct against the Collector of Wiscasset, made a general attack upon the Administration, in which he said, " Was not the late Secretary of War (Eaton) removed because of his attempt fraudulently to give to Governor Houston the contract for Indian rations?" Houston took fire at the allusion, and sent a note to Stanberry by his friend Cave Johnson of Tennessee, demanding to know if his name had been used, and if the remarks were correctly reported. To this note Stanberry replied to Johnson saying that he had received a note from his hands, signed Sam Houston, and that he could not recognize the right of Houston to any such information. Houston was excessively angry at Stanberry's refusal to reply to his demand, and particularly at that portion which said " a note signed Sam Houston," as though he was an unknown or insignificant individual, and said : " I will introduce myself to the damned rascal." He declared that he would whip Stanberry on sight, as he knew he would not accept a challenge. Johnson endeavored to persuade Houston to abandon his purpose, representing to him that an assault for words spoken in debate would be a breach of the privileges of the House. He then informed Stanberry of Houston's threats, and " washed his hands of the affair." Stanberry armed himself in anticipation of the assault, and Houston repossessed himself of a young hickory cane, which he had cut in the grounds of the Hermitage and given to a friend in Georgetown.

The encounter, when it actually took place, was apparently in a measure accidental, although both parties had been prepared for it. On the evening of April 13, Houston had been in the room of Senator Felix Grundy of Tennessee, in company with Senator Alexander Buckner of Missouri and Representative John C. Blair of Tennessee, and left it in company with the two latter. After walking up Pennsylvania

Avenue some distance "in light conversation," Blair
said they had gone half way with Houston, and that
to be polite he ought to turn about and go back with
them. Houston excused himself on the ground that
he had company. As they stood there a man was seen
crossing the avenue, and Blair, who had recognized
him as Stanberry, walked rapidly off. As the man
stepped on the sidewalk, Houston asked him if his
name was Stanberry, and, on the reply that it was,
said, "You are a damned rascal," and struck with his
stick. The affray lasted for several minutes, Houston
attempting to throw Stanberry, who dragged him about
the sidewalk, and finally succeeding in knocking him
down and beating him severely. As Stanberry lay
on his back under the blows of Houston, he drew a
pistol and aimed it at Houston's breast, but it snapped
without exploding, and Houston wrenched it from his
hands. Stanberry at length lay motionless, and Buckner, who had stood by while the beating was being
administered, said that he was about to interfere, when
Houston stopped of his own accord, and walked off.
It does not appear that Houston was armed.

The next day Stanberry addressed a note to the
Speaker, saying that he had been waylaid and beaten
the previous evening with a bludgeon, by Governor
Houston, for words spoken in debate, and that he was
confined to his boarding - house in consequence, and
asking that the information be laid before the House.
The note was read by the Speaker. A resolution was
offered for the arrest of Houston by the sergeant-at-

arms, which was opposed by Mr. Polk and others of
the Jackson party, who claimed that a committee of inquiry would be sufficient. The resolution was adopted
by a vote of 146 to 25. Houston was arrested by the
sergeant-at-arms, and brought to the bar of the House,
April 16. He was informed by the Speaker that he
could have time to procure counsel and witnesses.
Houston replied that he desired no counsel, but
twenty-four hours in which to prepare his answer.
He changed his mind about counsel, however, and appeared, accompanied by Francis Scott Key. In reply
to the interrogatory of the Speaker presenting the
charge, Houston admitted that he did assault and beat
Stanberry on accidentally meeting him, but denied that
the assault involved a breach of the privileges of the
House. The trial lasted for a month, including the
examination of witnesses and the debates. Houston's
counsel argued that the assault was not a breach of
legislative privilege, which could only protect a member when in the actual discharge of his functions.
Houston made a spirited and passionate speech in
defense of himself. It was evidently carefully prepared, and contained many allusions to Draco, Ca-
ligula, and other classical figures, in the oratorical
fashion of those days, and a good deal of bombastical
and theatrical rhetoric. But it was really vigorous
and eloquent, and, carried off by Houston's splendid
physique and commanding demeanor, doubtless produced a deeply sensational effect. He denied that he
had lain in wait like an assassin to commit the assault.

" If," said he, " when deeply wronged, I have followed
the generous impulses of my heart, have violated the
laws of my country and the privileges of this honorable body, I am willing to be held to my responsibility
for so doing." In regard to the charges that he was
a " man of ruined fortune and blasted reputation," he
said: " Though the ploughshare of ruin has been
driven over me, and laid waste my brightest hopes,
yet I am proud to think that under all circumstances
I have endeavored to maintain the laws of my country,
and to support her institutions. Whatever may be
the opinion of gentlemen in relation to these matters,
I am here to be tried for a substantive offense, discon-
nected entirely with my former life or circumstances.
I have only to say to those who rebuke me at this
time, when they see adversity sorely pressing upon
me, for myself,

> " ' I ask no sympathies, nor need ;
> The thorns which I have reaped are of the tree
> I planted. They have torn me, and I bleed.' "

He asserted that his attack upon Stanberry was not
for words spoken in debate, but for their publication
in the " National Intelligencer," and the refusal to answer his note demanding an explanation ; and argued
that a member forfeits the privilege "when he brands
a private citizen as a fraudulent villain in the face of
the whole world, and renders himself answerable to
the party aggrieved."

A resolution was offered that Samuel Houston be
discharged from the custody of the sergeant-at-arms,

and another that he had been guilty of a breach of
the privileges of the House. The debate lasted for
several days, turning mainly upon the cheap quibble of
whether the assault had been for the words spoken in
debate or for their publication in the newspaper. The
friends of the Administration rallied to the defense
of Houston, who had the outspoken approval of President Jackson, who said that "after a few more examples of the same kind, members of Congress would
learn to keep civil tongues in their heads;" but the
case was too flagrant, and a resolution that Samuel
Houston be brought to the bar and reprimanded by
the Speaker was passed by a vote of 106 to 89. An
addition that he be excluded from the privileges of
the floor as an ex-Representative was lost by a vote
of 90 to 101. On Monday, May 18, the day fixed
for the delivery of the reprimand, Houston presented
a paper protesting against the sentence as unconstitu-
tional, if not on the ground of an " unusual punishment," yet as inconsistent with our institutions and
unfit to be inflicted on a free citizen, but concluding
" that he would suffer in silent patience whatever the
House may think proper to inflict." The Speaker,
Hon. Andrew Stevenson, of Virginia, administered
the reprimand in a very mild and perfunctory manner, saying, " Whatever the motives and causes may
have been which led to this act of violence committed by you, your conduct has been pronounced
by a solemn judgment of the House to be a high
breach of their rights and privileges, and to demand

their marked disapprobation and censure . . . and
in obedience to the order of the House I reprimand
you accordingly."

A committee, of which Mr. Stanberry was a member, was appointed to investigate the affair of the
contract, and it made a report acquitting Houston
of any fraudulent intent. A charge of assault and
battery was brought against Houston in the courts,
and he was convicted and sentenced to pay a fine of
$500. This fine was remitted by President Jack-
son, — "divers good and sufficient reasons moving
me thereto," which were not given, — and this ended
the affair.

There is no doubt that Houston's assault on Stanberry, ruffianly and barbarous as it was, increased
his popularity in the Jackson party, and in the
frontier communities, who regarded violence as the
proper way in which to reply to insult. The vote
in the House showed how far the sentiment of
nearly a majority of the members was from being
in disapproval of such an act, although it was an
attack upon their own privileges of debate. Houston, on his return to the Indian Territory through
Tennessee, received an ovation, and was pressed to
remain and reënter public life. He never expressed
any regret for the occurrence, but, on the contrary,
said, in alluding to it: "I was dying out once, and
had they taken me before a justice of peace and
fined me ten dollars for assault and battery it would
have killed me; but they gave me a national tribu-

nal for a theatre, and that set me up again." This
remark might lead to the shrewd suspicion that
there was some calculation as well as anger in Houston's attack on Stanberry.

During Houston's residence in the Indian Territory,
he fell in love with a Cherokee woman, named Tyania
Rodgers. She was a half-breed, of great personal
beauty, and as tall and stately for a woman as Houston was for a man. He took up with her in the
Indian fashion as his wife, and, leaving the abode of
his friend, John Jolly, he established himself on the
west bank of Grand River, nearly opposite Fort Gibson. Here he made a small clearing and built a log
cabin. He established a small trading-post, and combined this occupation with some slatternly farming
and stock-raising. At this time Houston had sunk to
a low depth of degradation in personal habits. His
tall form was often seen stretched in a state of helpless intoxication in the paths about the cantonment
of Fort Gibson, and the Indians changed his name
of Co-lon-neh to the more expressive one of " Big
Drunk." One who was in his employ at the trading
post has said that Houston's life was marked by fits
of deep melancholy, which he would relieve by stupe-
fying indulgence in liquor ; after the effects of the
debauch had passed he would for a time be his ordinary cheerful self again. These fits of despondency
and excesses were the natural consequences of his
sense of degradation and failure in life, and showed
the stirrings of his better spirit, too strong and manly

to sink absolutely and hopelessly to the level of the border " squaw man." On one occasion Houston and his chief assistant quarreled, while under the influence of liquor, and the assistant challenged Houston. On being remonstrated with for accepting the challenge of an employee, Houston said that he had always treated him like a gentleman, and he was entitled to a gentleman's satisfaction if he considered himself injured. The duel took place, and several shots were exchanged, but the seconds had considerately failed to put any bullets in the pistols, and no one was injured. Houston had no children by his Indian wife. That he was sincerely attached to her was manifested by the fact that he sent for her to join him after his removal to Texas ; but she refused to leave her people, and died a few years afterward in the home which he had made.

Houston was justly regarded by the Cherokees as their sincere and efficient friend. He not only procured the removal of swindling agents, while living among them, but defended their rights by treaties when in power in Texas, and performed many valuable services in their behalf while a Senator of the United States. The delegations of the tribe were always welcome to his rooms in Washington, and he spent what were, doubtless, some of his pleasantest evenings, while they were seated around him on the floor in council and talk. His memory is still fresh among them, and his name is perpetuated as an honored patronymic like that of William Penn.

But from this scene of unworthy degradation he was summoned to take part in a noble and stirring drama, and to redeem his name and fame by services and achievements beyond even the brilliant promise of his early years.

CHAPTER V

THE vast territory of Texas, comprising 268,684 square miles, was very thinly peopled at the time of the beginning of the struggle for independence. The whole of the northern and the greater portion of the central part were still in the condition in which they were at the time of the arrival of La Salle on the shore of Matagorda Bay in 1685. This region was inhabited only by wandering tribes of Indians, some of them the native aborigines, Comanches, Wacos, Lipans and their congeners, and others fragments of the tribes, Cherokees, Choctaws, Delawares and Shawnees, who had been driven from their homes in the United States by the aggressions of the whites. Among the Indians were a few white hunters and trappers, scarcely less wild and uncivilized in their habits than the savages, the occasional wandering traders, who bartered ammunition and trinkets for furs at the risk of their lives, and the American and Mexican drovers, who chased and gathered in cavayards of the wild mustang ponies for the Louisiana and San Antonio markets. But permanent habitations there were none in all this vast region of prairie and forest, and the picket posts of civilization in the shape of settlers' cabins had not been planted beyond the boundaries of the empresario's colonies, and the sheltering timber of the principal streams. There were small towns in the interior, San Antonio, Nacogdoches, Goliad, and others, which dated from the time of the early Spanish colonization, or which had grown around the Missions established by the Franciscan friars for the conversion and civilization of the Indians; and there were seaports or landing places on the coast, Galveston, Brazoria, Velasco and Copano, which were the result of the necessity for sea communication for supplies and trade. There were agricultural colonies founded under grants of land from the Mexican government to empresarios or contractors, Austin's, De Witt's, De Leon's, and the Irish colony of McMullin and McGloire, of various degrees of strength and permanence, and others which were merely such in name, and were used for fraudulent speculation in land scrip, or merely the chimæras of over-sanguine projectors. In these colonies, and notably in that of Austin, were the germs of the Anglo-American occupation of Texas, and its conquest from the nominal domination of the Hispano-Mexicans.

In 1834 Colonel Juan Nepomuceno Almonte made a tour of inspection through Texas, by direction of the Mexican government, to report upon its population, trade, and general condition. Almonte was an officer of intelligence and good judgment. He was, according to tradition, the son of the patriot priest Moreles, the leader of the Mexican revolt against Spain, had been thoroughly educated in the United States, and was at that time thirty years of age, colonel and aid-de-camp to President Santa Anna. His report is the only statistical account of the condition of Texas at that period, and, although obviously imperfect, affords ground for reasonable estimate and conjecture.

Colonel Almonte estimated the total population of Texas at 36,300, of whom 21,000 were whites and negroes, and 15,300 Indians. It must be said, of course, that this estimate of the Indian population was the sheerest guess-work, and it might have been put at any merely arbitrary figure. Neither was there any means for an accurate census of the civilized population, and a variation of several thousands, either way, was quite possible. Texas at that time was divided into three departments, Bexar, Brazos, and Nacogdoches.

There were four municipalities or districts in Bexar, the western department, whose population was as follows: San Antonio, 2400; Goliad, 700; Victoria, 300; San Patricio, the Irish colony, 600. The population of Bexar, with the exception of the Irish colony, was exclusively Mexican, and it had diminished since the last report in 1806 from 6400 to 3400. There was but one school in the department, at San Antonio, and that was so miserably supported as to be practically of no value. There was but one priest in the whole region. The condition of the population of Bexar was evidently but little above barbarism, the people living by rude agriculture and their flocks and herds, and being less civilized and prosperous than under the Spanish dominion in the early part of the century. The whole export trade consisted of from 8000 to 10,000 skins and furs, and the imports were only a few supplies from New Orleans, exchanged for peltry at San Antonio.

The population of Brazos, the central department, which included the prosperous colony of Austin, was estimated at 8000, of whom 1000 were negroes, nominally only servants under the Mexican laws, but in reality slaves. The municipalities were San Felipe de Austin, the capital of the colony, with a population of 2500; Columbia, 2100; Matagorda, 1400; Gonzales, 900; Mina, 1100. The exports consisted of a yearly average of 5000 bales of cotton, returning, at New Orleans, $225,000; 50,000 skins, valued at $50,000; and a large quantity of beeves and other livestock driven to the market at Natchitoches, Louisiana, of which no estimate was given. The maize and other cereals were all consumed at home. The colonists owned large herds of cattle and droves of hogs, which fed wild on the prairie. There was but one school in the department, at Brazoria, with about forty pupils. The wealthier colonists sent their children to the United States to be educated, and "those, who

have not the advantages of fortune, care little for
the education of their sons, provided they can wield
the axe and cut down a tree, or kill a deer with dex-
terity."

The total population of Nacogdoches, the eastern
department, was estimated at 9900. It had four
municipalities, with the population as follows: Nachi-
doches, 3500; San Augustine, 2500; Liberty, 1000;
Johnsbury, 1000. The town of Anahuac had a population of 50; Bevil, 140; Tanaha, 100; Teran, 10.
In this department were about 1000 negroes, brought
by their masters from the United States. Colonization in Nacogdoches had not been prosperous, owing
to the fact that the empresarios, Burnett, Zavala, and
Vchlein, had sold their contracts to speculators in
New York and elsewhere, who made no attempt at the
settlement of immigrants, but simply disposed of the
land scrip to whomever they could persuade to buy
by means of flaming circulars and illusory promises.
There was a constant conflict of titles between the
immigrants and the original settlers or squatters, and
the consequences were very injurious to the growth
and prosperity of the colony. The trade of Nacogdoches was estimated at $470,000. The exports
consisted of 2000 bales of cotton, 40,000 skins, and
50,000 head of cattle. The imports were estimated
at $265,000.

The total trade of Texas for the year 1834, exports
and imports, was estimated at $1,400,000, which in-
cluded a contraband trade through the ports of Bra-

zoria, Matagorda and Copano, conjectured to amount
to $270,000. Says the report: " Money is very scarce
in Texas, not one in ten sales being made for cash.
Purchases are made on credit or by barter, which gives
the country the appearance of a continued fair."
Almonte declared Texas to be " the bravest of our
provinces," and urged retired army officers to capitalize
their pay and go and colonize the country. "There
they will find peace and industry, and that rest for
their old age, which, in all probability, they will not
find in the centre of the republic," — a remark which
indicated that Almonte had not formed a very accurate estimate of the prospects of an attempt to
Mexicanize Texas by colonization, however sound his
judgment of the prospects of tranquillity in the mother
country.

The real root and foundation of the prosperity and
growth of Texas was in the colony of Stephen F.
Austin on the Brazos.

The Mexican settlements in Bexar had none of the
elements of progress and civilization, and had rather
degenerated than advanced in the past half century.
It simply contributed an outlying and rural province
of Mexico, without the mineral riches and agricultural
development which had given wealth and a certain
amount of civilization to the central provinces.

The American settlements in Nacogdoches, although of older date than Austin's colony, had been
seriously injured by the fact that the " neutral
ground," which had existed beyond the Sabine be-

tween the boundaries of the United States and Mexico, had been the Alsatia of the criminal refugees of both countries, and the favorite retreat of the desperadoes of the Southwest. Once beyond the muddy waters of the Sabine, criminals were safe from all molestation, except at the hands of their fellows, and for many years they had dominated the country, making life and property unsafe for the travelers and settlers. Here were gathered the murderers and manslayers who had escaped from the hands of justice in the States, the bandits and robbers, banished members of gangs like that of the famous John A. Murrell which had exercised a reign of terror in Mississippi, fraudulent debtors who had chalked on their shutters the cabalistic letters " G. T. T." — Gone to Texas, — and the ruffians and desperadoes of every description who lived in an atmosphere of violence, and to whom all law was a mockery. These associates were equally lawless, if not equally criminal, and it was a society in which every one " fought for his own hand."

One of the notable and characteristic figures of this community was Colonel Martin Parmer, known as " The Ring Tailed Panther." Parmer had lived in Missouri in the Indian wilderness, among the Osages and Iowas, and his feats of savage daring and eccentricity were the gossip of the border. On one occasion he was said to have stood with a drawn knife over a savage named " Two Heart," who had devoured the heart of a white man he had killed, and compelled him to eat until he died of repletion. He sent fifty miles for a minister to preach a sermon over the body of a favorite bear dog. With all this he was a man of ability, had been a member of the Constitutional Convention of Missouri, and an efficient Indian agent.

The outlaws of the neutral ground organized themselves into bands, and fought over land titles and for political domination, and in 1826 commenced a war against the Mexican authorities under the leadership of Hayden Edwards, an empresario, whose contract had been annulled on account of the conflicts which had arisen between the claims of his colonists and the original Mexican inhabitants and squatters. This émeute, called " The Fredonian War," was easily suppressed, Austin and his colonists taking part with the Mexican authorities.

These troubles, the presence of a large body of Cherokee Indians, who had settled in the country under a concession of the Mexican government, and the difficulties arising from the sale of fraudulent and conflicting land titles, had been a serious drawback to the permanent and prosperous settlement of eastern Texas, which would naturally have been the first in growth, owing to its neighborhood to the United States. At this time it had recovered from the worst of its lawlessness, and was securing a better class of emigrants; but it was yet not attractive to the orderly and progressive colonists, such as had gathered under the government and direction of Austin.

Stephen F. Austin, who justly deserves the title given him by Houston, of " The Father of Texas," was born in Austinville, Virginia, in 1793. His father, Moses Austin, was a native of Durham, Connecticut, and had spent an enterprising and adventurous life in developing lead mines in Virginia and the Missouri Territory. His operations in the latter region proving financially unprofitable, he turned his attention toward Texas, of whose beauty and fertility he had heard much from explorers and Spanish traders. In 1820 he set out for Texas. He was at first coldly received by Governor Martinez of San Antonio, but by the aid of the Baron de Bastrop, a Prussian officer, who had served under Frederick the Great, and was then in the service of Mexico, he obtained a favorable hearing on his proposition to settle a colony of emigrants from the United States in Texas. Austin's petition was forwarded to the central government, and he returned home. On the route he was robbed and stripped by his fellow-travelers, and, after great exposure and privation, subsisting for twelve days on acorns and pecan nuts, he reached the cabin of a settler near the Sabine River. He reached home in safety, and commenced his preparations for removal to Texas; but his exposure and privations had weakened his vital forces, and he died from the effects of a cold in his fifty-seventh year, leaving his dying injunction to his son, Stephen, to carry out his project.

The response from Mexico was favorable. A concession was made for the settlement of three hundred families on the condition of their professing the Roman Catholic religion and promising fidelity to the Spanish government. The grants included 640 acres of land for each head of a family or single man, 320 acres for the wife, 160 acres for each child, and eighty acres for each slave. The premium to the empresario was five square leagues of grazing land and five labores (a labore consisting of 177 acres) for each one hundred families settled, the total number not to exceed 800. Austin visited the country for the purpose of exploration, and selected the country between the Brazos and the Colorado, then an uninhabited wilderness, as the site of his colony.

He returned to Louisiana, and advertised for emigrants. The terms and the adventure were attractive, and he set out with a considerable number of followers by land, having previously dispatched the schooner Lively to Matagorda Bay with supplies and agricultural implements. The schooner was lost, and the colony had to begin their settlement with only the means which they had brought with them.

In the mean time the revolution against Spain had been accomplished in Mexico. Austin was obliged to make the long and perilous journey of 1200 miles to the city of Mexico, which he accomplished on foot and in the disguise of a common soldier, in order to obtain a renewal of his grant. He obtained a renewal from the Emperor Iturbide, and was about to return home, when the revolution, headed by Santa

Anna, drove Iturbide from the throne, and he was
compelled to make another application to the Mexican
Cortes. In this he was also successful, and, in 1823,
after a year's absence, returned to his colony, which
had been nearly destroyed by the prolonged uncertainty and discouragement.

Austin renewed his efforts, and the settlers began
again to come in. There were the usual difficulties
and trials connected with a pioneer settlement. A
vessel with supplies was cast away, and another, having run aground, was plundered, and the crew massacred by the Carankawa Indians, a ferocious tribe of
the coast. The settlers had to import their seed-corn
from beyond the Sabine, or to buy it at San Antonio,
where it was scarce and dear. They were obliged to
live mainly on wild game, and, the deer and bears
being scarce, on account of the drought and failure of
the mart, they were reduced to killing the wild horses
for food. The women as well as the men were clad
in buckskin garments, and the advent of a stray pack-
peddler, with a few yards of flowered calico at fifty
cents per yard, was like the arrival of a ship with
a cargo of silks in an eastern port. The men were
engaged in building cabins and making clearings,
hewing down the trees and cutting the cane brakes.
In the blackened fields, after the burning of the
brush, they planted corn in holes made with sharp-
ened sticks. While at work they kept guard against
the Indians, who roved about stealing the stock, at
times making a night attack upon a cabin, or mur-

dering and scalping some solitary herdsman or traveler. The Mexicans did nothing to protect or govern
the colony. The settlers, with the Anglo-Saxon instinct for law and order, created a code of laws for
the administration of justice and the settlement of
civil disputes. The land titles were duly recorded,
and a local militia was organized. Austin was the
supreme authority, the judge and commandant, and
ruled the colony with fatherly kindness and practical
sagacity, like a tribal patriarch.

The characters of the settlers of Austin's colony
were of a much higher type than those of the desperate and criminal refugees in the eastern section.
They were sturdy and honest, the best representatives
of the hardy adventurers who have led the van of
civilization in its march across the American continent, and founded stable, orderly, and prosperous
communities. They were wild and adventurous in
spirit, with an irresistible longing for the life of the
wilderness, for the excitement of danger, and the
delight of vigorous achievement. To them the free
air of the prairie and the breath of the forest were like
the salt scent of the sea-breeze to the ancient viking.
Their blood was warm and flamed rapidly into combat; but they were kindly, hospitable, honest, and
above all things manly. There was no place among
them for the cowardly vices of an artificial society.
There is a universal testimony as to their honesty
and hospitality. Even a prejudiced observer, like
Charles Hooten, an English author of some tempo-

rary note, who wrote a vituperative book about Texas
in 1840, testifies that it was the common custom
to leave the doors unfastened when the house was
empty, and that seldom or never was anything disturbed. So late as after the close of the Mexican
war, Major Hutter, the United States paymaster,
detailed to settle the claims of the Texas soldiers,
traveled through the country with half a million
dollars in gold in his ambulance, without an escort, and met with no interruption or molestation.
The fact of his journey was well known, and the
places where he would pay the claimants were announced in the newspapers, so that robbers could
have had every opportunity to waylay him, while
there were often places on his route where the houses
were from fifteen to twenty miles apart. No man
took another's note for a loan, the verbal promise
of payment being considered sufficient, and all the
transactions of business were conducted on a fully
warranted trust in the general integrity. Even those
who had left the States on account of pecuniary failure or dishonesty came under the influence of the
standard of honesty about them, and in some instances
remitted the sums due to their distant creditors.
This was the case with Captain Moseley Baker, one
of the heroes of San Jacinto, who had fled from the
United States on account of a forgery, and who
afterward sent back the amount to the individuals
who had lost by it. There were some thefts and
depredations upon the colony by wandering rascals

and brigands, but they were dealt with very sternly and summarily. The marauders, when caught, were at first tied and whipped, but, this not proving effectual, recourse was had to Austin for advice. He said that as there were no courts of justice or jails in the colony, they had better follow the marauders, recover the property, but not bring back any of the thieves. The hint was taken. The next time there was a theft the robbers were followed, shot, and the head of one of them cut off and stuck on a pole by the roadside as a significant warning. The justice of Judge Lynch was served out for those crimes which affected the safety of the property, or outraged the sense of propriety in the community, while those which were merely the results of personal quarrel, were left to the arbitrament of the encounter.

As for hospitality, it was more than an obligation, it was an impulse. The saying, "The latchstring hangs out," was more than a proverb, it was a fact of common life. The traveler who rode up to the front fence was instantly invited to alight. His horse was staked out or hoppled to feed on the prairie grass, and the visitor sat down to exchange the news with his host. The coffee-mill was set going, if there were any of the precious grains in the house, and the hopper in the hollowed log to grinding the corn. The venison or bear meat was put on the coals, and the ash-cake baked. After the meal and the evening pipe, the visitor stretched himself on a buffalo robe on the floor with the members of the family, and slept the sleep of health and fatigue. In the morning the response to any inquiry as to the charge was, " You can pay me by coming again." The story that a certain hospitable settler used to waylay travelers on the road, and compel them to visit him at the muzzle of a double-barreled shot-gun, was only a humorous exaggeration of the instinct for hospitality which characterized the community. The visitor was a living newspaper, who brought the only news obtainable, and was a welcome relief to the monotony and loneliness of the wilderness. When times had changed and the new comers showed themselves more churlish, an old traveler in Texas said that he used to find his quarters for the night by inquiring of the man of the house, " How long have you been in this country? " If the answer was a considerable number of years, or that he " disremembered " just how long it was, the traveler used to alight sure of a hearty welcome.

These men, who were the early settlers of Texas, had in many instances traveled more than a thousand miles in ox-teams, from Missouri or beyond the Mississippi River, amid all the perils and hardships of the wilderness, crossing great tracts of prairie and forest, without a road or trail to mark the way, rafting their teams over swollen streams and surmounting all natural obstacles. They had sometimes been two or three years on the way, halting for a season to raise a crop of corn, and moving on when it was harvested. Children were born in the camps, and the dead were buried by the roadside, with no memorial but a pile of

rocks to preserve the body from being dug up by the
wild beasts. The ready rifle supplied game at every
halting-place, and insured safety from the wandering
savages. Cold and heat made no impression on their
hardened frames, and the accidents to flesh and limb
were treated with a rough and handy surgery. There
were some that perished. The blood-stained ashes of
the camp-fire and the plundered wagon showed where
the wanderers had been swooped upon by an over-
powering band of savages, and the various perils of
flood and field counted their victims. But the survivors were of the strongest type of manhood, hardened,
by every trial and peril, to the perfection of courage,
helpfulness and endurance, the fit kings of the wilderness and founders of great States.

The fascination of the life was irresistible to those
under its sway, and took possession of the ministers
and missionaries as well as the rough frontiersmen.
They fought the Indians, herded stock, and cultivated
the ground, when not preaching at neighborhood gath-
erings in the cabins or building their own churches of
logs or stone, and the inspired zeal with which they
pursued their sacred calling was stimulated by the
passion for the wild and free life of danger and adventure, and the intoxicating breath of the wilderness.
Men like the Rev. Z. N. Morrell, the Baptist "cane-
brake preacher," and the Abbé Domenech, the Catholic missionary, have testified to this in their written
volumes of reminiscences, and it was well-nigh universal with their class.

These pioneers wanted elbow-room and untainted air, and, like Daniel Boone, were uneasy when the smoke of a neighbor's chimney could be seen from their own cabin door. No age could tame their spirit of adventure, and the route of their pioneering sometimes extended half·across the continent. There is a story of a Tennessee planter, who removed from his native State to the Red River, from the Red River to Nacogdoches, from Nacogdoches to the Brazos, and from the Brazos to the Colorado. When seen at his last location by a friend he complained of being crowded, and said that he must move again. The settlements on the Colorado were then many miles apart, and the settler was in his eighty-fifth year.

Austin's colony continued to increase, and for a number of years was left undisturbed by the Mexican government, which was going through all the turmoils of the repeated revolutions which followed the overthrow of the Spanish domination. The ordinance requiring the colonists to profess the Catholic Apostolic religion remained a dead letter. No priests were sent into the country, and marriages were performed by the persons joining hands before the alcalde, and agreeing to live together as man and wife. Slaves were introduced under a special clause in Austin's contract, although slavery was not recognized by the Mexican laws. The colonists were exempt from taxation for a term of six years, and they had only to subdue the wilderness and fight the marauding Indians.

But this state of things could not last. It was inevitable that the progress of the American colony should arouse the jealousy of the Mexicans, and that the conflict of the antagonistic races for supremacy should begin. By the constitution of 1824, which made Mexico a republic, the territory of Texas was united with the province of Coahuila, under the title of " The State of Coahuila and Texas," and the capital established at Saltillo, five hundred miles from the Texan colony. The two provinces had nothing in common, the one being inhabited by a Mexican and the other by an American population. The government of the State was entirely in the hands of the Mexicans, the Texan representatives in the provincial assembly being limited to two. This created great dissatisfaction among the Texans, and the signs of a growing spirit of interference on the part of the Mexican government caused a feeling of uneasiness and resentment. The jealousy of the Mexican government in regard to the American occupation of Texas was still farther aroused by the proposition on the part of the United States for the purchase of the territory, which was made by the Administration of President Adams, and renewed by that of President Jackson.

In 1830, Anastasio Bustamente, the Vice-President of Mexico, organized a revolution and drove the President Guerrero from power. Bustamente was a sanguinary tyrant, and represented the centralist and anti-liberal party. He issued decrees, prohibiting farther immigration from the United States, forbidding the introduction of any more slaves, and establishing custom-houses at San Antonio, Nacogdoches, Copano, Velasco and Brazoria for the collection of imposts upon the trade. He also began preparations by making Texas a penal colony, by sending a thousand soldiers, mostly criminals and convicts, to stations in the country.

Bustamente's military commandants soon made themselves obnoxious by their tyranny and impositions. One Colonel John Davis Bradburn, a renegade Virginian, in command of the port of Anahuac at the head of Galveston Bay, proclaimed martial law, released slaves, arrested citizens, and exercised the annoying authority of a petty tyrant. At length all the ports were closed except that at Anahuac, which was very inconvenient for the settlers, as it was outside the limits of Austin's colony, and inaccessible to vessels drawing over six feet of water. An indignation meeting was held at Brazoria, and a committee of citizens appointed to procure a revocation of the order from Bradburn. This, after some equivocation and delay, was granted under the threat of armed resistance. Bradburn next sent a file of soldiers to arrest a number of citizens prominent in the insurrectionary movement. Among them was William B. Travis, the future hero of the Alamo, and Monroe Edwards, an extraordinary individual, who had been engaged in smuggling slaves landed from Africa on the Texas coast into Louisiana. He afterward figured as an abolitionist advocate in England, and, after a notorious and successful criminal career in Europe and the United States, was convicted of forgery and sentenced to Sing Sing prison, where he died in 1847. The citizens were aroused to resist the arrest, and a force was gathered for the purpose of attacking the fort at Anahuac. At this juncture the news arrived that Santa Anna had organized a revolt against Bustamente, and that another revolution was in progress in Mexico. Colonel Bradburn was deprived of his command by Colonel Piedras, the commandant of Nacogdoches, and retired to the United States.

On July 25 an attack was made on the fort at Velasco by a force of one hundred and twenty-five Texans under the command of Colonel John Austin. A small cannon was placed on a schooner and directed against the fort, and the Texan riflemen, behind a palisade of planks which had been erected during the night, picked off every Mexican soldier who showed himself above the walls. Colonel Ugartchea, who commanded the fort, signalized himself by an act of reckless bravery in standing at his full height upon the walls under fire. This so moved the admiration of the Texans that they did not shoot him. The fort was surrendered after a loss of thirty-five men on the part of the Mexicans, and eight on the part of the Texans. In a short time afterward, Colonel Mexia, an emissary of Santa Anna, arrived with four vessels at the mouth of the Brazos, having with him Stephen F. Austin, the Texan member of the Mexican Congress. Mexia's purpose was to obtain the adhesion of Texas to the revolutionary movement of Sànta Anna, and, after a meeting at San Felipe, it was decided that the troops should be withdrawn from the country. Colonel Piedras, the commandant at Nacogdoches, refused to give his adhesion to the party of Santa Anna, and, after a sharp skirmish in the town, was pursued to the banks of the Angelina River, where he gave up his command, the troops declaring in favor of Santa Anna. The garrison at San Antonio also joined the revolutionary party, and the troops all took their departure for Mexico to join in the warfare against Bustamente. The inhabitants of Texas gave their approval and adhesion to Santa Anna, who had announced himself in favor of the restoration of the Liberal Constitution of 1824, and there was a belief that, with his success, the troubles would be ended, and that Texas would enjoy peace and the privileges of self-government as one of the States of the Republic of Mexico.

CHAPTER VI

It is not probable that Houston's determination
to go to Texas was the result of any sudden purpose.
The future of that vast domain and the desire to
acquire it from the Mexicans had undoubtedly had a
place in his mind, as it had in those of other restless
and ambitious spirits in the United States and in the
schemes of the Federal Government. The story told
by a Dr. Robert Mayo, of Washington, in 1830, and
by him communicated to President Jackson, that
Houston had confided to him a scheme for the organization of an expedition to wrest Texas from the feeble
hands of Mexico, and that recruiting offices had been
established in the eastern cities, under the direction
of one Hunter, a discharged cadet from West Point,
must be regarded as an invention. Jackson satisfied
himself by inquiry that no such scheme was on foot.
Recruiting offices could not have been opened in the
eastern cities without the knowledge of the authorities, and the story evidently grew out of that element
of mystery and conjecture, which accompanied Houston's sensational disappearance into the wilderness.
At the same time some indefinite idea of an ambitious

future in connection with Texas must have crossed his mind in the intervals in which his better spirit stirred to lift him out of the degradation of Indian savagery. According to the Rev. Z. N. Morrell he had expressed a purpose to one Deacon McIntosh, of Nashville, to establish "a two-horse republic" in Texas, and to be its first president, as early as in 1830. There are letters which show that such a scheme was not only in his own mind, but in those of his friends, during his Indian exile.

It was in the nature of things that the settlement of Texas by colonists from the United States should create the belief that the country would come into their possession as an independent community, if not as a part of the Union, and restless and enterprising adventurers had been attracted there by more ambitious schemes than those of the agricultural colonists. Among those already in Texas were men of ability and energy, who were afterward distinguished in its military and political history. There was David G. Burnet of New Jersey, afterward the provisional president of the Republic, who had been a subordinate officer in Con Francisco de Miranda's unfortunate expedition for the capture of Venezuela in 1806, and who was at that time the nominal empresario of a grant of land in northeastern Texas; Dr. Branch T. Archer, of Virginia, the president of the revolutionary consultation of Texas citizens, who had intended to join Burr's expedition for the founding of an empire in the Southwest, and had fled to Texas after killing his antagonist in a duel; Thomas J. Chambers, the first chief justice of the State of Coahuila and Texas, who had made a study of Spanish laws and customs, and was already a man of influence in Mexican affairs; the brothers James and Rezin P. Bowie, of Louisiana, forceful and vigorous adventurers, who had been engaged in smuggling African slaves from the coast into the United States; Henry Smith, of Kentucky, the first provisional governor and Secretary of the Treasury under Houston; Thomas J. Rusk, of South Carolina, a youthful protégé of John C. Calhoun, afterward Secretary of War, commander of the Texan army, Chief Justice and Senator of the United States, a man of sound judgment, great force of character, and commanding ability; the brothers William H. and John A. Wharton, of Virginia, the first, President of the Convention which declared the provisional independence of Texas, and the second, a brilliant soldier at San Jacinto and Secretary of the Navy. These and many others were of a high order of ability, and ready to take the lead in developing the political as well as the material interests of the colony, and in organizing resistance against the aggressions of the Mexican government. In most instances it is probable they had from the first a purpose to bring about the independence of the country. The expectation that there would be a struggle with Mexico existed at an early day among the colonists, and at a meeting at Nacogdoches in 1832 it was proposed to invite General Sam Houston or General

William Carroll, of Tennessee, to settle among them, and take the lead in any revolutionary movement.

Houston went to Texas with a commission from President Jackson to arrange treaties with the Comanches and other wild tribes for the protection of the American traders and settlers on the border, and also to endeavor to persuade those Indians who had left the United States and settled in Texas to return. There was, in all probability, also a secret understanding that he was to examine into the condition of the country as to the power of the people to throw off the Mexican authority, and as to the feeling of the American colonists in regard to annexation to the United States. He was furnished with a passport from the War Department, recommending him to the friendship and good will of all the Indian tribes whose territories he should visit. He also had some private business as an agent of land claimants.

There are various stories told of the incidents of Houston's departure from the Indian Territory and journey to Texas. One, told by Major Elias Rector, known in the Southwest as "The Fine Arkansas Gentleman," is that Houston, a Major Arnold Harris, and himself traveled together through southeastern Arkansas. Houston was mounted on a little Indian pony very disproportionate to his stature. The constant subject of Houston's conversation was the ignoble appearance he would make on such an animal, and he earnestly appealed to Harris to exchange his fine large horse for it. Said he, —

"This d——d bob-tailed pony is a disgrace. He is continually fighting the flies, and has no means of protecting himself, and his kicks and contortions render his rider ridiculous. I shall be the laughter of all Mexico. I require a steed with his natural weapon, a flowing tail, that he may defend himself against his enemies as his master has done. Harris, you must trade."

The terms of the exchange were finally made, and Houston recovered his dignity and good humor as the possessor of the broom-tailed mare. When they came to part, Rector took a razor from his saddle-bags and presented it to Houston. Houston said, —

"Major Rector, this is apparently a gift of little value, but it is an inestimable testimony of the friendship which has lasted many years, and proved steadfast under the blasts of calumny and injustice. Good-by. God bless you. When next you see this razor it shall be shaving the President of a Republic, by G—d!"

Houston left the Indian Territory and crossed the Red River on the 10th of December, 1832. He went first to Nacogdoches, and from there to San Felipe, where he failed to meet Austin, who was absent. He journeyed from San Felipe to San Antonio in company with Colonel James Bowie, then a prominent figure in Texas affairs, and was by him introduced to Veramendi, the Vice-Governor of the State, Bowie's father-in-law, and to Ruiz, the Mexican commandant. Houston was cordially received by the

Mexican authorities, and by their consent held a council with the Comanche chiefs, distributed medals among them, and made arrangements to have them send a delegation to Fort Gibson to meet commissioners from the United States. This arrangement was not carried out by the Indians, owing to the jealousy of the Mexican officials, who apprehended the results of American influence on the tribes in their territory. Houston returned by way of San Felipe, where he met Austin. At Nacogdoches he was invited by the citizens to take up his residence among them, and promised to do so. He proceeded to Natchitoches, Louisiana, from whence he sent a report of his council with the Comanches to the War Department, and addressed the following letter to President Jackson, in which can be read the answer in regard to his secret mission to Texas: —

NATCHITOCHES, LA., *February* 13, 1833.
GENERAL JACKSON:

Dear Sir, — Having been as far as Bexar, in the province of Texas, where I had an interview with the Comanche Indians, I am in possession of some information, which will doubtless be interesting to you, and may be calculated to forward your views, if you should entertain any, touching the acquisition of Texas by the United States government. That such a measure is desired by nineteen twentieths of the population of the province, I cannot doubt. They are now without laws to govern or protect them.

Mexico is involved in civil war. The Federal Constitution has never been in operation. The Government is essentially despotic, and must be so for years to come. The rulers have not honesty, and the people have not intelligence. The people of Texas are determined to form a state government, and separate from Coahuila, and unless Mexico is soon restored to order, and the Constitution revived and reënacted, the province of Texas will remain separate from the Confederacy of Mexico. She has already beaten and repelled all the troops of Mexico from her soil, nor will she permit them to return. Her want of money, taken in connection with the course which Texas *must and will adopt*, will render the transfer of Texas to some power inevitable, and, if the United States does not press for it, England will most assuredly obtain it by some means. Now is a very important crisis for Texas. As relates to her future prosperity and safety, as well as to the relations which it is to bear to the United States, it is now in the most favorable attitude, perhaps, which it can be, to obtain it on fair terms. England is pressing her suit for it, but its citizens will resist, if any transfer is made of them to any power but the United States. I have traveled nearly five hundred miles across Texas, and am now enabled to judge pretty correctly of the soil and resources of the country, and I have no hesitancy in pronouncing it the finest country, for its extent, upon the globe; for the greater portion of it is richer and more healthy than West Tennessee. There can be

no doubt that the country, east of the River Grand of
the North, would sustain a population of ten millions
of souls.) My opinion is that Texas, by her members
in Convention, will, by the 1st of April, declare all
that country as Texas proper, and form a State Constitution. I expect to be present at the Convention,
and will apprise you of the course adopted, as soon
as the members have taken a final action. It is probable that I may make Texas my abiding-place. In
adopting this course *I will never forget* the country
of my birth. I will notify from this point the Commissioners of the Indians at Fort Gibson of my success, which will reach you through the War Department. I have, with much pride and inexpressible
satisfaction, seen your proclamation, touching the
nullifiers of the South and their "peaceful remedies."
God grant that you may save the Union! It does
seem to me that it is reserved for you, and you alone,
to render to millions so great a blessing. I hear all
voices commend your course, even in Texas, where
is felt the greatest interest for the preservation of
the Republic. Permit me to tender you my sincere
thanks, felicitations, and most earnest solicitation for
your health and happiness, and your future glory,
connected with the prosperity of the Union.

> Your friend, and obedient servant,
> SAM HOUSTON.

Houston returned to Nacogdoches, and was undoubtedly busy in consultation with the men who

were scheming for the acquisition of Texas from
Mexico. One G. W. Featherstonehaugh, an English
traveler, came across him in the little village of
Washington at this time. Says he, in his book, "A
Journey through the Slave States:" —

"I was not desirous of remaining long at this
place. General Houston was here, leading a mysterious sort of a life, shut up in a small tavern, seeing
nobody by day, and sitting up all night. The world
gave him credit for passing his waking hours in the
study of *trente et quarante* and *sept à lever*, but I
had been in communication with too many persons of
late, and had seen too much passing before my eyes
to be ignorant that the little place was the rendezvous where a much deeper game than faro or *rouge
et noir* was being played. There were many persons at the time in the village from the States lying
adjacent to the Mississippi, under the pretense of
purchasing government lands, but whose real object
was to encourage the settlers in Texas to throw off
their allegiance to the Mexican government."

The war between Santa Anna and Bustamente was
terminated by a compromise in which both generals
united to place President Pedraza, who had been
elected in 1828 and deposed, in nominal power.
Santa Anna retired to his princely estate, Manga del
Clavo, near Vera Cruz, as was his custom, to await
the disturbances under a weak government which
would again enable him to appear as the savior of
the state. Bustamente, having disbanded his troops,

was banished at the instigation of Santa Anna.
Pedraza's term having expired, Santa Anna was
elected President of the Republic without opposition
at the election on the 29th of March, 1833, and took
his seat on the 16th of May following. In his inaugural address he declared himself in favor of the
Liberal Constitution of 1824, and promised that his
administration, "like his own character," should be
mild and tolerant.

Antonio Lopez de Santa Anna was one of the most
remarkable figures who have appeared in the history
of this continent, and the vicissitudes of his prolonged
career included every variety of fortune and adventure. His head was constantly appearing above the
troubled waters of Mexican politics, and the civil
wars which were synonymous with them, from the
expulsion of the Spaniards in 1821 to the downfall
of Maximilian's empire in 1866. He was born in
Jalapa, February 21, 1795, and entered the army at
an early age. He was a lieutenant-colonel in the
Spanish service when he joined with Iturbide in the
revolution, and was made a brigadier-general and
commandant of Vera Cruz. In 1822 he organized
the revolt which overthrew Iturbide, and in 1828 deposed Pedraza and put Guerrero in his place. In
1829 he defeated and captured a division of Spanish
troops under General Barradas, who had landed at
Tampico for the purpose of repossessing the country.
In 1832 he outmanœuvred Bustamente, who had
usurped the presidency, and banished him. He was

elected President in 1833, abolished the Congress, and virtually made himself dictator. His defeat and imprisonment in Texas destroyed his influence, until it was restored by his attack upon the French in Vera Cruz in 1838, in which he lost a leg. He was again President, or the governing power behind the nominal occupant of the chair, from 1841 to 1844, when there was a revolution against him, and he went into banishment at Havana. From this he was recalled to be President and commander-in-chief of the army in the war between Mexico and the United States. After his series of defeats by Generals Taylor and Scott, he abandoned his office and retired from the country to Jamaica. Another revolution in 1852 recalled him to power, and in 1855 he was again driven into exile. He returned to Mexico when the French troops invaded the country in 1863, and was Grand Marshal of the Empire under Maximilian. He was banished by Marshal Bazaine for issuing proclamations and conspiring against the empire, and after its downfall was captured while attempting to make a landing in the country, and sentenced to death, but was pardoned by President Juarez on condition of leaving the country. In 1872 a general amnesty enabled him to return to Mexico, and he survived in harmless imbecility and contempt until the 20th of June, 1876. Santa Anna was a man of restless energy and ambition, and displayed considerable ability both as an administrator and a military commander. He lost his head in the Texas campaign, but he was invariably successful in the Mexican civil wars, and in the battles with the American armies showed a good deal of strategic skill. He was utterly unscrupulous and treacherous, and betrayed every party and every ally that put trust in him. He was vindictive and cruel even beyond the barbarous habits of Mexican warfare, and never spared a defeated enemy. In habits and tastes he was a thorough Mexican, his favorite amusements being cock-fighting and card-playing, and his personal vices were gross and notorious. In personal appearance he was about five feet five inches in height, of spare form, dark complexion, and with what the English traveler, Ruxton, described as "an Old Bailey countenance." But his manners were pleasing and insinuating when he chose to make them so, and his force of character was manifested in his speech and gesture. Up to the time of the invasion of Texas he had been successful in all his battles and schemes of ambition, and arrogated to himself the title of the "Napoleon of the West."

The legislature of the State of Coahuila and Texas had passed a law forbidding the further settlement of American colonists, and limiting future grants to Mexicans. This and the general inconvenience and disorganization resulting from the enforced union of the two provinces determined the colonists in Texas to demand the organization of the territory into a State by itself. They elected delegates to a Convention for this purpose, and it met at San Felipe on April 1, 1833. Houston was one of the delegates from Nacogdoches. William H. Wharton was elected President, and committees were appointed to frame a state Constitution, and draw up a memorial to the Mexican Congress setting forth the reasons why a separation from Coahuila was asked for. Houston was chairman of the committee to frame a Constitution. The one reported was formed on the model of those of the States of the Union. It contained provisions for a trial by jury, the writ of habeas corpus, the right of petition, the freedom of the press, universal suffrage, and other essentials of a republican form of government. On the subject of the freedom of religion the Constitution was silent. Resolutions offered by Burnet, and supported by Houston, condemning and prohibiting the African slave trade, which had been carried on through the ports of Texas since the time of the settlement of the pirate Lafitte at Galveston, were adopted by the Convention. A debate arose on the question of incorporating banking institutions. This was opposed by Houston, on the ground that it was unwise in itself and calculated to prejudice the Mexican government against the acceptance of the Constitution. Houston prevailed, and a clause was inserted in the Constitution prohibiting the creation of any banking institution for the term of ninety-nine years. An able memorial was drawn up by Burnet, setting forth the reasons why Texas was entitled to an independent organization; Stephen F. Austin, William H. Wharton, and James B. Miller were appointed delegates to present the petition to the Mexican Congress; and the Convention adjourned after a session of fifteen days.

Austin was the only one of the delegates who went to Mexico. When he arrived at the capital, he found that Gomez Farias, the Vice-President under Santa Anna, was exercising the executive power, Santa Anna having retired in one of his mysterious seclusions at Manga del Clavo. Great confusion prevailed in the Mexican government. The finances were disorganized, and Congress, under the instigation of Farias, had passed laws disbanding a portion of the army and levying taxes on the property of the church. These caused great dissatisfaction among two powerful elements in the State, and revolutionary movements, probably instigated by Santa Anna, were continually breaking out in the capital and in the provinces. Austin could get no hearing on his petition, and, in despair of obtaining any action, he wrote, on the 2d of October, 1833, to the municipal council of Bexar, recommending that all the districts in Texas should unite, and organize a State in accordance with the provisions of the Constitution of 1824, without waiting for the sanction of the Mexican Congress. In the mean time Austin had obtained the abrogation of the law, passed by the Coahuila legislature, prohibiting immigration from the United States, and started to return home. But his letter to the municipality of Bexar had been sent to Vice-

President Farias, who considered it treasonable, and had Austin intercepted and arrested at Saltillo. Austin was taken back to the city of Mexico, and imprisoned in one of the dungeons of the old Inquisition, where he was treated with great rigor, and denied the use of books or writing materials.

On the 13th of May, 1834, Santa Anna reappeared from his seclusion, and resumed his office as President. He dismissed the Congress, and promulgated a "Plan," which is the Mexican phrase for an alteration in the form of government, by which the laws for the taxation of church property and the banishment of monarchists were abolished, and a special Congress called to frame a new Constitution. Santa Anna released Austin from his dungeon, and professed great friendliness to him. But he was still detained at the capital, while the charges against him were transferred from one court to another with the obvious purpose of delaying his return. In the mean time the legislature of Coahuila and Texas had been disposing of enormous tracts of land at a nominal price, under the pretext of providing a fund for the payment of troops to repress the Indian raids; and a quarrel, followed by an émeute, had arisen over the removal of the provincial capital from Saltillo to Monclova. On the 5th of October, 1834, Santa Anna called a council, consisting of the four Secretaries of State, the representatives of Coahuila and Texas, Austin, and Lorenzo de Zavala, Governor of the province of Mexico, to take into consideration the question in dispute, and the petition of Texas for a separate organization. Santa Anna decided that Texas could not be separated from Coahuila, as there was no provision in the Constitution authorizing such actions, but held out hopes that it might be organized as a Territory. He, however, ordered a new election for Governor and Legislature, and Austin wrote advising the people of Texas to accept the decision. Austin was satisfied, or professed to be, with Santa Anna's promises of liberal treatment to the Texan colonists; but, as he was still detained as a prisoner, it is possible that he expected that his correspondence would be opened and examined. The people of Texas were at once alarmed and angered at the arrest and imprisonment of Austin. A meeting was held at San Felipe to protest against it, but the petition for his release had no effect.

There were some abortive attempts at insurrectionary movements in Bexar and San Felipe during the fall of 1834, while Austin was imprisoned. But they were discouraged, as premature and jeopardizing Austin's safety, by the Central Committee appointed by the April Convention, and came to nothing. In the mean time the subservient Mexican Congress was carrying out the dictatorial purposes of Santa Anna. The province of Zacatecas, which had not acquiesced in the revolution, was declared to be in a state of rebellion, and Vice-President Farias, who was a sincere republican, was banished. The most important action, and one which made a revolution in Texas

inevitable was the passage of a decree reducing the
number of the militia to one for every five hundred
inhabitants, and ordering the rest to give up their
arms. The arms of the Texans at that period were
a part of their daily means of existence, as well as
the protection of their lives and property, and to take
them from the people would be to deprive them of
an essential aid to their support, as well as to leave
them and their families at the mercy of the marauding Indians. There could be but one answer in such
a community to a demand for the surrender of its
arms, and the refusal would be justified by the fun-
damental law of self-preservation.

The legislative and executive government of the
State of Coahuila and Texas was in a condition of
anarchy. Augustin Viesca, a republican, had been
elected Governor, but the people of Saltillo, angry at
the removal of the capital to Monclova, had declared
in favor of Santa Anna and raised the standard of
revolt. The legislature had sold another large tract
of Texas land at the price of two cents per acre, and,
although professing to be liberal toward the American colonists, had done nothing for their government
or protection. Santa Anna advanced at the head of
an army for the subjugation of the rebellious province of Zacatecas. On the 11th of May, 1834, a
bloody and decisive battle was fought on the plain of
Guadelupe between the army of Santa Anna and that
of Don Francisco Garcia, the Governor of Zacatecas.
The latter was routed with great slaughter, and the

city of Zacatecas given up to pillage. After having subjugated Zacatecas, Santa Anna returned to the capital, leaving behind him General Martin Perfecto de Cos, his brother-in-law, to regulate matters in Coahuila. Governor Viesca fled to Bexar, but afterward returned to Coahuila and was captured by the troops of Cos. Viesca, and with him Colonel Benjamin F. Milam, a Texan empresario, who had taken part in the brilliant and daring expedition of Xavier Mina against the Spanish government of Mexico in 1817, were sent as prisoners into the interior. The legislature of Coahuila was dispersed by Cos.

These events deprived the colonists in Texas of even the semblance of a government, and they organized themselves into committees of safety for protection against the Indians, who had become very troublesome, and had attacked and murdered a party of traders near Gonzales. These committees of safety had no design of resistance to the Mexican authorities, but there was an element among the colonists in favor of an immediate movement for independence. In June a meeting was held at San Felipe, at which resolutions were adopted in a war spirit, and an address was issued by R. M. Williamson, known as "Three-Legged Willie," calling upon the people to arouse themselves to resistance, and declaring that "Our country, our liberty, and our lives are all involved in the present contest between the State and the military." Early in the same month, William B. Travis, at the head of a party of fifty colonists, made a descent upon the post at Anahuac, commanded by Captain Tenorio, and disarmed and drove out the soldiers. This act was disavowed by the municipal council of Liberty, and Captain Tenorio and his soldiers were forwarded to Bexar by the citizens of San Felipe. Various attempts were made by representatives of the peace party to arrange terms of conciliation with General Cos, and two commissioners, Edward Gritton and D. C. Barrett, were appointed to wait on him for that purpose. Cos professed liberal and pacific intentions, but, in the mean time, dispatches from him to the commandant at Anahuac, announcing the departure of troops from Mexico "to regulate matters" in Texas, had been intercepted. Early in July, Lorenzo de Zavala, a prominent Mexican republican, who had been governor of the province and city of Mexico, and ambassador to France, arrived in Texas. He had refused to acquiesce in the despotic movements of Santa Anna, and fled to escape proscription. An order was at once sent to Colonel Ugartchea, in command at Bexar, for the arrest of Zavala, and also Travis, Williamson, Johnson, and other leaders of the war party. Ugartchea's requisition for the arrests was refused or evaded by the civil authorities, and, pending the abortive communications of the peace commissioners with General Cos, no attempt was made to capture them by military force. The order for the arrests caused great excitement among the colonists, and greatly stimulated the war feeling. At a meeting at San Augustine resolutions were introduced by Houston, and adopted, declaring that the arrest of Governor Viesca and the intended introduction of the military were evidences of tyranny and a violation of the terms on which the colonists had been invited to Texas. They also provided for the appointment of a committee of safety, the organization of the militia, and for treaties of alliance with the neighboring Indians. It was also declared that those who should desert the country in the crisis should forfeit their lands. Houston and Rusk visited the Indians, and secured their alliance by promising that the surveyors should make no more marks on their lands. Further trouble had occurred on the coast. After the ejection of Captain Tenorio and his troops from Anahuac, Santa Anna sent Captain T. M. Thompson, an Englishman known as "Mexican" Thompson, in the schooner Correo to collect the revenue. Thompson, who was a desperado of buccaneering proclivities, conducted himself in a very high-handed manner. He captured the American brig Tremont, with a supply of goods for the Texas trade, and attempted to seize the schooner San Felipe, Captain Hurd, but was beaten off. Subsequently the Correo was captured by the San Felipe and the small steamer Laura, and Thompson was taken to New Orleans, where he was tried for piracy.

Early in September, Stephen F. Austin returned to Texas, after more than two years' detention in Mexico. He was released by Santa Anna, with strong protestations of friendship for himself and the people of Texas. Austin's arrival caused great rejoicing in his colony, and he was given a public dinner at Brazoria, at which he addressed a gathering of more than a thousand citizens on the condition of affairs. His speech was moderate in tone, and repeated Santa Anna's professions of good will toward the people of Texas. But it declared that liberal institutions were being overthrown in Mexico, and a centralized and despotic government established, and recommended the calling of a consultation of the people of Texas to "decide what representations ought to be made to the general government, and what ought to be done in the future." The moderation as well as the strength of Austin's character gave unity and confidence to the people, and hereafter public sentiment was organized into a harmonious and definite form. Every one realized that a contest was inevitable, and the peace party gave way to that in favor of resistance. On September 13, a circular was issued by Austin, representing the committee of San Felipe, recommending the election of delegates to a General Consultation, and the organization and equipment of military companies.. It declared that the peace negotiations with General Cos were useless. It concluded with the emphatic words, "War is our only resource. There is no other remedy. We must defend our rights, ourselves, and our country by force of arms." About the middle of September, General Cos had landed at Copano and started to march to Bexar with five hundred troops.

On the 2d of October occurred the first clash of
arms in the war of independence. In accordance
with the decree for the disarmament of the Texans,
Colonel Ugartchea, in command of the troops at
Bexar, sent a demand to the people of the little town
of Gonzales for a six-pounder cannon which had been
supplied them by the authorities of Bexar for defense
against the Indians. They refused to give it up,
and Ugartchea dispatched Captain Castenada with
a troop of a hundred cavalry, to .demand it of the
alcalde, and, if it was refused, to take it by force.
When Castenada arrived at the west bank of the
Guadelupe River he found that the ferry boat had
been removed to the east side. He made his demand
across the river for the cannon, but was answered
that the alcalde was absent. As soon as the first
requisition had been made for the cannon the people
of Gonzales had sent messages to the neighboring
colonists asking for help, in expectation that the demand would be renewed by force. An armed party
had been gathered at San Felipe for the purpose of
attempting to intercept the march of General Cos to
Bexar, but on the receipt of this appeal it hurried by
forced marches to Gonzales. A reinforcement of
volunteers also arrived from Bastrop. On the 30th
Castenada made one or two attempts to cross the
river, but, finding the fords guarded by the Texans,
withdrew. The next day the Texan force, which had
been increased, by the arrivals, from eighteen to a
hundred and sixty-eight men, organized by the choice

of John H. Moore, a distinguished Indian fighter, as colonel, and crossed the river at seven o'clock in the evening. Their advance was discovered by the Mexican pickets, who gave the alarm by firing. Both parties formed in array of battle and rested on their arms during the night. At four o'clock in the morning, under cover of a dense fog which had sprung up, the Mexicans retreated to a mound on the prairie. When this movement was discovered at daylight by the Texan scouts, they fired upon the Mexicans, who pursued them to the main body, but were driven back by a discharge of the six-pounder. The Texans then advanced with their cannon, and prepared to give battle. Castenada attempted a parley with the evident purpose of gaining time for the arrival of reinforcements. Moore met him, and demanded that he should declare in favor of the Liberal Constitution and join the Texans, or surrender. Castenada refused and the battle was opened. The six-pounder, loaded with grape, was fired, and the Texans charged with a yell upon the Mexicans, who broke at the first onset, and galloped away to Bexar. The Texans did not lose a man. The Mexicans had a small number killed. This was the response to the first attempt to carry out the decree for the disarmament of the colonists, and an evidence of the kind of fighters Santa Anna would have to meet in attempting to subdue Texas to the condition of a Mexican province.

CHAPTER VII

BATTLE OF CONCEPCION — CAPTURE OF SAN ANTONIO

THE news of the fight at Gonzales kindled the spirit of the Texan colonists into open flame. On the 3d of October, the committee of San Felipe issued an address calling upon each man in Texas to decide for himself whether he would submit to the destruction of his rights and liberties by the Central Government of Mexico. "If he will not submit, let him give his answer by the mouth of his rifle." It concluded by announcing that "the citizens of Gonzales have been attacked, the war has begun," and appealing to every citizen to march to the assistance of his fellow-countrymen now in the field. Meetings were held in all the townships, and bodies of armed men gathered together, and took their departure for the seat of war. At a meeting at San Augustine, October 5, Houston, Rusk, and other leading men were present, and a company of volunteers was raised, which left at once for the scene of action. At a general meeting of the committees of the township of Nacogdoches, Sam Houston was elected commander-in-chief of the forces in Eastern Texas, and at once engaged in organizing and forwarding the volunteers.

The leaders of the colonists gathered at San Felipe to consult with Austin. Among them was Zavala, who left his estate on the San Jacinto River to cast in his lot with the American colonists, and was welcomed as representing the liberal sentiment in Mexico, as well as for his own ability and reputation. On October 8, Austin issued a general appeal to the citizens of Texas to hurry by forced marches to Gonzales, "without waiting for cannon or anything." The gathering at San Felipe formed a temporary government by electing a council of representatives from each municipality. The council elected R. R. Royall President, and Austin left to join the forces at Gonzales. He arrived on the evening of the 10th of October, and was at once elected commander-in-chief by general consent. He sent off messengers to hasten the arrival of the volunteers. Houston received the call at San Augustine, and took out his last five-dollar bill to give to the express rider, whom he dispatched to summon the citizens. The purpose of the army was the capture of San Antonio, and Austin marched on the 13th at the head of 350 men to a point on the San Antonio River about eight miles below the town. Here he encamped, and awaited reinforcements. General Cos had reached San Antonio on the 9th with 500 men, and immediately dispatched Colonel Ugartchea to the Rio Grande for a body of additional troops.

Previous to Austin's advance a force of 110 men had been sent under the command of Captain Benjamin Fort Smith to take possession of Victoria. In the mean time the colonists in the neighborhood of Goliad had rallied for the capture of that place, where the Mexican commandant had been exercising an oppressive tyranny. They were only forty in number, but set out on the march for the town under the command of Captain George Collingsworth. They reached the ford on the San Antonio River below the town about midnight on the 9th of October, and sent forward scouts to reconnoitre. As the main body was feeling its way toward the town it came upon a man hiding in a thicket of mesquite bushes. It was Colonel Milam, who had made his escape from Monterey, through the connivance of his jailer, and ridden day and night for six hundred miles. Utterly exhausted, he had thrown himself down to rest, when he was aroused by the voices. He at first supposed the party to be Mexicans, and was preparing to defend himself, when he discovered them to be Americans and made himself known. He joined the ranks, and the party penetrated into the town. As they reached the quarters of Lieutenant-Colonel Sandoval, the commandant, they were discovered and fired upon by the sentinel. He was killed by a shot, and the door of the house was broken in with axes. Sandoval was made prisoner, and the garrison, taken by surprise, offered no resistance. A portion of them escaped in the darkness, but twenty-five remained prisoners. Only the sentinel was killed in the affair. The spoils included supplies and munitions of war to the value of $10,000, two or three pieces of artillery, and 500 stand of arms. The capture of Goliad also broke up the communication of the Mexican troops with the Gulf, which was never afterward regained. The troops under Captain Smith found that the Mexicans had abandoned Victoria, and returned to join in the attack on Goliad, but only arrived the day after its capture.

On the 20th, the forces under Austin moved up to the Salado Creek, about four miles from San Antonio, and a flag was sent to General Cos with a demand for the surrender of the place. Cos refused to receive it, and gave warning that he would fire on a second one. Austin remained in camp at the Salado, awaiting the arrival of reinforcements and artillery, and Cos busied himself in barricading the streets and building breastworks. While the army was encamped on the Salado, Houston arrived with a contingent of troops from eastern Texas. Unlike most of his associates, who took to fighting as readily as to any other occupation, Austin was diffident and uneasy in his position as commander-in-chief. He felt his incapacity in military affairs, and his health had also suffered from his long confinement in Mexico. On Houston's arrival Austin urged him to take the command. Houston declined, saying that the volunteers, who had gathered at Gonzales, had elected Austin as commander-in-chief, and that it would cause dissatisfaction if another should take his place. Austin argued that, as Houston had already been elected to the command of the troops in eastern Texas, there would be no objection to his becoming the general-in-chief. Houston, however, persisted in his refusal, but offered to serve under Austin's orders. Houston was, doubtless, wise in refusing to take the command at the risk of causing dissatisfaction by seeming to displace Austin, but it is known that he did not approve the movement for the capture of San Antonio, and had already written to Fannin and others advising the concentration of the army behind the Guadelupe. He did not as yet appreciate the fighting capacity of the Texan volunteers as compared with the Mexican conscript soldiers, and, perhaps, did not fully realize it until he saw it under his own eyes at San Jacinto.

San Antonio was one of the oldest as well as the largest and most important of the Spanish settlements in Texas. It had been founded in 1715 as a military post in consequence of the French schemes for the occupation of Texas from the colony of Louisiana, and to afford protection to the Missions of the Franciscan friars, which were being planted in the valley of the San Antonio River. It had grown through various vicissitudes, and several captures by American filibusters and Mexican revolutionists, to a town of about 2500 inhabitants, and was the depot of a considerable trade with the Indians and the northern Mexican provinces. Its situation was a lovely one, in the valley of the head-waters of the San Pedro Creek and the San Antonio River, whose limpid, green

waters wound their way through the town under a
sheltering fringe of luxuriant foliage. Around it was
a gently rolling prairie, whose elevations bounded the
horizon. Noble groves of lofty pecan-trees filled the
river bottoms and shaded the gushing springs. To
the south, for a distance of ten miles, extended the
stations of the stone churches and buildings of the
Missions, each with its surrounding wall for a protection against the Indians. The buildings were elaborate and strongly built, and some of the churches were
decorated with fine and costly carvings, but at this
time they were abandoned and falling to ruin. The
colonies of Indian proselytes had disappeared under
the attacks of the savage Comanches and Apaches,
and the friars had withdrawn to Mexico. The great
irrigation ditches, which had been dug to fertilize the
broad valley, were filled up and choked, and the rich
fields, which had flowered with tall maize, were over-
grown with rank grass and mesquite bushes. The
town was mostly on the west bank of the river, extending into a deep indentation toward the east. It
was grouped around two large squares, the Main and
Military Plazas, which were separated by the church
of San Fernando. The houses and main buildings
were of stone, many of them strong and substantial,
with thick walls and embrasured windows. But scattered among them, and extending into the suburbs,
were the jacals or huts of the poorer Mexicans, con-
structed of adobe, the sun-dried brick, or simply of
wattles and mud. The inhabitants were almost alto-|

gether Mexicans, with a few American traders, and, although the town had considerably decayed since the early part of the century, there were a number of wealthy families, and a society which preserved the traditions of Spanish luxury and hospitality. The Indians professed a nominal friendship for the people, and frequented the place for trade. But they conducted themselves with a barbaric insolence and sense of mastery. They invaded the houses and helped themselves to articles without resistance, and a Mexican soldier would often be seen humbly holding the horse of a Comanche brave. On the east side of the river, about three fourths of a mile from the plaza, was the Mission of San Antonio de Valero, or the Alamo, with its church, convent, and walled inclosure.

On the 27th of October, Austin sent a party of ninety men, under the command of Colonel James Bowie and Colonel James W. Fannin, to reconnoitre and select a position for the army nearer San Antonio, with instructions to return before night. This, however, they did not do, but encamped near the Mission Concepcion, about a mile and a half below the town, in a bend of the river, about a hundred yards wide, called the "Horseshoe." It was a strong position, the river and a skirt of timber protecting the rear, while in front the bottom sunk below the level of the prairie to the depth of from six to ten feet in the form of a semicircle open to the front, the steep bluff forming a protection to those behind it. The Mexicans discovered the camp, and made preparations to surround it during the night, crossing the river at a ford about two hundred yards above it. Colonel Bowie was alarmed by the creak of an artillery wheel, and aroused the men, who lined the parapet on both sides of the semicircle, and waited for · daylight. The advance of the Mexicans came upon Henry Karnes, an outpost sentinel, in the darkness. He fired upon them and fell back into the camp. The dawn was darkened by a heavy mist, and the Mexicans commenced the attack by harmless volleys in the obscurity. As soon as it was light the Texan troops were drawn together on the south side of the angle, so as to avoid the danger of a cross-fire, and occupied themselves in clearing a path through the vines and underbrush, so as to readily rally upon an attacked point, and in cutting steps in the bluff, so as to fire over its edge. Before this work was completed the Mexicans advanced with trailed arms and formed a line about two hundred yards from the bluff on the right flank of the Texans. Five companies of cavalry surrounded the whole front of the Texan position. The engagement opened with the deadly crack of a rifle from the extreme right of the Texan line. The fire of the Mexican infantry was in heavy and continuous volleys, which did no execution, while the Texans fired with single shots and an accurate aim, each man yielding his place to another at the parapet while he dropped back to reload. About ten minutes after the beginning of the engagement the Mexicans brought up a four-pounder cannon, which opened a harmless fire on the Texan right flank, and the trumpets sounded for a cavalry charge. The charge was broken by a volley from the Texan rifles, which emptied the foremost saddles, and the artillerymen were leveled around the gun. Twice the cavalry was re-formed under blows from the flats of the officers' swords, only to break under the Texan fire as it charged; and three times the gun was cleared, the last man falling in a vain attempt to spike it. It was fired only five times, and was left in the hands of the victors. During the engagement the mules attached to the caisson were wounded, and tore through the line of the infantry, throwing them into confusion. After the third attempt to charge, the Mexican troops were re-formed on the prairie out of the reach of fire, and withdrew to San Antonio. The number of the Mexican troops was estimated at 400. Their loss was sixty-seven killed and forty wounded, the proportion showing the deadly accuracy of the Texan fire. Sixteen men were found dead around the cannon. The Texans had but one man, Richard Andrews, killed, and none wounded. A messenger had been sent to Austin, and he hurried up with the main army, but did not arrive until about half an hour after the fight was over.

After the battle of Concepcion Austin moved his troops, who had now increased to about one thousand men, to a position north of San Antonio, and settled down into a sort of blockade of the town. At a council of war it was decided that it would be impossible to capture the place without siege guns to batter down the walls and barricades. Houston and other delegates to the Convention left the camp for San Felipe in order to organize the civil government. Cos continued to fortify himself, and dispatched a messenger to Laredo to hasten the reinforcements. On November 25, Austin, who had been elected by the Convention as one of the commissioners to solicit aid in the United States, resigned as commander-in-chief, and left the army. General Edward Burleson, who had won distinction as an Indian fighter, was elected in his place.

Various skirmishes took place between the Texan and Mexican forces, one of which was celebrated as the "Grass Fight." One of the principal scouts in the Texan army was Erasmus, or "Deaf" Smith, as he was called from his infirmity. Smith was a native of New York, where he was born in 1787, and had been one of the early adventurers in Texas. He had taken part in Long's filibuster expedition in 1819, and married a Mexican woman of San Antonio. He was a notable type of the wandering hunter and frontiersman, thoroughly at home in the wilderness, with a passion for solitude and the loneliness of the prairie and forest. He was celebrated among all his fellows for his skill in woodcraft, his coolness and daring, and was the most efficient scout of the army during all its campaigns. He was of medium size, with black hair and eyes, and a dark and leathery countenance. On November 26, Smith had been out on a scout, and discovered a body of about one hundred cavalrymen, who had been sent out by Cos to cut grass for his starving horses. Smith supposed them to be the reinforcements under Ugartchea, who was reported to be on his way from Laredo, and that the panniers of the mules were loaded with silver to pay off the Mexican troops. He galloped into the camp, and gave the alarm. The men instantly swarmed out at the cry of "Ugartchea," and Bowie dashed off at the head of one hundred mounted men to intercept the convoy. He came upon the Mexican cavalry about a mile from the town, and they took refuge in the dry bed of a creek. Bowie's movements had been seen from San Antonio, and a party of the garrison sallied out to the relief of the foragers, bringing with them two pieces of artillery. They attacked Bowie as he was about to charge upon the cavalry in the ravine, and he wheeled to meet them. There was a brisk fight for some minutes, the Mexicans falling back. In the mean time the main body of the Texan army arrived on the ground, drove the foragers out of the ditch, and followed the retreating Mexicans to the town. The mules, with their panniers of grass, were captured. The Mexicans had about fifty killed and some wounded. The Texans had one killed and one missing.

Meanwhile, the Texan troops, as is usual with all volunteer soldiery, had become impatient and dissatisfied with the long and apparently fruitless service, and were continually drifting away from the camp. There was no regular term of enlistment and no rigid rule of discipline. Every one came and went as he pleased. The army had gathered under a sudden impulse, and in the disappointment at the failure to immediately attack San Antonio many went home. Two companies of fifty men each arrived from the United States. They had been recruited in New Orleans, fitted out by subscriptions of the citizens, and were called the "Grays." A company of volunteers also arrived from Mississippi, and another from eastern Texas. But, in spite of these additions, Burleson's army, on the 1st of December, did not amount to over eight hundred men. There was great dissatisfaction among the volunteers at the prospect of continued inaction. One Dr. James Grant, a Scotchman, who had large estates in Coahuila, and had been driven out by the troops of Santa Anna, was active in endeavoring to induce a movement upon Matamoras, asserting that it would be supported by an expedition from the United States, and a revolutionary movement in Mexico.

On December 3, three Americans, Messrs. Smith, Holmes, and Maverick, who had been detained as prisoners in San Antonio by General Cos, made their escape and came into the Texan camp. They gave such an account of the condition of the garrison and the defenses that it was decided to attack the town at daybreak the next morning. During the night one of the Texan scouts disappeared, and it was appre-

hended that he had deserted to the enemy with information of the intended attack. A council was hastily
called in Burleson's tent, and it was decided to give
up the venture and raise the siege. When this decision became known to the troops there was almost a
mutiny, and every indication that the army would
disperse and fall to pieces. At this juncture the suspected scout returned, bringing with him a Mexican
lieutenant who had deserted. The deserter confirmed the accounts of the discouragement among the
garrison and the weakness of the defenses. Colonel
Milam urged Burleson to authorize an attack, and
received permission to call for volunteers. Stepping
out in front of Burleson's tent, he waved his hat, and
shouted to the angry and disorganized men, "Who
will go with old Ben Milam into San Antonio?"
An eager crowd took up the cry, and gathered about
him. Milam was elected the commander by acclamation, and the men were directed to meet at night
at the old mill on the banks of the river between the
camp and the town.

At the meeting of the volunteers, 301 in number, at the mill, the plan of attack was arranged.
The force was divided into two battalions, the first
under the command of Colonel Milam, and the second under that of Colonel Frank W. Johnson, who
had been prominent in the disturbance on the
coast, and was on Santa Anna's proscribed list.
The force moved to the attack just before dawn,
and penetrated into the town, the division of Milam

entering by Acequia street, and that of Johnson
by Soledad street. These streets led directly to
the plaza, and at the upper ends were defended by
barricades and swept by artillery. As they moved
along in the darkness between the low walls of the
houses, a sentinel gave the alarm, and was shot by
Deaf Smith, who was leading Johnson's force as a
guide. The drums beat the alarm in the garrison,
and the divisions rushed forward and broke into two
houses for shelter. Milam's division took possession
of the house of De La Garcia, and Johnson's that of
the Vice-Governor, Veramendi. These houses were
opposite to each other on the two streets, and about
a hundred yards from the plaza. In the mean time
Colonel Neill, who had been dispatched from Burleson's camp to make a feint on the Alamo, opened
fire, withdrawing after the engagement became general in the town. The Mexicans, as usual, fired
furiously and wildly with cannon and small arms.
The Texans waited for daylight, and then through
the windows and the loop-holes, which they had made
in the walls of the houses, picked off the cannoneers
at the barricades, and every Mexican soldier who
showed himself. They had brought with them two
cannon, a twelve and a six pounder, but the first was
dismounted, and the second could not be served without a breastwork for the protection of the gunners.
The streets were swept by the Mexican fire, so that
there could be no communication between the two
divisions. The battle lasted in this way all day, the

Texans having one man killed and fifteen wounded, among the latter two colonels and a lieutenant. Deaf Smith and some others were wounded on the top of Veramendi's house, which they endeavored to hold, but from which they were driven by the Mexican fire. In the night the Texans succeeded in opening communication between the two divisions by digging a trench across Soledad street under the enemy's fire, which was kept up during the darkness. The Mexicans spent the night in strengthening their barricades, and in cutting holes for musketry fire through the parapet walls of the houses which commanded the street. During the following day the Texans succeeded in mounting their twelve-pounder, and it was fired a few times without much effect. A party under Lieutenant William McDonald broke into a house adjoining that of Garcia, extending the line of attack toward the plaza. During the night the Mexicans kept up a feeble fire, and dug a trench on the Alamo side of the river for the purpose of opening a crossfire. On the morning of the third day of the siege the Mexicans opened fire from the trench, but it was soon silenced by the Texan rifles. At noon Henry Karnes dashed forward at the head of a party, and broke down the door of a house still farther toward the plaza. It was occupied and held by Captain York's company. In the evening Colonel Milam was killed. He had crossed the lines to Colonel Johnson's position, and was just entering the courtyard of the Veramendi house, when he was struck in the head by a musket ball. A consultation of the officers was held, and the chief command was conferred upon Colonel Johnson. The body of Colonel Milam was buried where he fell. At ten o'clock that night the Texans broke into and occupied the house of Antonio Navarro, adjoining the Military Plaza and one block from the Main Plaza, and stormed a redoubt, which had been erected in the same street. The Mexicans attempted to dislodge them from the Navarro house by firing through loopholes made in the roof, but the Texan rifles had a quicker and surer aim, and soon cleared the roof. On the fourth day of the siege the Texans attacked a row of houses adjoining the Navarro house, known as the "Zambrano Row." The houses were of stone with thick partition walls, which the Texans broke down with crowbars, clearing each room as they advanced. The Mexicans resisted stoutly, but were finally driven out, and the Zambrano Row, which extended to one corner of the Main Plaza, was occupied by the Texans. During the day a small party of Mexicans from the Alamo advanced upon General Burleson's camp, but were driven off. In the evening Colonel Ugartchea arrived in town with a nominal reinforcement. It consisted of 500 convict soldiers, who had been marched in chains from the Rio Grande under the guard of 100 regulars. They brought no provisions with them, and their arrival was only an additional weakness. On the last night of the siege the Texans captured a building known as the "Priest's House," which fronted upon the centre of the Main Plaza, and commanded the interior of the Mexican defenses. At ten o'clock a hundred men, by a quick rush from the Garcia house, gained the entrance to the Priest's House, and, under a heavy fire from an adjoining outbuilding occupied by the Mexicans, broke into and held it. They spent the night in barricading the doors and windows and in cutting loop-holes through the walls, the enemy keeping up a heavy and noisy fire. But the Mexicans did not wait to be exposed to the fire of the Texan rifles in the interior of their works, and withdrew before dawn to the Alamo. It is asserted that General Cos intended to make an attack upon General Burleson's camp from the Alamo, but there was great confusion and some insubordination among the troops. The Alamo was crowded with women and children, who had fled from San Antonio. They were panic-stricken on the arrival of the retreating troops, and there was a commotion in which all order was lost. Some of the troops deserted and fled toward the Rio Grande. In the morning General Cos sent in a flag of truce to General Burleson proposing terms of capitulation.

General Burleson repaired to San Antonio, and the terms were arranged. The articles were creditable to the moderation of the victors. General Cos and his officers were allowed to retain their arms and private property on giving their parole of honor not to oppose the reëstablishment of the Constitution of

1824; the regular soldiers were to be allowed to return to Mexico, or to remain, according to their own choice; the convict soldiers were to be conducted across the Rio Grande under guard; the troops returning to Mexico were to be supplied with provisions to last them on their march as far as the Rio Grande at the ordinary prices; the sick and wounded were to be left to the care of the victors; the public property and arms, of course, came into the possession of the Texans. On the 14th of December, General Cos set out on his retreat with 1105 men, two cannon, and sufficient arms for protection against the Indians and to guard the convicts.

The Texan loss at the capture of San Antonio was only two killed and twenty-six wounded. The loss of the Mexicans was not reported, and is variously estimated at from 100 to 300. Twenty-one pieces of artillery, a large quantity of small arms and munitions of war fell into the hands of the Texans.

On December 15, General Burleson resigned the command of the army and returned to his home, leaving a force under the command of Colonel Johnson to hold the Alamo. The larger part of the volunteers left the camp for their homes, and the army was practically disbanded. During the siege of San Antonio a slight engagement took place near the town of Lipanititlan on the Nueces. The garrison at Lipanititlan under orders from General Cos had marched to attack Goliad, while the garrison of Goliad advanced by another road and captured Lipanititlan.

Both parties retraced their steps and met on the prairie. The Mexicans were defeated and compelled to surrender. They were released on the condition that they should leave the country, and not bear arms against the Texans. After General Cos's retreating forces had crossed the Rio Grande, there was not an armed Mexican soldier left in the territory of Texas.

Just after the capture of San Antonio a very painful and disgraceful affair occurred at Tampico. General Mexia, a leader of the Liberal party in Mexico, fled from the country, and went to New Orleans. There he concocted a plot to force a party of emigrants to Texas to join in a descent upon Tampico. On November 6, the emigrants, to the number of 130, embarked on the schooner Mary Jane, bound, as the greater part of them supposed, to Matagorda. When they had been six days at sea they were informed that the vessel was bound to Tampico, and that they were expected to take part in a revolutionary movement. About fifty, who were probably privy to the plot, consented to enlist. The rest were confined in the hold. In attempting to enter the harbor of Tampico the schooner struck on the bar and was wrecked. The party got ashore in their boats. The officer in command of the fort on the north of the town, who was probably in collusion with Mexia, surrendered it at the first demand. The next day, Sunday, December 15, arms were forced into the hands of those who had previously refused to serve, and an advance was made upon the town. Mexia expected that a party of the inhabitants would declare in his favor, but they rallied unanimously in defense of the Central Government, with shouts of "Viva Santa Anna!" and "Death to the Foreigners!" A feeble attack on the plaza was repulsed, and Mexia and a portion of the troops escaped on board a small vessel in the harbor, which landed them at the mouth of the Brazos. Thirty-one were taken prisoners. Three died of their wounds, and twenty-eight were shot, in spite of heavy ransoms offered for their release.

The Mexicans had two armed vessels upon the coast, the Bravo and the Montezuma, which caused considerable annoyance to the Texas trade. Early in November, the Bravo pursued and drove ashore near Pass Caballo the schooner Hannah Elizabeth, laden with arms and ammunition for the Texan troops and a private consignment of goods. The Bravo took off the crew and passengers, and left a prize crew on board the stranded Hannah Elizabeth. The Bravo was driven off by a gale, and the citizens of Matagorda manned the schooner William Robbins, which sailed out and recaptured the Hannah Elizabeth. The Mexican vessels disappeared from the coast.

CHAPTER VIII

ORGANIZATION OF THE PROVISIONAL GOVERNMENT — HOUSTON ELECTED COMMANDER-IN-CHIEF

A MEETING of the delegates to form a provisional government had been held at San Felipe on the 16th of October, but no quorum was present, and it adjourned until the 1st of November. A number of the leading delegates had accompanied Austin's force in its advance to San Antonio, and, while it was encamped before that place, a council was held to consider the question of whether they should remain, or return and organize the civil government. There was then no prospect of any decisive operation in the immediate future, and it was decided that they should return.

The Consultation met at San Felipe on November 3. It consisted of fifty-five delegates, representing all the municipalities in Texas, except Bexar and Goliad. Branch T. Archer was elected President. The sessions were held in a small frame house, consisting of one room without ceiling or plaster, and many of the delegates, doubtless, camped out at night by the side of the horses which brought them. Houston still wore his Indian dress of blanket and buckskin, and it was in reply to some comment on his

appearance at this occasion that Jackson is reported
to have said he "thanked God there was one man,
at least, in Texas, whom the Almighty had the making of, and not the tailor." The remark, if made,
was as affected as Houston's costume, for Jackson
knew as well as anybody that Houston's Indian dress
was only a part of his theatrical vanity, and as much
a piece of dandyism as if it had been the most ultra-
fashionable civilized costume. The convention appointed a committee of twelve, of which John A.
Wharton was chairman and Houston a member, to
prepare a declaration of the causes which induced
Texas to assume its attitude of revolt against the
Central Government, and a committee of five to prepare a constitution for a provisional government.
The committee on the declaration reported November
7 the following vigorous and concise decree of provisional independence under the Mexican Constitution of 1824: —

"Whereas General Antonio Lopez de Santa Anna
and other military chieftains have, by force of arms,
overthrown the federal institutions of Mexico, and
dissolved the social compact which existed between
Texas and the other members of the Mexican Confederacy, now the good people of Texas, availing
themselves of their natural rights, solemnly declare:

"1. That they have taken up arms in defense of
their rights and liberties, which were threatened by
the encroachments of military despots, and in defense of the Republican Principle of the Federal

Constitution of Mexico of eighteen hundred and twenty-four.

"2. That Texas is no longer, morally or civilly, bound by the Compact of Union; yet, stimulated by the generosity and sympathy common to a free people, they offer their support and assistance to such members of the Mexican Confederacy as will take up arms against military despotism.

"3. That they do not acknowledge that the present authorities of the nominal Mexican Republic have the right to govern within the limits of Texas.

"4. That they will not cease to carry on war against the said authorities while their troops are within the limits of Texas.

"5. That they hold it to be their right, during the disorganization of the Federal system and the reign of despotism, to withdraw from the Union, to establish an independent government, or to adopt such measures as they may deem best calculated to protect their rights and liberties; but that they will continue faithful to the Mexican government so long as that nation is governed by the Constitution and laws, which were formed for the government of the Political Association.

"6. That Texas is responsible for the expenses of her armies now in the field.

"7. That the public faith of Texas is pledged for the payment of any debts contracted by her agents.

"8. That she will reward by donations of land all who may volunteer their services in her present struggle, and receive them as citizens.

"These declarations we solemnly avow to the world, and call God to witness their truth and sincerity; and invoke defeat and disgrace upon our heads should we prove guilty of duplicity."

The proposed declaration caused a warm debate, a considerable number of the delegates being in favor of a decree of absolute independence. A resolution in favor of absolute independence was actually carried, but Houston prevailed upon one of the members, who voted for it, to move a reconsideration, and, after a powerful speech, succeeded in having the declaration adopted. Houston and those who acted with him were evidently of the opinion that the Liberal party in Mexico might possibly regain power by a revolt against Santa Anna, or at least that they would be able to check any repressive action on the part of the Central Government so long as Texas professed a willingness to remain as a Mexican state. There was still a party in Texas in favor of peaceful measures, and, while there could be little doubt that the ultimate tendency of events would bring about complete independence, it was thought prudent to hold to the previous declaration of adherence to the Constitution of 1824. It is likely, also, that it was believed that this course would have a good effect upon public opinion in the United States, and remove the conception that the revolt of the Texans was a filibuster movement originating in a conspiracy.

The Constitution for a provisional government was adopted November 13. It provided for the election of a governor and lieutenant-governor, and an advisory council to consist of one member from each municipality. The government was authorized to contract for a loan of $1,000,000, on the security of the public lands, to arrange for treaties of friendship and alliance with the Indians, to establish a postal service and courts of justice and admiralty. The land commissioners were ordered to cease their functions during the interregnum, and the recent sales of lands by the Legislature of Coahuila and Texas were repudiated. It was decreed that all male citizens, capable of bearing arms, who should leave the country while Texas was in revolt, should forfeit their lands. Provision was made for the creation of a regular army of 1120 men, to be subject to the same rules and regulations as those of the army of the United States, and for the election of a major-general commanding. Austin would have been the natural choice of the delegates for Governor, but it was considered that his services would be more valuable as a commissioner to solicit aid in the United States. Henry Smith was elected Governor, and James W. Robinson, Lieutenant-Governor. Stephen F. Austin, Branch T. Archer, and William H. Wharton were appointed commissioners to the United States. Sam Houston was elected commander-in-chief with but one dissentient vote. The Consultation adjourned to meet at Washington on the 1st of March, provided the provisional government should still be in existence.

Houston appointed his staff, and drew up a plan for

the organization of the army. But the Council delayed in passing the necessary ordinances for the recruiting service and the election of officers. There was a good deal of confusion and some disturbance in popular feeling. Some of the restless and ambitious adventurers, discontented at their exclusion from office and authority, denounced the Council, and endeavored to subvert the government. A meeting was held at San Felipe at which a series of resolutions were offered by Moseley Baker, declaring the Council imbecile, and calling for the establishment of a more energetic government. Baker supported the resolutions in a violent speech. Houston again demonstrated the power of his impassioned and forcible eloquence upon the turbulent spirits. Having obtained permission to address the meeting, he pointed out the folly of discord in such a crisis, when their liberties were at stake. The Consultation had been appointed by the sovereign will of the people, and could not abandon their trust with honor. To advocate its dissolution and plunge the country into anarchy at such a time would be worse than the act of a midnight incendiary. Drawing up his figure to its full height, and pointing his finger at Baker, he said, "I had rather be a slave and grovel in the dust all my life than be a convicted felon." Baker, although a brave man, was thoroughly cowed, tore up the manuscript of his resolutions, and endeavored to excuse himself by saying that he had been put forward by others to make the movement.

Houston addressed several letters to the Governor and Council, pointing out the necessity of more thorough and rapid action for the organization of the army, and warning them that the enemy would undoubtedly advance with a large force for the subjugation of Texas. But the Governor and Council were more engaged in wrangling over the distribution of the offices than in taking means for the effectual defense of the country. Finally the necessary ordinances were adopted, and on December 13, Houston issued a proclamation, from his headquarters at Washington on the Brazos, calling for recruits for the regular army and for the volunteer service. For all who enlisted for two years, or during the war, a bounty of $24 and eight hundred acres of land were offered. To the volunteers for two years, or the war, was offered a bounty of six hundred acres, and for one year, a bounty of three hundred and twenty acres. No bounty was offered for lesser terms of service. The rights and privileges of citizenship were promised to all who would unite with the people in defending the republican principles of the Constitution of 1824. It concluded: "The services of five thousand volunteers will be accepted. The 1st of March next, we must meet the enemy with an army worthy of our cause, and which will reflect honor upon freemen. Our habitations must be defended; the sanctity of our hearths and homes must be preserved from pollution. Liberal Mexicans will unite with us. Our countrymen in the field have presented an example

worthy of imitation. Generous and brave hearts
from a land of freedom have joined our standard
before Bexar. They have by their heroism and valor
called forth the admiration of their companions in
arms, and reflected honor on the land of their birth.
Let the brave rally to our standard."

　The quarrels which broke out between the Governor and Council paralyzed all Houston's efforts, and
prevented the organization of any adequate force to
resist Santa Anna's expected invasion. The first
difficulty arose over the appointment, by the Council,
of Thomas F. McKinney, as a special agent to borrow
$100,000 on behalf of Texas. The appointment was
vetoed by the Governor, on the ground that the commissioners to the United States had already been
empowered to contract a loan. The Council unanimously passed the ordinance appointing McKinney
over the veto. General Mexia, on his return from his
disgraceful expedition to Tampico, made application
to the Texan government for aid in organizing an
invasion of Mexico. The Council passed a resolution
to assist him, which Governor Smith vetoed, declaring that Mexia was an adventurer, who was only
desirous of recruiting his own desperate fortunes by
robbery, and announcing his opposition to any connection with the Mexicans in the struggle, as he
believed that they would be found hostile and treacherous. The Council passed the resolution over the
veto, and invited General Mexia to join the forces
before San Antonio. This he declined to do, and

the Council withdrew their promise of aid. The Council elected D. C. Barrett, one of their number, to be judge advocate-general, and Edward Gritton to be collector of the port of Copano. Barrett and Gritton had been the peace commissioners to General Cos, and their fidelity to the Texan cause was suspected. Governor Smith vetoed both the appointments, making strong charges against the personal character of Barrett; but the Council voted that both the commissions should be issued. The Council assumed a hostile attitude toward Houston, and he complained that the Committee of Correspondence had thrown obstacles in the way of recruiting. Not only were the colonists discouraged from enlisting by these quarrels of the authorities, but the foreign volunteers, who had begun to arrive from the United States, were disgusted at the lack of any organization to receive and provide for them. Houston found at Washington a company from Kentucky and one from Alabama who were threatening to return home.

In the mean time, after the capture of San Antonio, Dr. Grant had renewed his schemes for the invasion of Mexico. He had fought bravely during the attack on the town, been severely wounded, and gained the confidence of the volunteers. He had never been a citizen of Texas, and was not interested in securing its independence, so much as in recovering his own rich estates and mines at Parras. He doubtless believed that the people of Coahuila would be ready to revolt against Santa Anna at the first opportunity, and excited the minds of the volunteers with visions of the easiness of the conquest and the prospects of rich rewards in booty and lands. The volunteers from the United States, who had come to Texas for war and adventure, were disappointed at being left in inactive occupation of San Antonio, and were eager for the expedition. They did not consider the lessons of failure that had followed every attempt at the invasion of Mexico by a foreign expedition, in the expectation that it would receive the support of any portion of the inhabitants. Mexican jealousy had always been aroused by the appearance of any foreign force, and all parties had united to oppose it. The capture of Matamoras itself, even if it could be accomplished, would have been of little value, for the customs' revenue would have been immediately withdrawn. Houston and Governor Smith did not favor Grant's scheme, but it was necessary to do something to occupy the attention of the American volunteers, and preserve the direction of affairs which would otherwise have been taken out of their hands. On December 17, Houston sent an order to Colonel James Bowie to organize and take command of an expedition for the capture of Matamoras. If he did not consider this to be practicable he was to secure a position on the frontier, and annoy the enemy by all the means possible in civilized warfare, and under all circumstances to hold the port of Copano. Bowie had left Goliad for San Antonio, and did not receive the order. Houston also sent orders to the quartermaster-general at New Orleans that volunteers from the United States, sailing from that port, should land at Copano or Matagorda, and rendezvous at Refugio and Goliad. It is not probable that Houston, in concentrating his troops in the West, had any other purpose than to head off Grant's expedition, and to have them ready to meet the invasion of Santa Anna. The troops in the service of Texas at that time amounted to only about 750 men; 400 at San Antonio; 200 at Velasco; 70 at Washington, and 80 at Goliad. And with the best results of recruiting and the expected arrivals from the United States, no force could be gathered which would be at all adequate for the invasion of Mexico.

While Houston had been issuing these orders the Council had proceeded to supersede his authority. Colonel F. W. Johnson, who had been left in command of the Alamo, favored the project of Dr. Grant, and went to San Felipe, where he received authority from the Council to take command of the expedition. Meantime, Grant had collected his volunteers at San Antonio to the number of between three and four hundred, seized the arms and munitions of war belonging to the State, pressed horses and supplies from the inhabitants, and set out on his march. Colonel Neill was left in defense of the Alamo with only about sixty men. The Council authorized Colonel J. W. Fannin, who had been appointed by Houston colonel of artillery, and sent to Velasco on recruiting service, to act as its "agent" to collect

and organize the troops now in the State, or expected
to arrive, at Copano, for the expedition to Matamoras, with authority to contract a loan of $3000,
and appoint "sub-agents." He was also directed to
hold an election for commander of the forces after
they should be concentrated. All this was a direct
supersession of the authority of the Governor and
the commander - in - chief. Houston was profoundly
affected by these miserable intrigues, which threatened the destruction of Texas, and wrote to Governor
Smith in very impassioned terms on receipt of the
report of Colonel Neill as to the condition of affairs
at the Alamo: —

HEADQUARTERS, WASHINGTON, *January* 6, 1835.

SIR, — I have the honor to inclose to your excellency the report of Lieutenant-Colonel J. C. Neill of
the artillery; and most respectfully request that you
will render to the cause of Texas and humanity the
justice of bestowing upon it your serious attention, and
referring it to the General Council of the provisional
government in secret session. There, I may be permitted to hope, you will attend in person, that all the
essential functionaries of the government may deliberate and adopt some course that will redeem our
country from a state of deplorable anarchy. Manly
and bold decision alone can save us from ruin. I
only require orders and they shall be obeyed. If the
government now yields to the unholy dictation of
speculators and marauders upon human rights, it

were better that we had yielded to the despotism of a single man, whose ambition might have been *satisfied* by our unconditional submission to his authority, and a pronouncement, for which we are asked, in favor of his power.

In the present instance the people of Texas have not even been consulted. The brave men, who have been wounded in the battles of Texas, and the sick from exposure in her cause, without blankets or supplies, are left neglected in her hospitals; while the needful stores and supplies are diverted from them, without authority and by self-created officers, who do not acknowledge the only government known to Texas and the world.

Within thirty hours I shall set out for the army, and repair there with all possible dispatch. I pray that a confidential dispatch may meet me at Goliad, and, if I have left, that it may pursue me wherever I may be.

No language can express my anguish of soul. Oh, save our poor country! — send supplies to the wounded, the naked, the sick, and the hungry, for God's sake! What will the world think of the authorities of Texas? Prompt, decided, and honest independence is all that can save them and redeem the country. I do not fear, — I will do my duty!

I have the honor, etc.,

SAM HOUSTON.

Governor Smith shared Houston's indignation,

but, in place of meeting and conferring with the Council, he sent them a message couched in the most violent language. He denounced Grant's expedition as piratical, and accused members of the Council of conniving at it. He applied to these members the epithets of "Judases," "parricides," and "wolves," and called upon the honest men to drive out the scoundrels, whom they would detect by "the contraction of the eyes, the gape of the mouth, the vacant stare, the hung head, the restless, fidgety disposition, the sneaking, sycophantic look, the natural meanness of countenance, the unguarded shrug of the shoulders, a sympathetic and tickling contraction of the muscles of the neck anticipating the rope, a restless eagerness to adjourn, dreading to face the storm themselves have raised." After this extraordinary appeal to their sensibilities, he declared the Council adjourned to March 1, unless it immediately and publicly renounced its errors. The Council appointed a committee to confer with the Governor, and attempted some peaceful arrangement; but he was inexorable. On January 11 the Council adopted a resolution declaring his language "low, blackguardly, and vindictive," ordered his message to be returned to him, and declared him deposed from office. Governor Smith at first endeavored to conciliate the Council, apologizing for the harshness of his language, and expressing the desire that there might be harmony between the two branches of the government for the common welfare; but no arrangement resulted. The

Governor retained possession of the archives, and
issued orders to such officers as would obey him, ful-
minating from time to time an address or a handbill
against the Council. The Council issued an address
to the people vindicating its course, but soon ceased
its meetings for want of a quorum. Before it dispersed, upon the advice of Austin and others, it appointed an election for February 1, for delegates to
a general convention to be held March 1. Fannin
and Johnson continued to exercise the authority
given them by the Council, and both claimed the
supreme direction of the proposed expedition to
Matamoras. Fannin called upon the troops concentrated at Copano to hold an election of officers.
Fannin was chosen colonel, and Major William
Ward, who had arrived from Georgia at the head of
three companies of volunteers, lieutenant-colonel.

Under orders from Governor Smith to establish
headquarters at Bexar or elsewhere on the frontier,
and commence active hostilities as soon as possible,
Houston left Washington on the 8th of January, and
reached Goliad on the night of the 14th. He found
great confusion among the troops on the frontier.
Dr. Grant had passed with his volunteers from San
Antonio, and, styling himself "acting commander-in-
chief," had seized a *caballada* of horses belonging to
citizens of Goliad. Captain Dimitt, in command of
the regular forces at Goliad, had been superseded
by Captain Wyat of the volunteers from Alabama.
There was a want of food among the troops, and the

supplies expected from New Orleans had not arrived
at Copano. Houston issued orders for the concentration of the troops at Refugio, where beef at least
could be obtained, but had great difficulty in per-
suading the men to march on account of their discontent at the failure of the government to provide them
with either food or clothing. A message was received
from Colonel Neill, in command at San Antonio, that
he expected to be attacked by a large force of the
enemy, and Houston dispatched Colonel Bowie to his
assistance. He ordered Colonel Neill to demolish
the fortifications of the Alamo, and bring off the
artillery. Colonel Neill replied that he had no teams
with which to move the guns, and the garrison remained in the Alamo. Governor Smith sent Lieutenant-Colonel Travis, who had been stationed on
recruiting service at San Felipe, with a small party
to reinforce the garrison. Colonel Neill returned to
his home, and Travis assumed the command. While
Houston was at Refugio endeavoring to bring some
order out of the confusion and disorganization, Colonel Johnson arrived and exhibited the resolutions of
the Council empowering him to take command of the
expedition against Matamoras. Houston at the same
time was informed of the deposition of Governor
Smith. He considered that it would be useless to
attempt to accomplish anything in such a conflict of
authority, and that by remaining with the army he
would be simply held responsible for the failures
which would inevitably follow, without any power to

prevent them. He addressed the volunteers, discouraging the expedition against Matamoras, and returned to his headquarters at Washington, from whence he forwarded a communication to Governor Smith, giving an account of his proceedings, and arguing strongly against the competency of the Council to depose the Governor. While at Refugio he had been elected by the citizens a delegate to the Convention to be held March 1.

The proposed expedition to Matamoras came to nothing. Johnson and Fannin were unable to agree as to who should have the command, and the volunteers were so much discouraged by Houston's speech, pointing out the folly and inevitable failure of the expedition, that they refused to march. Johnson was left with only sixty men, and abandoned his enterprise. Fannin remained with the volunteers from the United States for the defense of Goliad, but attempted no active operations. Grant and his men occupied themselves with raids for the stealing of horses.

The commissioners to solicit aid in the United States met with a good deal of success. Austin made addresses in some of the principal cities, and the moderation as well as earnestness of their tone had a good effect upon the conservative opinion of the country, and relieved the revolt of the Texans from the imputation of being a filibuster enterprise. Subscriptions of money and arms were given to some extent, and there was a warm feeling of sympathy for the success of the colonists in the struggle. The commissioners succeeded in negotiating a loan of $200,000 in New Orleans, Austin pledging his private fortune as security. Of this they obtained $20,000 in cash, and later they effected a loan of $50,000 in cash. With these funds they purchased supplies, which kept the army from entirely falling to pieces.

While Houston had virtually given up the command of the army, he was enabled to perform an important service for the success of the colonists in their struggle. The Indians in eastern Texas, who included the Cherokees and other fragments of tribes driven from the United States, constituted a very formidable body. They were jealous of the aggressions of the colonists upon the lands, which had been granted them by the Mexican government, and were on friendly terms with the Mexican agents stationed among them. It was highly important that they should be conciliated and rendered passive, if not actively friendly, to the colonists. On November 13, the Consultation adopted a "Solemn Declaration" in regard to the rights of these Indians, to which each member subscribed his name. The declaration is in the handwriting of Houston, and was undoubtedly adopted by his influence. It reads: —

"We solemnly declare that the boundaries of the claims of the said Indians are as follows, to wit, being north of the San Antonio road and the Neches, and west of the Angelina and Sabine rivers. We solemnly declare that the Governor and General Council immediately on its organization shall appoint commissioners to treat with the said Indians to establish the definite boundaries of their territory, and secure their confidence and friendship. We solemnly declare that we will guarantee to them the peaceable enjoyment of their rights and their lands as we do our own. We solemnly declare that all grants, surveys, and locations within the bounds hereinbefore mentioned, made after the settlement of the said Indians, are and of right ought to be utterly null and void, and the commissioners issuing the same be and are hereby ordered immediately to recall and cancel the same, as having been made upon lands already appropriated by the Mexican government. We solemnly declare that it is our sincere desire that the Cherokee Indians and their associate bands should remain our friends in peace and war, and if they do so we pledge the public faith to the support of the foregoing declaration. We solemnly declare that they are entitled to our commiseration and protection, as the first owners of the soil, as an unfortunate race of people, that we wish to hold as friends and treat with justice."

Samuel Houston, John Forbes, and John Cameron were appointed commissioners to treat with the Indians on this basis.

After Houston's return to Washington he was given a furlough by Governor Smith until March 1, and directed to carry out his instructions as one of the commissioners to treat with the Indians. Houston and Forbes visited the Indians, and held a grand council of the tribes at the village of Bowles, the chief of the Cherokees, where a treaty was concluded February 23, on the basis of the "Solemn Declaration." This kept the Indians quiet during the struggle, and it is perhaps needless to say that the treaty was repudiated by the Texan Congress after it was over.

CHAPTER IX

FALL OF THE ALAMO — CREATION OF THE REPUBLIC

WHILE the government and military organization of Texas had fallen into a condition of confusion and anarchy, Santa Anna had been consolidating the power in Mexico. The new Constitution abolished the state legislatures, and preserved only the forms of a federal government in a department council and governors of provinces appointed by the President. The President was the supreme authority and absolute dictator in all but the name. The republican party was completely cowed, and the majority of the people of Mexico accepted the destruction of their liberties without a murmur, and even apparently with approval. Having completed this work, Santa Anna turned his attention to the subjugation of Texas, where alone his authority was resisted. He commenced the concentration of troops at San Luis Potosi early in December, and dispatched the first brigade under the command of General Sesma for the relief of General Cos, then besieged in San Antonio. Cos's retreating forces were met at the Rio Grande, and Sesma halted there to await the arrival of the remainder of the army. The other two brigades, with the cavalry and artillery, were concentrated at Saltillo, and Santa Anna took the command in person. General Vincente Filisola, an Italian, who had been for some time in the service of Mexico, and was the empresario of a grant of land in Texas, was appointed second in command. General Castrillon commanded the artillery, and General Audrade the cavalry. Generals Tolsa and Gaona commanded the second and third brigades. The troops were the best in the Mexican army, veterans of the civil war, and disciplined so far as the system of service was capable of doing it. From Saltillo Santa Anna dispatched General Urrea with 200 cavalry to Matamoras, with instructions to take command of the troops there, and move north to attack Refugio and Goliad. Early in February, Santa Anna reached Monova with his army, consisting of about 4000 men, and set out with an escort of fifty cavalry to join General Cos and General Sesma on the Rio Grande. When the army was consolidated with the troops under Cos and Sesma it numbered between 6000 and 7000 men. The march of the Mexican army from Monova to San Antonio, a distance of nearly 600 miles, was a most painful and trying one. The greater portion of the country was almost a desert, without inhabitants, except a few scattered villages, a barren plain without shelter and almost without water. It was the dead of winter, and the snow and sleet and piercing "northers" swept down upon the thinly clad and unacclimated troops. In accordance with the Mexican custom, a great crowd of women, wives of the soldiers, and camp followers accompanied the march, and added to the distress and difficulty. In spite of rapacious demands upon the inhabitants of the villages, food fell short, and the army was put on half rations. The animals died in great numbers, and it was with extreme difficulty that the cannons and wagons were dragged along. But the imperious energy of Santa Anna whipped the army along, and the advance guard appeared before San Antonio on February 22.

The garrison was taken by surprise. No scouting parties had been sent out, and so careless were the Texans that they had been attending a fandango two nights before, while Santa Anna was encamped on the Medina. He was informed of the condition of the garrison, and attempted to move forward for the surprise of the place during the night. But the ammunition wagons were on the west side of the river, the stream was swollen, and a heavy norther was blowing, so that he gave up his design. The first knowledge of the approach of the Mexican army was from the sentinels on the roof of the church. Their alarm was disbelieved at first, and two horsemen were sent out to reconnoitre. They came upon the enemy at Prospect Hill, an eminence a short distance west of the town, and were pursued by the Mexicans, one of them being thrown from his horse and breaking his arm. The garrison hastily retreated across the river to the Alamo, Lieutenant A. M. Dickenson catching up his wife and child on his horse at the door of a Mexican house. As the garrison crossed the plain they swept up with them thirty or forty beef cattle, and drove them into the plaza of the fortress. When Santa Anna reached San Antonio he sent a flag with a demand for the immediate surrender of the Mission. Travis dispatched Major Morris and Captain Marten to meet the flag, and on the return of his messengers gave his answer by an emphatic "no" from a cannon shot. The blood-red flag of "no quarter" was hoisted on the tower of the church of San Fernando, and the siege was begun by a cannonade from the Mexican guns.

The Mission of the Alamo, which signifies the cottonwood-tree, was established, where it then stood, in 1722. It had been founded by the Franciscan friars from the college at Queretaro in 1710, in the valley of the Rio Grande, and after several removals on account of the scarcity of water and the attacks of the Indians, it had been finally located at San Antonio. The buildings of the Mission consisted of a church in the usual form of a cross, with walls of hewn stone, five feet thick, and twenty-two and a half feet high. The church faced to the westward, toward the river and the town. The central portion of the church was roofless at the time of the siege; but arched rooms on each side of the entrance and the sacristy, which was used as a powder magazine, were strongly covered with a roof of masonry. The windows were high up from the floor, and close and narrow, to protect the congregation from the flights of Indian arrows. The front was decorated with battered carvings and stone images, and the entrance was barred by heavy oaken doors. Adjoining the church on the left and touching the wing of the cross formed by its walls was the convent yard, an inclosure about a hundred feet square, with walls sixteen feet high and three and a half feet thick, strengthened on the inside with an embankment of earth to half their height. At the farther or southeastern corner of the convent yard was a sally port, defended by a small redoubt. The convent and hospital building, of adobe bricks, two stories in height and eighteen feet in width, extended along the west side of the yard to the distance of 191 feet. It contained one long room in the hospital, and a number of small rooms and cells. The main plaza extended in front of the church and convent in the form of a parallelogram, with its side toward the river, and covered between two and three acres. It was inclosed by a wall eight feet high and thirty-three inches thick. On the southern end of the plaza were buildings used as a prison and barracks, and a heavy stockade of cedar logs had been planted from this corner of the plaza, which extended some twenty yards beyond the line of the church, diagonally to the corner of the church, and protected the entrance. Other buildings and houses occupied places on the inside of the wall of the plaza, but were not of much strength or consequence. The Mission was entirely isolated

from the town, which was wholly on the west bank
of the river, with the exception of a few miserable
jacals on the eastern bank. There was a plentiful
supply to water from the acequias, one on the south
connecting with a ditch through the plaza, and the
other skirting with its shallow, greenish stream the
east end of the church.

To defend this extensive place Travis had fourteen
pieces of artillery. These were mounted on the walls
of the church fronting north, south, and east; two
were planted at the stockade, and two at the main
entrance to the plaza; four defended the redoubt at
the entrance to the convent yard, and others were
placed at various points along the walls. There were
no redoubts or bastions, except the single outwork in
front of the sally port to the convent yard. It was
evidently impossible to defend so wide a space with
so small a garrison, and the defense was mainly concentrated about the church and convent. Travis had
been as careless about his supply of provisions as
about his guard. Only three bushels of corn were at
first found in the Alamo, but some eighty or ninety
bushels were afterward discovered in one of the
houses.

The garrison, when it entered the Alamo, consisted
of 145 men. The garrison comprised the men who
had remained after the departure of the expedition
under Grant, and such volunteers as had since strag-
gled in. They had no training in arms, except in
the use of the rifle, which was a necessity of their

daily existence. They were without definite military organization, and were only held together by a common heroic purpose. The commander, Lieutenant-Colonel William Barrett Travis, was a native of North Carolina, twenty-eight years of age, and by profession a lawyer. He had taken a prominent part in the early troubles with the Mexican authorities, and was on the proscribed list of Santa Anna. In appearance he was six feet in height, erect and manly in figure, with blue eyes, reddish hair, and round face. The second in command was Colonel James Bowie, famous all over the West as the inventor of the terrible knife which bore his name. He was a native of Georgia, but removed to Chatahoula parish in Louisiana. While there he fought a desperate duel with one Norris Wright on a sand bar in the Mississippi. Bowie was shot down, and Wright bent down to dispatch him, when Bowie drew his knife and stabbed him to the heart. Bowie accompanied Long's filibuster expedition to Texas, and afterward remained in the territory, engaged in smuggling African slaves from Galveston and in various adventures. He had a prolonged and desperate fight with the Comanches, while at the head of a party in search of the old San Saba gold mines, and his hardihood and courage had become proverbial. He was a large, fair man, and, like many of the early Texans, occasionally worked off the fervor of his animal spirits by tremendous debauches of drinking. Another very notable figure among the defend-

skin, carried his favorite long rifle "Betsy," and was conspicuous by his coonskin cap. Another man of distinction among the defenders of the Alamo was Colonel J. B. Bonham, of South Carolina, who had responded to the call of Texas for volunteers, and arrived in San Antonio shortly before the commencement of the siege.

Santa Anna commenced his operations by erecting batteries for his fieldpieces, but did not make a complete investment of the Mission. The defenders occasionally replied with their cannon, but in the main depended upon their rifles, which seldom missed their mark. General Castrillon, under orders from Santa Anna, attempted to build a bridge across the river from the timbers of the houses. The party was within the reach of the rifles of the Texans, and in a few minutes thirty were killed. The survivors were withdrawn.

Travis sent the following appeal for assistance to the government, which has a stirring and heroic ring: —

TO THE PEOPLE OF TEXAS AND ALL AMERICANS IN
THE WORLD.

COMMANDANCY OF THE ALAMO,
BEXAR, *February* 24, 1836.

FELLOW-CITIZENS AND COMPATRIOTS, — I am besieged by a thousand or more of the Mexicans under Santa Anna. I have sustained a continued bombardment for twenty-four hours, and have not lost a man.

The enemy have demanded a surrender at discretion; otherwise the garrison is to be put to the sword if the place is taken. I have answered the summons with a cannon shot, and our flag still waves proudly from the walls. *I shall never surrender or retreat.* Then I call on you in the name of liberty, of patriotism, and of everything dear to the American character, to come to our aid with all dispatch. The enemy are receiving reinforcements daily, and will no doubt increase to three or four thousand in four or five days. Though this call may be neglected, I am determined to sustain myself as long as possible, and die like a soldier who never forgets what is due to his own honor and that of his country. Victory or death!

W. BARRETT TRAVIS,
Lieutenant-Colonel, Commanding.

P. S. The Lord is on our side. When the army appeared in sight we had not three bushels of corn. We have since found in deserted houses eighty or ninety bushels, and got into the walls twenty or thirty beeves.[1]

---

[1] The letter, in a firm and bold handwriting, now among the state archives at Austin, has the following indorsements on the back by the couriers, who forwarded it : —

"Since the above was written I heard a very heavy cannonade during the whole day. Think there must have been an attack on the Alamo. We were short of ammunition when I left. Hurry all the men you can forth. When I left there were but 150 men determined to do or die. To-morrow I leave for Bexar with what men I can. Almonte is there. The troops are commanded by General Sesma.

ALBERT MARTIN."

Colonel Bonham was also dispatched with a message to Colonel Fannin at Goliad asking him to come to the assistance of the garrison.

On the 25th Santa Anna endeavored to erect a battery 300 yards south of the main entrance to the plaza, and a sharp skirmish took place in which eight Mexicans were killed. The enemy succeeded in erecting the battery during the night, and also one near the old powder house to the southeast. The same night the Mexican cavalry were stationed on the road leading to the east. On the 26th there was a skirmish between the Texans and the Mexican cavalry on the eastern road, and during the night a party sallied out and burnt the jacals on the east side of the river, which had afforded shelter to the enemy. Santa Anna's troops continued to arrive, and the investment of the Mission was made more complete. But it was not close enough to prevent the entrance of a party of thirty-two men from Gonzales, under Captain J. W. Smith, who stole their way through the enemy's lines, and joined the garrison on the night of March 1. On March 3, Colonel Bonham returned with a message from Colonel Fannin that he would march at once for the relief of the garrison. Fannin started on the 28th of February with 300 men and four pieces of artillery. His ammunition

" I hope that every one will Rendeves at Gonzales as soon Possible as the Brave soldiers are suffering ; don not forget the powder is very scarce and should not be delad one moment.

L. SMITHER."

wagon broke down, and he had not oxen enough to get his cannon across the river. The troops had no provisions except some rice and a little dried beef, and, after a council with his officers, Fannin decided to return to Goliad. On the 3d of March, Travis sent off his last message to the government: —

"I am still here in fine spirits and well-to-do. With 145 men, I have held the place against a force variously estimated from between 1500 to 6000, and I shall continue to hold it until I get relief from my countrymen, or I will perish in its defense. We have had a shower of bombs and cannon balls continually falling among us the whole time; yet none of us have fallen. We have been miraculously preserved. . . . Again, I feel confident that the determined spirit and desperate courage heretofore exhibited by my men will not fail them in the last struggle; and although they may be sacrificed to the vengeance of a Gothic enemy, the victory will cost that enemy so dear that it will be worse than a defeat. . . . A blood-red flag waves from the church of Bexar and in the camp above us, in token that the war is one of vengeance against rebels. . . . These threats have had no influence upon my men but to make all fight with desperation and with that high-souled courage which characterize the patriot who is willing to die in defense of his country; liberty and his own honor; God and Texas; victory or death!"

The enemy had effected but little by their cannonade, their guns being only fieldpieces of light calibre.

The garrison, however, was worn down by constant vigilance night and day, and frequent alarms in expectation of an attack.

After Santa Anna's troops had all arrived on March 2, they were given three days in which to rest after their weary march. On the 5th, Santa Anna held a council of war on the question of an immediate assault of the Alamo. A portion of the officers were in favor of awaiting the arrival of siege artillery, but Santa Anna determined on an assault the next day. On the morning of the 6th of March, Sunday, the forces for the assault were formed at four o'clock. The troops numbered 2500, and were divided into four columns. The first was under the command of General Cos, the second under Colonel Duque, the third under Colonel Romero, and the fourth under Colonel Morales. The columns were supplied with scaling ladders, crowbars, and axes. The cavalry were drawn around the fort to prevent any attempt at escape. In the gray light of the morning the bugle sounded, and the bands struck up the Spanish air of Deguelo (Cut-throat), the signal of no quarter. Santa Anna witnessed the attack from the battery in front of the plaza. The troops dashed forward at a run, and were received with a deadly fire from the artillery and rifles. The column attacking the northern wall recoiled, and Colonel Duque was desperately wounded. The attacks on the eastern and western walls also failed, and the columns swarmed around to the north side. Here in a dense mass they were driven forward by the blows and shouts of their officers. Once more they recoiled before the fire, but at the third trial they scaled the wall, "tumbling over it like sheep." They carried the redoubt at the sally port, and swarmed into the convent yard, forcing the Texans into the convent and hospital. The captured cannon were turned against the flimsy adobe walls, and the Mexicans stormed the breaches. The Texans fought from room to room, using their clubbed rifles and bowie knives so long as they had life left to strike. Colonel Travis and Colonel Bonham fell here. The Mexicans fired a howitzer loaded with grape twice into the long room of the hospital. Fifteen Texans were found dead in the room, and forty-two Mexicans on the outside. The last struggle took place in the church. The column attacking on the south side carried the stockade and poured into the church. Major T. C. Evans, the commander of the artillery, started for the magazine to blow up the building, as the defenders had agreed should be done at the last extremity, but was struck down by a musket shot as he was entering the door. Crockett was killed near the entrance, with his clubbed rifle in his hand. Bowie was lying, disabled by a fall from a platform, on a cot in the arched room to the left of the entrance. He was shot through the door as he lay on his bed firing his pistols. Mrs. Dickenson, wife of Lieutenant Dickenson, and her infant child had been placed in the opposite room for safety. A wounded man by the name of Walters fled into the room. He was pursued by the Mexicans, who shot him, and then raised his body on their bayonets, "as a farmer does a bundle of fodder," until the blood ran down upon them. Mrs. Dickenson was protected by the interposition of Colonel Almonte. Mrs. Alsbury, a Mexican woman, niece and adopted daughter of the Vice-Governor Veramendi, and her little sister had gone to the Alamo with their brother-in-law, Colonel Bowie, and waited upon him after his injury. When the slaughter was over they came out of their hiding-place, and were protected by a Mexican officer. They were afterward recognized by a friend among the spectators, and taken to their home in San Antonio. Mrs. Alsbury and her sister, Mrs. Dickenson and her child, a negro boy, servant of Colonel Travis, and a Mexican woman were the only persons spared by the Mexicans.

At nine o'clock the Alamo had fallen. Santa Anna left the shelter of the battery and came upon the scene. Five persons, who had hid themselves, were brought before him. General Castrillon interceded for their lives, but Santa Anna turned his back upon him with a reprimand for his weakness, and the Mexican soldiers dispatched them with their bayonets.

After the slaughter the bodies of the dead Texans were collected by the order of Santa Anna, and piled together with alternate layers of wood. The mass was then heaped with dry brush and burned. The ashes and bones were left to the dogs and the vultures. A year later, what remained were placed in a coffin by order of Colonel John Seguin, mayor of San Antonio, and buried with military honors. The number of the dead cannot be known with absolute accuracy. It was probably in the neighborhood of 180, of whom the names of 166 are known. Several couriers had been sent out during the siege, all of whom did not return. Captain J. W. Smith, of the Gonzales party, escaped with Travis's message of March 3, and it is possible that there were other messengers, who were cut off by the Mexican cavalry. All the garrison were Americans except three Mexicans who had joined them from the town.

The loss of the Mexicans in the assault has never been ascertained. Santa Anna, in his official report, said that there were only 70 killed and 300 wounded. But this was obviously an outrageous lie, as he also said that the Texans numbered 400, and that the attacking party consisted of only 1400. Various estimates give the loss of the Mexicans at between 300 and 500 killed, or who afterward died of their wounds. Dr. Bernard, who was taken prisoner at Goliad, and sent to attend the sick at San Antonio, said that the Mexican surgeons told him that over 400 wounded soldiers were brought into the hospitals after the assault. Sergeant Bercero, one of the attacking party, in giving his reminiscence of the assault, said: "There was an order to gather our dead and wounded. It was a painful sight. Our lifeless soldiers covered the ground surrounding the Alamo.

They were heaped inside the fortress. Blood and brains covered the earth and floor, and were spattered on the walls. The killed were generally struck on the head. The wounds were generally in the neck or shoulders, seldom below that."

The defense of the Alamo was a mistake in strategic warfare. It was impossible that the small garrison could successfully defend the post against the overwhelming force of Santa Anna's army. The defenders undoubtedly knew it. It is said that Travis drew them together, and addressed them in terms that could have left no doubt in their minds; but whether that was so or not, they were aware that there was very little chance of their receiving succor from the Texan army. They could have made their escape, even after the investment of the Alamo, as easily as the party from Gonzales made their way into the fort. They could have found refuge in the timber of the streams, and with their skill in woodcraft have made their way safely south to the forces under Fannin at Goliad, or east to the settlements of the colonists. Their determination to remain was the impulse of their invincible courage, the strong vigor of their cool and desperate natures. They were ready to die in their tracks sooner than give way before an enemy they hated and despised, and they counted on the fight as only one of the many desperate chances of their lives. The lesson of the cost of taking the Alamo, and overwhelming its handful of defenders, would have warned Santa Anna, if he had been less headstrong and vainglorious, that the task of subduing the Texan colonists was an impossible one. But with its capture he seemed to think that the conquest of Texas was already accomplished. He sent off bombastic dispatches to the authorities in the city of Mexico, and, after giving orders to his subordinates to complete the campaign, made preparations to return. Mrs. Dickenson was furnished with a horse, and made the bearer of a proclamation to the colonists, announcing the capture of the Alamo, and calling upon them to submit to the Mexican authority. She crossed the prairies alone, with her child in her arms, until she reached the Salado Creek, where she came upon the negro servant of Travis, who had made his escape from the Mexicans, hiding in the woods. They made their way together to Gonzales.

A change had taken place in the minds of the leading men in Texas in regard to the policy of a total separation from Mexico. It was discovered that the Liberal party in Mexico was utterly powerless, and that the people, almost without exception, were hostile to the American colonists, and wished them subdued. As early as January 7 Houston wrote to Major John Forbes, saying, "I now feel confident that no further experiment need be made to convince us that there is but one course left for Texas to pursue, and that is an unequivocal declaration of independence, and the formation of a constitution to be submitted to the people for their rejection or ratification." Austin wrote a letter from New Orleans, which was published in the newspaper, stating that when he left the country he considered it premature to stir the question of independence, but the news from Vera Cruz and Tampico was that the Liberal party had united with Santa Anna to put down the Texans. Public opinion in the United States was strongly in favor of a declaration of independence by Texas, and he could not have obtained the loan without the belief that the Convention would take such a course. Whatever difference of opinion there might have been as to the time for such action he hoped there would be none now. The colonists were thoroughly disgusted with the quarrels of the Governor and Council, and anxious to have a new and more rigorous government. It is likely that the majority of them would have been ready at any time to throw off the Mexican authority, and separate from a country with which they had no natural affiliation, and whose government they tolerated only so long as it left them practically alone.

The General Convention called by the Council met at Washington, March 1, 1835. Fifty-eight delegates were present. Richard Ellis, of the Red River district, was elected president, and H. S. Kimble secretary. On the following day the declaration of independence was adopted. In its preamble it set forth the grievances of the people of Texas. It declared that the Federative Republic of Mexico had been changed without their consent to a consolidated military despotism, in which every interest was disregarded except that of the army and priesthood; that their agents bearing petitions had been thrown into dungeons; that the Mexican government had failed to maintain the right of trial by jury; denied the right of worshiping the Almighty according to the dictates of conscience; had made piratical attacks upon the Texan commerce; commanded the colonists to deliver up their arms necessary for their defense against the savages; had invaded their territory by sea and land; and had incited the merciless savages to massacre the defenseless inhabitants of the frontiers. It concluded: —

"These and other grievances were patiently borne by the people of Texas until they reached the point at which forbearance ceases to be a virtue. We then took up arms in defense of the National Constitution. We appealed to our Mexican brethren for assistance; our appeal has been made in vain; although months have elapsed, no sympathetic response has yet been heard from the interior. We are therefore forced to the melancholy conclusion that the Mexican people have acquiesced in the destruction of their liberty, and the substitution therefor of a military government; that they are unfit to be free and incapable of self-government.

"The necessity of self-preservation, therefore, now decrees our eternal political separation.

"We, therefore, the delegates, with plenary powers, of the people of Texas, in solemn Convention assembled, appealing to a candid world for the necessities of our condition, do hereby resolve and declare that our political connection with the Mexican nation has forever ended, and that the people of Texas do now constitute a free, sovereign, and independent Republic, and are fully invested with all the rights and attributes which properly belong to independent nations; and, conscious of the rectitude of our intentions, we fearlessly and confidently commit the issue to the Supreme Arbiter of the destinies of nations."

On the 4th of March, Sam Houston was unanimously reëlected commander-in-chief with authority over all the forces, regulars and volunteers. Ordinances were adopted for the reorganization of the army, and for the enrollment of all citizens between the ages of seventeen and fifty to be subject to drafts. Increased bounties of land were offered to volunteers: 1280 acres for those already enlisted, who should serve during the war, 640 acres for six months' service, and 320 acres for three months; 960 acres were offered for the new recruits who should serve during the war.

There was great excitement over the news of the beleaguerment of the Alamo. On March, 2 Houston issued the following appeal to the people of Texas: —

CONVENTION HALL, *March* 2, 1836.

War is raging on the frontiers. Bexar is besieged by two thousand of the enemy under the command of General Sesma. Reinforcements are on their march to unite with the besieging army. By the last report our force at Bexar was only one hundred and fifty men. The citizens of Texas must rally to the aid of our army or it will perish. Let the citizens of the East march to the combat. The enemy must be driven from our soil or desolation will accompany their march upon us. *Independence is declared.* It must be maintained. Immediate action, united with valor, can alone achieve our great work. The services of all are forthwith required in the field.

SAM HOUSTON,
Commander-in-Chief of the Army.

P. S. It is rumored that the enemy are on their march to Gonzales, and that they have entered the colonies. The fate of Bexar is unknown. The country must and shall be defended. The patriots of Texas are *appealed to in behalf of their bleeding country.*

A hundred or so of men were gathered about Washington, but there was no organization, and no attempt to march to the relief of the Alamo. On Sunday, March 6, the day of the fall of the Alamo, the letter of Colonel Travis making a last appeal for aid was handed to the president of the Convention. He hastily summoned the members together, and read it to them. There was a scene of intense feeling. Robert Potter moved that the Convention adjourn, arm, and march for the relief of the Alamo. Houston declared the resolution to be folly and treason to the people. He urged the Convention to remain and finish its work of organizing the government, without which the declaration of independence would be a vain fulmination. He promised that no enemy should approach them, and announced his intention to start at once for Gonzales. The Convention recovered from its excitement, and within an hour Houston was on his way to Gonzales, accompanied only by Colonel George W. Hockley, his chief of staff, and one or two others. While on his way he dispatched a letter to the Convention advising it to declare Texas a part of Louisiana under the treaty of 1803, and therefore belonging to the United States. The advice was not adopted, and it is not likely that it would have made any difference in the action of the United States, as that country had abandoned any such claim from Mexico.

The Convention continued its work, and adopted a series of ordinances for the formation of a provisional government. David G. Burnet was elected President, and Lorenzo D. Zavala Vice-President. Samuel P. Carson was appointed Secretary of State, Baily Hardiman, Secretary of the Treasury, Thomas J. Rusk, Secretary of War, Robert Potter, Secretary of the Navy, and David Thomas, Attorney-General. The government was authorized to contract for a loan of $1,000,000, to enter into treaties with foreign nations, and to decide upon the time for the election of permanent officers. The President issued a fervent appeal for sympathy and aid to the people of the United States. On the 16th, the Constitution of the

Republic of Texas was adopted, and signed the following day. It provided for the establishment of an Executive, a Legislature to consist of two bodies, Senate and House of Representatives, and a Judiciary to be governed by the common law of England. Slavery was established, and owners were forbidden to manumit their slaves without the consent of Congress. Free negroes were forbidden to reside in the territory. The importation of slaves, except from the United States, was punishable as piracy. The head rights of settlers were fixed at one league and a labor for each head of a family, and one third of a league to each single man of seventeen years of age or upwards, but the location of grants was suspended until the men serving in the army could have an equal choice. Freedom and equality for all forms of religious belief were decreed; the rights of trial by jury and writ of habeas corpus, except in cases of treason, and the freedom of the press were established. No man was to be imprisoned for debt, and titles of nobility and monopolies were forbidden. The Constitution was signed by fifty members, three of whom were Mexicans, and the Convention adjourned on the 17th. The provisional government at once removed its headquarters to Harrisburg on the Buffalo Bayou.

CHAPTER X

THE MASSACRE OF GOLIAD

TRAVIS'S morning and evening guns had ceased to send their signals over the prairie to the ears of the listening scouts from Gonzales five days before Houston's arrival, and on the 11th of March, when he reached the town, definite news of the fall of the Alamo had been received from the mouth of Antonio Borgaro, a Mexican from San Antonio. Houston instantly sent off a swift dispatch with the news to Colonel Fannin at Goliad, with orders to blow up the fort and evacuate the place. He was directed to bring away as many pieces of artillery as he could, and sink the rest in the river. He was to march to Victoria on the Guadalupe River, intrench himself, and await further orders. Every facility was to be afforded to the women and children who wished to leave the place. Prompt action was urged, as the enemy were reported to be advancing, and there was likely to be a rise in the waters. On the 13th, Mrs. Dickenson reached Gonzales, and brought a confirmation of the news of the capture of the Alamo, and the slaughter of its defenders. There was a scene of wild grief and panic in the little town. The larger portion of its male citizens had formed the party which had joined the defenders of the Alamo, and perished with them. Twenty women were made widows by the slaughter, and almost every family had lost one of its members. There were rumors that the Mexican troops had reached the Cibolo Creek on their way to Gonzales, and preparations were made for immediate flight. Those who had wagons loaded them with such things as they could carry, and women mounted on horseback with their children in their arms for a wild flight across the prairie. One woman, who had lost her husband in the Alamo, rushed frantically about the streets with disheveled hair, screaming for the Mexicans to come and kill her and her children. Houston exerted himself to calm the violence, and bring some order out of the panic. When Houston reached Gonzales he found about 300 militia men gathered there without organization, and about a hundred more had come in since. It was useless to attempt to resist the advance of Santa Anna with any such force, and Houston determined to fall back to the line of the Colorado, and await the junction of the troops under Fannin. That night the troops were gathered together and, escorting the wagons containing the women and children, set out on the forlorn march over the wet prairie. Two small cannon were thrown into the river for the want of means to bring them away, and a single wagon, drawn by four feeble oxen, contained all the munitions and supplies of the army. After leaving the town it was set on fire, and as the band struggled on

in the darkness their backward glances could see the
lights of their blazing homes on the horizon. Deaf
Smith and Henry Karnes were left behind as scouts
to watch for the approach of the Mexicans. The next
day, at Peach Creek, fifteen miles from Gonzales, a
party of 125 volunteers was met, twenty-five of whom
left on hearing the news of the fall of the Alamo.
Thirty-five more joined them during the day, making
the number remaining with the force 474. When the
party reached Nevada Creek, fifteen miles from the
Colorado, Houston learned that a blind widow with
six children had been ignorantly left at a house some
distance from the road. He sent a party back to
bring them in, and delayed his march until they arrived. He sent Major William T. Austin, his aid-
de-camp, to the mouth of the Brazos for six cannon
which were supposed to be there, and pushed on to
the Colorado, which he reached on the 17th. He
made his camp on the west bank of the river at a
place known as Burnham's Crossing, and awaited the
news from Fannin.

While Santa Anna had been advancing upon San
Antonio, General Urrea, with his escort of cavalry,
had proceeded to Matamoras, and taken command of
the troops there for an advance to the north. He
left Matamoras on February 18 with a force of between 900 and 1000 men, and reached San Patricio
on the 27th. He immediately asaulted the barracks
in a storm of rain. The garrison of forty men, under
Captain Peirce, made a desperate resistance, but the

building was taken. The prisoners, to the number of twenty-four, were shot by order of General Urrea. Colonel Johnson and three companions, who were in a house in the town, made their escape through the back door, and found their way to Refugio. Dr. Grant and a party of forty men were out on a horse-raiding expedition toward the Rio Grande. They had previously captured Captain Rodriguez and sixty-six Mexicans with a *caballada* of horses. The party was released under parole, but broke their parole, and joined the forces under Urrea. After the capture of San Patricio, Urrea set out in pursuit of Grant. He discovered Grant's party on the 2d of March near the Aqua Dulce, returning with a herd of captured horses. He set an ambush, and the Mexicans charged upon Grant's party from two belts of timber through which they were passing. The greater portion of Grant's men were killed in the charge. But he and a man named Reuben R. Brown fled across the prairie. They were pursued, and, after a desperate race of seven miles, Grant was killed by a lance thrust. Brown was lassoed from his horse, and made a prisoner.

When Fannin received Houston's dispatch ordering him to abandon Goliad and fall back upon Victoria, he was in command of about 500 men. They consisted almost entirely of volunteers from the United States. Fannin, in his letter to the Council, had complained that there were less than half a dozen Texans in his ranks. They were divided into two

battalions, known as the "Georgia" and the "La
Fayette." The first consisted of Ward's, Wads-
worth's, and Tucker's companies from Alabama and
Georgia. The second included the New Orleans
"Grays," Captain Pettes; the "Mustangs" of Kentucky, Captain Duval; the Mobile "Grays," Captain
McManeman; a company from Louisville and Huntsville, Tennessee, Captain Bradford; Captain King's
company from Georgia; and the "Red Rovers" of
Alabama, Captain Shackleford. There was also a
small squadron of cavalry under Captain Horton, and
a detachment of artillery under Captain Westover.
Colonel Fannin had built an earthwork around the
old Mission church, which he called Fort Defiance,
and prepared to defend the place. Learning of the
advance of Urrea he sent an order to the garrison of
San Patricio to join him, but had been disobeyed.
He then sent Captain King with twenty-eight men to
bring in the families from Refugio. Captain King
arrived at Refugio on the 12th of March. Before he
could remove the families he was attacked by the advance guard of Urrea's cavalry, and took refuge in
the old stone church of the Mission. He dispatched
a message to Colonel Fannin for assistance, and Fannin sent Lieutenant-Colonel Ward with 120 men.
King defended the church until the arrival of Ward
on the evening of the 13th, and preparations were
made for a retreat the next day. But in the morning Urrea arrived with the main body of his force.
On the news of his approach, Captain King was sent

out with a party of thirteen men to reconnoitre, and was attacked by a strong force of cavalry. Ward sallied out to his assistance, but was beaten back, and compelled to retreat to the church. Captain King was cut off, and compelled to surrender. He and his men were tied to post oak-trees and shot. Their bodies were left unburied, and their skeletons were afterward found fastened to the trees. Ward and his party were besieged in the Mission church. The building was in ruins, but its walls were strong. Urrea brought up a four-pounder to batter in the door, and attempted to take the church by assault. The attack was repulsed by the deadly fire of the rifles, and in the evening the enemy withdrew to their camp, leaving pickets around the building. The Texans, finding their ammunition nearly exhausted, determined to escape during the night. There was the painful necessity of leaving behind three of the comrades who had been disabled during the fight. They filled the canteens of the wounded with water, and left them to the mercy of the Mexicans, who afterward butchered them. The party broke through the patrol guard, and started to find their way to Victoria, where they expected to meet Fannin. They took a circuitous route through swamps and forests, so as to avoid the pursuit of the enemy's cavalry, and reached Victoria on the 20th. They found Victoria in possession of the enemy, and were attacked by a force of cavalry. They retreated into the swamps of the Guadalupe, where they spent the night. In the morning, having not a single round of ammunition left, they surrendered, and were marched back as prisoners to Goliad.

Fannin waited six days for the return of Ward and King, sending off courier after courier in a vain attempt to obtain news. On the 18th he received definite news that the church was taken, and that Ward had retreated in the direction of Victoria. A scouting party of cavalry was sent out under Captain Horton, who reported that a large force was advancing slowly from the direction of San Antonio. Some skirmishing took place during the day with advance parties of Urrea's cavalry. In the evening a consultation of the officers was held, and it was decided to retreat the next day. The heavy pieces of cannon were buried, the fort was dismantled, and the provisions and supplies, which could not be taken with the force, destroyed. The force set out on its march toward Victoria on the morning of the 19th. It numbered about 350 men, and had nine fieldpieces and a howitzer, and a number of wagons drawn by oxen. The morning was extremely thick and foggy, and it took until ten o'clock to get the train across the San Antonio River. The march was begun across an open prairie, skirted with belts of timber, toward the Coleto Creek, about ten miles from the town. Not a Mexican had been seen, except a couple of mounted videttes, and when within about three miles of the sheltering timber of the Coleto, Fannin ordered a halt at a place where the grass had sprung up green after being burned over, to allow his cattle to graze. It was a fatal error. Fannin was remonstrated with by some of his officers, and urged to push on to the timber. But he appears to have held the Mexicans in contempt, and imagined that they would not dare to molest him.

After a halt of about an hour and a half, and just as the order had been given to hitch up the teams to resume the march, a dark line of cavalry was seen coming from a skirt of timber to the right of the Texan force, and about two miles distant. They advanced at a gallop, and formed in a mass between the Texans and the Coleto. A large body of infantry followed the cavalry, and took a position in the rear, rapidly advancing lines on both sides. The Texans were caught in a trap. The train had been halted in a depression of the prairie six or seven feet below the general surface, and in an attempt to reach an eminence an ammunition wagon broke down. The lines were then drawn in a hollow square, three ranks deep. The wagons were pushed in the centre, and the artillery stationed at the corners. After the Mexican forces had been posted so as to surround the Texans, their cavalry advanced and opened a harmless fire with their *escopetos*. Fannin ordered his men to lie down, and not to fire until the enemy came within certain range. When they did so, the Texan rifles emptied the foremost saddles, and drove them back. Captain Horton, who had been sent forward with the cavalry to examine the crossing over the

Coleto, hearing the firing, galloped back to rejoin the main body. But his party was attacked by the cavalry, and compelled to take flight through the woods toward the settlements. The enemy appeared at two o'clock, and at three, having made all his dispositions, Urrea ordered a general charge upon the lines from the two sides and the rear. They were received with a withering fire from the artillery and the rifles, each Texan being supplied with two or three loaded guns, and firing with great coolness and precision. The Mexicans came on with great impetuosity, until their front ranks were almost at the bayonet push. The Texan fire, however, was so rapid and deadly that they were compelled to fall back. The infantry were ordered to lie down within range, and fire from that position, but were picked off by the Texans whenever they raised their heads, and were compelled to withdraw. Urrea endeavored to break the Texan lines by a cavalry charge led by himself, but it was broken by a discharge of grapeshot from the howitzer and a volley from the rifles. For the third time the assault was made, the officers pricking on the men from behind with their swords. The infantry were driven up close, but the cavalry broke when scarcely within range. The plain was strewn with the bodies of men and horses, and riderless horses charged through the lines of infantry, throwing them into still greater confusion, "until their retreat resembled the headlong flight of a herd of buffaloes." The Mexican troops were finally rallied, and drawn up around the Texan lines out of range. Colonel Fannin was severely wounded in the thigh in the early part of the engagement, but continued to command with great coolness and courage. The Texan cannon were useless after a few discharges, from becoming heated and clogged, there being no water with which to sponge them.

After the assault had been given up the cavalry were drawn around the lines in open order. They kept up a harmless fire with their muskets and *escopetos*, to which the Texans responded with more deadly effect. There were about a hundred Campeachy Indians with the Mexican forces. They crept up around the Texan lines, taking advantage of every hillock and tuft of thick grass, and opened a much more deadly and accurate fire upon the besieged force, killing and wounding a number of the Texans. Four of them crept up to within a hundred yards, and were firing with deadly effect, when Captain Duval, an excellent marksman, undertook to dislodge them. Taking a position behind a gun carriage he fired every time an Indian showed his head, and silenced them in four shots. As he fired his last shot the forefinger of his right hand was taken off by a rifle ball. After the battle the four Indians were found where they fell, each with a hole in his head. During the fighting one of the wounded was Harry Ripley, a youth of eighteen or nineteen, the son of General Ripley, of Louisiana. He had his thigh broken shortly after the Indians took to the grass.

He asked Mrs. Cash, a lady of Goliad, who had accompanied the retreat, to help him into her cart. She fixed a prop for him to lean against, and a rest for his rifle. He was seen to bring down four Mexicans before he received another wound, which broke his right arm. He said to Mrs. Cash, "You may take me down, now, mother. I have done my share. They have paid exactly two for one on account of the balls in me." The Indian firing began at dusk, but as soon as the darkness rendered the flashes of the guns more plainly visible, the Texan rifles were instantaneously aimed at the spots, and soon put an end to the discharges. Urrea drew off his troops, and surrounded the Texan lines, his camp fires gleaming redly in the darkness, and his guards keeping up a continual cry of "*Sentinela alerte.*"

The night was one of extreme darkness and a heavy fog. Colonel Fannin addressed the men, saying that the only chance of escape was by a retreat during the night to the timber of the Coleto. He said that there was no doubt of their ability to do so, as the enemy was much demoralized by the failure of their attacks, but in the morning it would be too late, as the Mexicans would undoubtedly receive reinforcements. If the majority of the men were in favor of the attempt it should be made. But this would have necessitated the abandonment of the wounded. There were sixty of the men who had been hit, about forty of whom were disabled. The men refused to abandon their wounded comrades to the mercy of the Mexicans, and it was decided to remain. The lines were contracted to the centre from the original area in which they had fought the battle, and the night was spent by the Texans in throwing up an earthen breastwork, which was still further barricaded by the wagons and the dead bodies of the oxen killed during the afternoon's fight. It was so dark that the surgeons were unable to attend to the wounded, who suffered intensely from thirst. By an oversight the provisions had been left behind, and the night wore away for the besieged without food, or drink, or sleep. During the night three men deserted, and attempted to reach the timber of the Coleto. But the reports from the muskets of the Mexican patrols showed that they had been intercepted and killed.

In the early morning, before it was fairly light, reinforcements of 300 or 400 men were seen coming to the enemy. They had with them two pieces of artillery, and a hundred pack mules laden with ammunition and supplies. The pieces were soon trained, and the Mexicans opened fire with grape and canister, shattering the wagons and ploughing through the camp. The position of the Texans was untenable. Their cannon were useless, and there were but two or three rounds of ammunition left for the small arms. A consultation of the officers was hastily called, and the question was discussed of a surrender. Fannin opposed it, saying, "We whipped them off yesterday, and can do it again to-day." But the majority were in favor of a surrender, if honorable and safe terms of capitulation could be obtained. The question was submitted to the men by the commanders of the companies, and they agreed that it was impossible to attempt to resist any longer. The white flag was hoisted, and responded to by the enemy. Colonel Fannin and Major Wallace, accompanied by Captain Durangue, as interpreter, went out from the encampment. They were met halfway between the lines by Colonel Salas, Lieutenant-Colonel Holzinger, and Lieutenant Gonzales, the officers sent by Urrea. After a conference the Texan officers returned, and announced that articles had been agreed on by which the besieged should surrender as prisoners of war, and be treated according to the usages of civilized nations. The wounded were to be taken back to Goliad and properly cared for. Private property was to be respected. Dr. Joseph H. Bernard, one of the surgeons, said that he saw what he supposed to be the articles signed by Colonel Fannin, and delivered to a Mexican officer, and believed that each commander had a duplicate. It was rumored about the camp that it was agreed that the men should be sent to New Orleans at the first opportunity, under parole not to serve any more during the war in Texas. This was confirmed by the saying of Lieutenant-Colonel Holzinger, the Mexican officer appointed to receive the surrendered arms. As they were delivered up he said, "Well, gentlemen, in ten days liberty and home." The officers' arms were received separately, nailed up in a box, and put on one side, with the assurance that they should be delivered to them on their release.

The loss of the Texans in the battle, called by the Mexicans "Encinal del Perdido," was seven killed and sixty wounded, of whom some died before the removal of the prisoners. The loss of the Mexicans is not known with any accuracy. General Urrea reported only eleven killed and fifty-four wounded, which was a manifest absurdity. Dr. Bernard says that he assisted in attending over a hundred of the wounded Mexicans. The total Mexican loss in killed and wounded can hardly have been less than between 200 and 300. The most reasonable estimate of the number of Urrea's troops on the morning of the surrender is that of about 1200.

The prisoners were put under a strong guard of cavalry, marched back to Goliad, and confined in the old church. The wounded were brought in carts the next day, and placed in the barracks' hospital. The church, which was of limestone, gloomy and vaulted, was not large enough to comfortably contain the prisoners. They were huddled together, and given as rations only four ounces of fresh beef, which they were obliged to cook as they could. Hospital dressings and surgical instruments were wanting for the wounded, and the surgeons complained to Colonel Fannin, who addressed a note to General Urrea calling attention to the terms of the capitulation in regard to the treatment of the wounded. Urrea set out in pursuit of Ward's party, and they were brought in prisoners a few days afterward. He also dispatched a force to Copano, who returned with Major Miller and eighty-two volunteers from Nashville. They were captured by Colonel Vara immediately upon landing, and surrendered without resistance. They arrived on the 25th, and were confined in the church, being distinguished from the rest of the prisoners by pieces of white cloth tied around their arms.

Meantime the news had reached Santa Anna at San Antonio of the capture of Fannin and his force. He instantly dispatched an order to Lieutenant-Colonel Portilla, the commandant of Goliad, to have the prisoners all shot. The Mexican Congress the previous year had passed a law that all foreigners making an armed invasion of the country should be dealt with as pirates.

Colonel Portilla received the order for the execution of the prisoners on Saturday evening, the 26th. On that same evening Colonel Fannin and Lieutenant-Colonel Holzinger returned from Copano, where they had been to see if a vessel could be obtained to take the men to New Orleans; but they could find none in the harbor. Colonel Fannin was very cheerful, and spoke of his wife and child, whom he expected soon to see. The prisoners were encouraged by the apparent purpose of the Mexicans to send them home, and spent the evening in singing, one of the men who had retained his flute playing "Home, Sweet Home." Portilla was much agitated and distressed by the receipt of the order from Santa Anna, and the news soon spread among the Mexican officers, causing horror and indignation among the more humane. Urrea was absent in the direction of Victoria, and the news did not reach him until after the execution had taken place.

In the early morning of Palm Sunday the prisoners were awakened and formed into three divisions. One was led out on the road to San Antonio, one on the road to San Patricio, and the third on the road to Copano. One party was informed by the Mexican officers that it was marching to be sent home, another that it was being taken out to kill beeves, and the third that the church was required for Santa Anna's advancing troops. As they passed through the town the Mexican women, gazing at them from the doors of the houses, exclaimed, "*Pobrecitos!*" (poor fellows) but the exclamation aroused no suspicion. They were marched in double file with Mexican soldiers on each side of them, and cavalry squads in the rear. When about half a mile from the town, in different directions, the divisions were halted, and one line of the Mexican soldiers passed around to the other side. There was hardly time for the exclamation, "Boys, they are going to kill us!" when the order was given to fire, and the volleys were poured in at close range. The lines of prisoners fell in heaps. Some few, who were unwounded, struggled to their feet, and dashed toward the timber out upon the prairie, pursued by the cavalry, and shot at as

they ran. The guards stabbed the wounded to death
with their bayonets. Many of the fugitives were
shot down, or stabbed with lances, and some of those
who reached a temporary shelter in the river timber
were afterward intercepted and killed by the cavalry
pickets. Twenty-seven finally escaped by reaching
the woods and swimming the river. They made their
way by long and painful journeys over the prairies,
hiding by day and moving on by night, and, after
incredible sufferings and perilous adventures, reached
places of safety in the settlements, or joined the
Texan army in its advance after the battle of San
Jacinto.

Before daylight in the morning, Dr. Bernard and
Dr. Shackleford, who was a surgeon as well as captain of the "Red Rovers," were aroused by Colonel
Garay with a serious and grave countenance, and
directed to go to his headquarters, which were in a
peach orchard, two or three hundred yards from the
church. They found that Captain Miller's company
had also been ordered there, and followed them on,
supposing that their services were required for some
wounded. Drs. Bernard and Shackleford were called
inside of Colonel Garay's tent, where they found two
men lying completely covered up with blankets, so
that they could not see their faces, and whom they
supposed to be the patients they were called to attend.
While waiting a lad named Martinez came in, and
addressed them in English. They chatted for some
time, but, becoming impatient at the non-appearance

of Colonel Garay, they were about to return to the church, when Martinez told them that the directions for them to remain were positive. Just then they were startled by a volley of firearms from the direction of the fort, and Dr. Shackleford exclaimed, "What's that?" Martinez replied that it was the soldiers discharging their guns for the purpose of cleaning them. But yells and cries were heard, which were recognized as being the voices of Americans, and through the openings in the trees some prisoners were seen running at their utmost speed with Mexican soldiers in pursuit of them. Colonel Garay then entered the tent with a distressed countenance, and said, "Keep still, gentlemen, you are perfectly safe. This is not from my orders, nor do I execute them." He then told them of the orders which had been received from Santa Anna to shoot the prisoners, and that he had taken upon himself the responsibility of saving the surgeons, and the others, who had been taken without arms in their hands. The men under the blankets were two who had been employed by Colonel Garay as carpenters, and whom he had resolved to save. In the course of five or ten minutes as many as five distinct volleys were heard in the tent, and occasional shots followed for more than an hour. Dr. Shackleford had recruited the "Red Rovers" from among his friends and neighbors in Alabama, and his eldest son and two of his nephews were in their ranks. Señora Alvarez, the wife of one of Urrea's officers, having been informed of the approaching massacre, withdrew a few of the Texan officers during the night, and concealed them in her house until the slaughter was over. They joined Miller's men, and were released after the retreat of the Mexicans from San Jacinto.

Fannin and Ward were not shot with the rest of the prisoners, but taken out later. Fannin received the order for his execution with a calm countenance. He handed his watch to the officer commanding the firing party, with the request that it be sent to his family. He asked that he be not shot in the head, and that he should be decently buried. It is said that he was shot in the head, and at any rate his body was thrown in the heap with the rest of the prisoners. Ward refused to kneel at the word of command, and was shot while denouncing the Mexicans as cold-blooded murderers. Fannin was a native of Georgia, and had come to Texas in 1834. At the outbreak of the revolution he had enlisted a company called the "Brazos Volunteers," and joined Austin's army. He had sided with the Council in the difficulties between it and Governor Smith, but the charge that he refused to obey the orders of General Houston to retreat from Goliad is an error. But his delays in executing them promptly were as fatal as disobedience. Ward was a native of Georgia, where he had recruited a company at the call of Texas for volunteers, and reached the country a few months previous to his death. The wounded were butchered in their beds in the hospital. Toward evening the bodies were piled in heaps, and some brushwood was piled over them and set on fire. It was not sufficient to consume them, and the next day the vultures were seen feeding on the scorched and mangled remains. When the Texan army advanced after the battle of San Jacinto to follow General Filisola's retiring march, it halted at Goliad, and the bones of the victims of the massacre were gathered and placed in a grave, at which General Rusk delivered a feeling address. The number of men killed in the massacre was 320. Twenty had been previously killed with Captain King, or butchered in the church at Refugio. The massacre was as bunglingly executed as it was cruel, and included all the horrors of cowardly treachery and clumsy butchery more befitting a band of savages than a disciplined military. The troops departed for the east the next day, leaving seventy or eighty men to guard the hospital. Miller's men were allowed at large on their parole. Drs. Bernard and Shackleford were taken to San Antonio to attend the Mexican soldiers wounded in the assault on the Alamo.

Some controversy arose as to whether Fannin had surrendered under an agreement of capitulation or at discretion. The copy of the agreement, if there was one, was never found, and General Urrea declared that the surrender was without conditions. The presumptive evidence, however, is strongly in favor of a capitulation. Fannin and his men were well aware of the cruelty of the Mexicans, and would have pre-

ferred to have died fighting rather than to have trusted
to their mercy, without some definite guarantee that
they would be treated as prisoners of war. All the
circumstances go to show that they laid down their
arms upon such a pledge. There is nothing in the
character of Urrea to vindicate him from the charge
of the falsehood and treachery too common among his
military associates, and his previous butchery of Captain King's men and the garrison at San Patricio
showed that he was ready to carry out the orders for
treating the invaders from the United States as
pirates. There is a further presumption that there
was a capitulation in the fact that he sent Fannin and
his men to Goliad, instead of executing them on the
spot. There is reason to believe that Urrea informed
Santa Anna that Fannin had surrendered upon
terms, although the latter denied it when a prisoner
at San Jacinto, for the order to shoot the prisoners
was sent not to Urrea, but to Colonel Portilla. The
odium of the butchery rests entirely upon Santa
Anna. He was responsible for the decree of the
Mexican Congress that invaders should be treated as
outlaws, for the Congress was entirely his creature.
He was undoubtedly deeply enraged at the slaughter
of his troops by the defenders of the Alamo, and perhaps counted on striking terror into the Texan colonists by an example of merciless severity. If so, he
was mistaken in the character of the men he had to
deal with. They were simply aroused to a pitch of
fury by his cruelty, and the cry of "Remember La

Bahia!" nerved the arms that struck down his fleeing soldiers at San Jacinto. Like all such deeds, it was a blunder as well as a crime. When he received the information that Miller and his company had been spared, he directed the preparation of an order for their execution, but Captain Savageiro, the bearer of the dispatch from Goliad, manfully remonstrated. He was reprimanded by Santa Anna, but the order was withdrawn to permit an investigation into the circumstances of the capture. To the credit of most of the Mexican officers, they were shocked at Santa Anna's barbarity, and some of them had the courage to express their shame and indignation.

Santa Anna was confirmed in his belief that the war was practically over by the capture of the garrison of Goliad. He divided his troops into three columns to complete the work of occupying the country. The first, under General Gaona, was to proceed by a northerly route to Nacogdoches. The second, under General Sesma, was to advance upon San Felipe, and thence by way of Harrisburg to the coast at Anahuac. The third, under General Urrea, was to sweep the country between Goliad and the mouth of the Brazos, and drive out all the colonists on the southern border. The orders to these commanders were to shoot all prisoners. He ordered a brigade of cavalry, with a portion of the artillery and military stores, to be ready to return to San Luis Potosi, and prepared to set out for Tampico himself by sea from Copano or Matagorda. But upon the remonstrances of General Filisola and Colonel Almonte, that the Texans were by no means yet subdued, and the receipt of a dispatch from General Sesma that a force of 1200 had gathered to dispute the passage of the Colorado, Santa Anna changed his mind, countermanded the order for the withdrawal of the troops to Mexico, and set out with General Filisola, under an escort of cavalry, to join the column under General Sesma.

CHAPTER XI

HOUSTON remained at Burnham's Crossing for two days, until all the fugitives and their families had been passed over, and then crossed to the east bank of the Colorado. He moved down to a place known as Beason's Crossing, where he remained until the 26th. The artillery which he expected did not arrive, and he complained that his orders for its transmission from the mouth of the Brazos had been countermanded by the government. The news of the fall of the Alamo and the retreat of Houston, combined with the withdrawal of the government to Harrisburg, created a thorough panic among the settlers. It was one of those alarms which are liable to seize any community on the receipt of sudden and terrifying news. The deserters from the army spread the panic from house to house with wild exaggerations as to the nearness and magnitude of the Mexican forces. Families packed their goods into wagons and started in frantic haste toward the eastern settlements, and men who should have joined the army took the backward instead of the forward trails. The flight and panic which spread through Texas were afterward known as "The Runaway Scrape." Nevertheless, the colonists rallied to some extent to join Houston's army. He declared, subsequently, that at no time had he over 700 men; but well-informed authorities assert that before he fell back from the Colorado his forces numbered between 1200 and 1400. His dispatches to the government, while urgently calling upon the people to rally to his standard, indicated a purpose to fight on the line of the Colorado. He said, "Fifteen hundred men can defeat all the troops Santa Anna can send to the Colorado. Let all the men east of the Trinity rush to us. Let all the disposable forces of Texas fly to arms. Rouse the Redlanders to battle." He reported his men as in fine spirits, under good discipline, and eager to engage the enemy. On the 19th, Generals Sesma and Woll arrived with a Mexican force, estimated at between 500 and 600, and took a position on the west bank of the Colorado about two miles above Beason's Crossing, under orders from Santa Anna not to cross the river unless the enemy had retired. Houston sent up a small force to dispute Sesma's crossing, and some skirmishing took place, but the Mexicans made no attempt to cross. He sent out spies to ascertain the number of Sesma's forces, and, according to his dispatches, it was correctly reported to him. He could have fallen upon and destroyed Sesma's force, but he waited for his artillery and for news of the movements of the troops under Fannin.

On the 25th, a fugitive named Peter Kerr arrived in camp with the news of the capture of Fannin's force. Houston, afraid of the effect of the news upon the spirits of his men, fell into one of his feigned rages, declared Kerr to be a traitor and a spy, and ordered him to be put under guard for execution the next morning. Of course he did not carry out his threat. He examined him privately at night, and was satisfied of the truth of the report. The destruction of Fannin's force left Urrea free either to form a junction with Sesma or to pass to Houston's rear. It is probable that Houston came to the conclusion, after the news of the defeat of Fannin, that an attack upon Sesma would lead to the concentration of the entire Mexican army upon the Colorado, which he would be unable to meet with a chance of success, while a defeat and the destruction of its only army would be fatal to the cause of Texas. It would be wiser to induce the enemy to divide their forces, and scatter through the country, so that they could be struck in detail. He made up his mind to fall back to the Brazos. He kept his own counsel, and took no one into his confidence except Colonel Hockley, his chief-of-staff. He began his retreat on the evening of the 26th, and fell back about five miles on his first march. The movement caused great dissatisfaction and some insubordination among the members of his little army. They wanted to fight, and, like all volunteers, could see nothing in a retreat but evidence of timidity on the part of the commander. It is the greatest test of the power and personal influence of a commander to keep a force of undisciplined soldiery together and in heart on a retrograde movement. Furloughs were given to some to remove their families from the country between the Colorado and the Brazos, and others departed without leave, so that the force was reduced to 750 men. Fiery and insubordinate spirits advocated revolt, and even the deposition of the commander. But Houston was indefatigable, and never was his power over men more thoroughly demonstrated than in keeping the confidence and control of the lawless, passionate, and undisciplined elements that composed his retreating force. He was the first in the morning to rally the troops and start the wagons, and by jest and good humor, by objurgation and appeal, pushed the march over every obstacle, and kept the men in hearty spirits. He put his own shoulder to the bemired wheels, and his persuasive presence was everywhere up and down the line. It was a very trying time for Houston. He wrote to Rusk, the Secretary of War, after reaching the Brazos: "I hope I can keep them together. I have thus far succeeded beyond my hopes. I will do the best I can, but be assured the fame of Jackson could never compensate me for my anxiety and mental pain." The weather was very depressing. Continued storms and heavy rains beat down upon the unsheltered troops, and tried even their seasoned hardihood. The streams were swollen beyond their banks, and the prairie, which at that season of the year was usually an elastic carpet of green grass and blooming flowers, was a dismal :

miry morass in which the wagon wheels sank up to
their hubs. But the line struggled on, sweeping up
the families along its line of march, and sending out
scouting parties to bring away the inhabitants of the
outlying cabins. There were many painful scenes of
distress and suffering. While the army was crossing
the Colorado, two women were seen sitting on a log
near the bank. The husband of one of them had
been killed at the Alamo, and she was utterly abandoned and destitute. Houston gave her fifty dollars
out of the two hundred which was all that he had for
any purpose. It is an evidence of the vigorous character of the pioneer settlers, that she afterward wrote
him that she had invested the money in cattle, and
had made herself comfortable and independent. The
army was increased during its march by three companies of 130 men, who had been brought from the
mouth of the Brazos by Major John Forbes. It
reached San Felipe, on the west bank of the Brazos,
on the 28th.

From this point Houston determined to march up
the river. It is difficult to understand why he took
this course, unless, as he afterward said, he intended
to fall on the enemy by surprise, when they arrived
at San Felipe. The movement caused more insubordination in the ranks of the army. Captain Moreley
Baker, with his company of 120 men, insisted on remaining to defend the crossing at San Felipe, and
Captain Wylie Martin, with his, in going below to
guard the ferry at Fort Bend. These withdrawals

left Houston with only 520 men. He marched up the river to Mill Creek, and then to Groce's Ferry, where he found the steamer Yellowstone, partially loaded with cotton. The steamer was seized by his order, and held to take the troops across the river if necessary. The army was encamped in the Brazos bottom. Heavy rains continued to fall, and the encampment was entirely surrounded by water. The valley of the Brazos became a running torrent, and any scheme to attack the Mexicans on their arrival at San Felipe was out of the question. The army remained at its camp, shelterless and with no food except the beeves they could kill, until April 12. In the mean time, President Burnett had issued a proclamation calling upon the people to rally to the army, and endeavored to allay the panic. But a universal alarm had seized upon the people. The fugitives from the region west of the Brazos, streaming across the country, spread the contagion of fear from settlement to settlement clear to the border of Louisiana. Samuel P. Carson, the Secretary of State, wrote from Liberty to President Burnett: "Never, until I reached the Trinity, have I desponded, I will not say despaired. If Houston has retreated or been whipped, nothing can save the people from themselves; their own conduct has brought this calamity upon them." On the 29th, Captain Baker burned the town of San Felipe on the mistaken supposition that the enemy were approaching, but it proved to be only a herd of cattle. On April 2,

Vice-President Zavala joined Houston, and a company of eighty men from Eastern Texas also arrived. On the 4th, Secretary of War Rusk came to give his counsel and assistance.

General Sesma, having been reinforced by the arrival of the troops under General Tolsa so that his force amounted to 1400 men, crossed the swollen Colorado with great difficulty on rafts. Santa Anna did what it was expected he would, and ordered a concentration of his columns. Generals Urrea and Gaona were ordered to move upon San Felipe to form a junction with Sesma. Santa Anna himself hastened forward to take command of Sesma's column. He arrived with escort at San Felipe April 7. Finding that Houston had vanished in the woods, he countermanded Urrea's advance, and directed him to proceed to Matagorda. In the mean time, General Gaona had lost his way in marching from Bastrop, and did not arrive at San Felipe until April 17. Santa Anna evidently believed that the Texan army had fallen back out of his path, and that all he need to do to finish the war was to push on and capture the members of the government at Harrisburg. He was probably also informed of the flight and panic of the people. Baker's small force remained to dispute the passage at San Felipe, and after some exchange of shots across the river, Santa Anna moved with a portion of his force down to Fort Bend. All the boats had been removed from the west bank of the river, but Colonel Almonte, hailing in English a negro ferryman on the east bank, persuaded him to bring over his boat, which was seized. Captain Martin's force was kept occupied at the upper ferry by a demonstration while the main body of the Mexicans crossed at the lower. The crossing was effected on the 13th, and on the afternoon of the 14th, Santa Anna pushed on with a column of about 700 men and one cannon, with the hope of surprising Harrisburg. He left Sesma with the remainder of the troops and the baggage, and announced that he would be back in three days. He forced his troops through the heavy timber of the Brazos bottom and across the miry prairie with impatient energy, and arrived in the vicinity of Harrisburg at eleven o'clock on the night of the 15th. He entered the town on foot with sixteen men, and found it deserted by all except three printers in the "Telegraph" office. He made them prisoners, and learned that the members of the government had left that morning for Galveston Island. He halted until the afternoon of the next day for the stragglers to come in, and, having set fire to the buildings of Harrisburg, pushed on for New Washington on the border of the bay, where he hoped to catch the fugitive members of the government before they could make their escape to Galveston. An advance guard of cavalry under Colonel Almonte nearly captured President Burnett, who had delayed to remove his family from his residence in the neighborhood. He had just pushed off in a small sailing vessel as they arrived, and stood exposed to their fire for some minutes, but fortunately escaped unharmed. Santa Anna arrived at New Washington on the 18th, and sent orders to General Cos, who was with Sesma's force, to join him by forced marches with 500 men. He intended to proceed to Anahuac, and from thence to Galveston.

The news that the Mexican advance had reached the Brazos was communicated to Houston by his scouts. On April 7, he issued an order to the army saying that "the moment we have waited for with anxiety and interest is fast approaching. The victims of the Alamo and the masses of those who were murdered at Goliad call for cool, deliberate vengeance. The army will be in condition for action at a moment's warning." On the 11th, two six-pounder guns, named "The Twin Sisters," which had been sent by the citizens of Cincinnati, arrived from Harrisburg. There was no ordnance with them, and horseshoes and old pieces of iron were cut up and tied in bags for canister. On the 12th, Houston became convinced that Santa Anna had crossed the Brazos, and determined to follow him. The army was taken over on the Yellowstone, and encamped at Groce's plantation, where it was joined by Baker's and Martin's companies. Baker and Martin were in a refractory temper. They asked if there was to be any fighting, and were informed by Houston that there would be. The companies at first refused to fall into line, and Martin was so insubordinate that he was sent to the Trinity to keep the Indians quiet, if they should prove turbulent, and protect the families of the settlers. On the 14th, the army commenced its march to the south. The roads were in a terrible condition, the streams swollen and the prairies quagmired. Houston pulled off his coat, and put his shoulder to the wheels of the cannon. On the 18th, the army reached Buffalo Bayou, opposite the ruins of Harrisburg. Deaf Smith and Karnes, who had been sent out as spies, returned with a prisoner bearing a buckskin bag full of dispatches to Santa Anna from General Filisola and the City of Mexico. There was no longer any doubt that the Mexican commander-in-chief was with the force below them. Houston and Rusk had a brief conference. "We need not talk," said Houston. "You think we ought to fight, and I think so, too." Up to that time Houston had kept his own counsel, and a good many of the officers and men believed that they would take the Liberty road toward the Trinity. He then called them together and addressed them. His brief words were: "The army will cross, and we will meet the enemy. Some of us may be killed, and must be killed. But, soldiers, remember the Alamo, the Alamo, the Alamo!" Said Major Somerville, "After that speech there will be damned few prisoners taken, that I know." Colonel Rusk began an eloquent speech, but stopped in the middle of it, saying, "I have done," as if he realized that it was useless to inspire men for a battle which they were eagerly longing for. The dogged courage which had

held up the retreat now flamed into the fierce energy
and lust for victory and vengeance.   Buffalo Bayou
is a narrow but deep stream, and was then running
bank-full.   Rafts were built of timber and rails, and
were pulled across on a rope stretched from tree to
tree, the horses swimming.   Houston stood on the
farther bank, and Rusk on the other, until the men
were across.   It was evening when the crossing was
finished, but the troops pushed on, until they became
so utterly exhausted that they were stumbling against
each other in the ranks and falling down.   They were
given a rest for two hours, and again resumed their
march, which they kept up until morning.   At sunrise on the morning of the 20th they were halted.
They had shot some wandering cattle, and were cooking their breakfast, when an alarm was given that the
scouts had encountered the enemy.   Leaving their
half-cooked meat on the sticks, they hastened forward
to Lynch's Ferry at the junction of Buffalo Bayou .
and the San Jacinto River, where it was expected that
Santa Anna would cross on his way to Anahuac.   No
enemy was in sight, but they found a flat-boat loaded
with provisions for Santa Anna's army, which they
seized.   They then fell back about half a mile to a
grove on the banks of the bayou.   The grove was of
heavy live oaks, hung with the weeping Spanish
moss, and free from underbrush.   Before it was a
stretch of gently rolling prairie, some two miles in
extent.   Upon the farther edge of the prairie were
the marshes of the San Jacinto River, which swept

around it to the southward, and whose timber
bounded the horizon. In front were two small
islands, or "motts" of timber, a few hundred yards
out on the prairie. In the rear were the turbid waters of the bayou, there broadened to a stream of
considerable width. The two cannon were planted
on the edge of the grove, and the men encamped
within its shelter. The grass on the prairie had already grown up tall, and the vegetation was in the
full leaf and luxuriance of the early Texas summer.

On the morning of the 20th, Santa Anna had
burnt the warehouses of New Washington and a vessel lying at the wharf, and his troops were in line for
the march to Lynch's Ferry, when Captain Barragan,
who had been sent out on a scout the previous day,
dashed up at full speed, and announced that Houston's army was close at hand, and had captured and
dispatched some of the stragglers. At the entrance
to New Washington there was a lane some half mile
in length, which was filled with the baggage mules
and the troops who had them in charge. When Santa
Anna, who had not left the town, received the report
of Captain Barragan, he dashed off at full speed
through the lane, thrusting aside and knocking down
the men and animals, and shouting at the top of his
voice, "The enemy are coming! The enemy are coming!" This mad conduct excited and frightened the
troops, and for some time there was an absolute confusion, the troops being on the verge of scattering in
flight. Finally, they were formed in line on the

prairie beyond the lane, and a scouting party was sent out. No enemy was in sight, and the troops were formed into ranks and advanced. About two o'clock in the afternoon Houston's pickets were discovered on the edge of the grove, and Santa Anna again formed his troops in line of battle. He brought up his cannon, and fired a few shots, which did no execution, except in wounding Colonel J. C. Neill, in command of the Texan artillery. The Mexican skirmish line of infantry advanced, but was received with a fire which drove it back in haste amid the wild shouts of the Texans. After some harmless exchanges by the artillery, Santa Anna drew off, and established his camp with very poor judgment. Its front was open to the prairie without defense, and in its rear were the deep marshes of the San Jacinto River. In fact, Santa Anna appears to have lost control of his faculties since the surprise of the morning and the realization that he had cut himself off from the main body of his troops. His officers perceived and spoke of the weak situation of the camp, but no one dared to remonstrate with him in his half-frantic state of mind. Late in the afternoon a slight skirmish took place. Colonel Sherman obtained permission to take out the Texan cavalry to reconnoitre, and endeavored to bring on a general engagement. He encountered the Mexican cavalry, and some shots were exchanged by which two Texans were wounded, one of them mortally. Some infantry was sent to his assistance, but Houston refused to advance for a battle, and the Texans retired. In this skirmish Mirabeau B. Lamar, afterward President of the Republic, distinguished himself. He had joined the army at Groce's, having walked nearly all the way from Velasco, and was serving as a private in the cavalry. During the skirmish a young man named Walter P. Lane was cut off and was in danger of being captured or killed. Lamar dashed forward, killed one Mexican, upset another, and disarmed a third, and brought Lane in safe. For this dashing feat he was given the command of the cavalry the next day. The Texans rested under double guard during the night, but there was nothing to break the silence except the voices of the night birds.

The morning sun of April 21 rose bright and cloudless. Santa Anna fortified his camp to a slight extent by piling up a barricade of boxes, baggage, and pack-saddles in front of his lines with an opening in the centre for his cannon. Boughs of trees were also cut and piled up as a sort of abatis. The Texans cooked their breakfast and waited for the orders of their commander. Houston was awake during the night, but slept for two hours in the morning with his head on a coil of rope used in dragging the cannon. At nine o'clock a body of Mexican troops were seen advancing over the prairie from the north. It was General Cos with a force of 500 men from Sesma's division. He had hastened by forced marches on the receipt of Santa Anna's orders to join him, and his men arrived so utterly exhausted that they threw themselves down as soon as they had stacked arms. Houston said that they were not new men, but merely a body of the old ones, which had been marched around behind a rise in the prairie to give the impression of a reinforcement. But it is doubtful if his explanation deceived anybody, or if the Texans were at all discouraged by the addition to the enemy's forces. In the morning Houston had directed Major Forbes to provide a couple of axes, and summoned Deaf Smith. He ordered him to select a trustworthy companion, and hold himself in readiness for special service, and not to leave the camp. Smith selected Denmore Reeves, a fellow-scout, as his companion, and waited for his orders. Houston made no sign of opening the engagements, and the men became impatient. About noon some of the officers waited upon him, and asked for a council of war. Houston consented. The council consisted of Colonels Burleson and Sherman, Lieutenant-Colonels Millard and Bennett, Major Wells, Secretary Rusk, and the commander-in-chief. The question was put, "Shall we attack the enemy in his position, or await his attack in ours?" The two junior officers were in favor of attack. The four seniors and Secretary Rusk were in favor of awaiting the attack of the enemy. Rusk said that "to attack veteran troops with raw militia was a thing unheard of; to charge upon the enemy without bayonets in the open prairie had never been known; our position is strong; in it we can whip all Mexico." Houston expressed no opinion, and dismissed the council. After the council had been dismissed Houston called Deaf Smith and his companion, and ordered them to take the axes and cut down Vince's bridge. The bridge was over Vince's Bayou, a stream running into Buffalo Bayou to the north about eight miles above the camp, and over which both armies had passed on their way into the *cul de sac*. Its destruction cut off the only means of retreat for either army, and made the coming battle a struggle for life or death. As Smith and his companion started with the axes over their saddle-bows, Houston told them that they must hurry if they would be back in time for what was about to take place. Smith smiled and said, "This looks a good deal like a fight, general."

At half past three o'clock Houston gave orders for the troops to be formed in line of battle. The only music which the Texan army had was a solitary drum and fife. As the troops were forming they struck up the air, "Will you come to the bower?" The lines were drawn up behind the mott of timber in front of the camp. Colonel Burleson occupied the centre with the first regiment. Colonel Sherman, with the second regiment, formed the left wing. The two pieces of artillery, under the command of Colonel Hockley, were stationed on the right of the first regiment, supported by four companies of infantry under command of Lieutenant-Colonel Millard. The squadron of cavalry, sixty-eight in number, under command of Colonel Lamar, completed the line on

the right. Houston was with the centre, Rusk with
the left. At four o'clock the order of "Forward!"
was given. The afternoon sun was shining full in
their eyes, lighting up the strong, eager faces and
the stained and ragged garments, as the line moved
forward with trailed arms. As they approached the
enemy's camp their pace was quickened to a run,
Houston dashing up and down behind the lines, waving his old white hat, and shouting, "G—d d—n
you, hold your fire!" When within about sixty
yards of the barricade Deaf Smith dashed up on his
horse, flecked with foam, and yelled, "You must
fight for your lives! Vince's bridge has been cut
down!" Where the guns were within point-blank
distance they were wheeled and fired, smashing into
the barricade. The Texans halted at close 'range,
and delivered a volley, and then dashed forward with
terrific yells, "Remember the Alamo! Remember
La Bahia!" The Mexicans were taken entirely by
surprise. Santa Anna had given up all idea of expecting a battle that day, and was enjoying his siesta
in his tent. Many of the other officers and men
were also stretched out in a doze. Some of the men
were cooking, and others were in the woods cutting
boughs for shelter. The lines were composed of
musket stacks. The cavalrymen were riding bare-
back to and from water. When the Texan line was
seen approaching there was the greatest alarm and
confusion. General Castrillon shouted on one side,
and Colonel Almonte was giving orders on the other.

Some of the officers cried out to the men to fire, and others to lie down and avoid the shots. Santa Anna ran out of his tent and yelled to the men to lie down. General Castrillon endeavored to rally some men to work the gun, but the cannoneer was shot down, and the men ran back, as they saw the charging line. General Castrillon himself soon fell dead, struck with a rifle ball. The Mexicans had barely time to seize their muskets, and give a scattering volley at the charging line, when it burst over the feeble barricade upon the frightened and disorganized crowd. The Texans clubbed their rifles or drew their bowie knives, and plunged into the mass. Some of the Mexicans tried to use their bayonets, but the brawny arms of the Texans struck them down, and, after a quarter of an hour of confused and desperate struggle, the Mexican army was in full flight over the prairie or running into the morass, pursued by the shouting and yelling Texans. Santa Anna, after running frantically about, wringing his hands, sprang upon a splendid black stallion furnished by one of his aids, and led the flight toward Vince's bridge. The Mexicans who fled into the morass were bogged in the quagmire, and shot down as they struggled. Some of them were intercepted by a deep and muddy bayou at the rear of the right of their camp, and were killed on its banks or shot as they endeavored to flounder across. Those who fled over the prairie were pursued by fleeter footsteps than their own, and struck down or shot. The cavalry pursued those who fled on horseback toward Vince's bridge. They found it destroyed, and only a few of them were able to cross the steep banks of the bayou. The Mexican soldiers, appalled by the fury of slaughter, threw up their hands and cried, "Me no Alamo! Me no Alamo!" The Texans executed a full vengeance. Six hundred and thirty were killed and 208 wounded out of a total of between 1300 and 1400 Mexicans. Colonel Almonte managed to rally 300 or 400 men beyond the camp, and make a formal surrender. The rest threw down their arms as they ran, and were herded into the Texan camp after the slaughter. Houston received a ball in his ankle which shattered the bone, and his horse was shot in several places as he followed the charging line on the breastworks. He remained upon the field, however, until the Mexican army was in full flight. While riding over the prairie endeavoring to stop the slaughter, his horse sank under him, and he fell to the ground. He turned over the command to Colonel Rusk, and was taken back to the camp. Deaf Smith charged on horseback ahead of the infantry. When close to the breastwork his horse stumbled and threw him over his head. Smith lost his sword in his fall, and drew his pistol to kill a Mexican soldier who was advancing to stab him with his bayonet, but the cap snapped. He threw his pistol at the Mexican, and staggered him back. He then wrenched the soldier's musket from his hands and defended himself until the infantry came up.

When darkness fell the prisoners were put under

guard. Bright fires were lit, and the Texans gave themselves up to wild rejoicings. They yelled and pranced around the prisoners, shouting to every officer, "Santa Anna? Santa Anna?" until some of them pulled off their shoulder-straps to escape the annoyance. There was a grand illumination of candles, which the Texans had procured from the Mexican baggage, and carried about in their hands. The dark arches of the grove echoed with the wild tumult until nearly morning. The prisoners, however, were not maltreated, but only made subject to a fire of chaff in a language which they did not understand. It was merely the effervescence of vigorous animal spirits working off the intoxication of victory.

The number of Texans in the battle which achieved their independence was 743. Of these only six were killed in the engagement, and twenty-five were wounded, of whom two afterward died. The losses were almost all in the scattering volley fired against them before they crossed the breastwork. After that the Mexicans were helplessly slaughtered. The Mexican loss was 630 killed, 208 wounded, and 730 prisoners. As an illustration of the fury of the Texan blows, many skulls have been picked up on the battle-field which showed where they had been struck in the back with bowie knives and sprayed, as a pane of glass is sprayed by a blow. A large quantity of arms, baggage, and camp equipage fell into the hands of the victors, including 900 English muskets, 300 sabres, and 200 pistols. There were 300 mules and 100 horses, clothing, tents, and camp equipage. Among the spoils was the sum of $12,000 in silver. The soldiers voted that $2000 of this should be devoted to the support of the navy. The rest was distributed among them, making $7.50 each, which was all the money they received during the campaign.

The next day parties were sent out to bury the dead Mexican soldiers, in whose bodies decomposition set in so rapidly as to cause the more superstitious among the prisoners to attribute their disaster to a supernatural visitation. The plunder of the Mexican camp was brought in, and the Texans amused themselves by decorating the mules with officers' sashes and ribbons, and in all kinds of rude horse-play. In the mean time, parties were scouring the country in search of Santa Anna and other fugitives. Houston had prophesied that Santa Anna would be found making his retreat on all fours, and in the dress of a common soldier. About two o'clock a little man was brought in behind a soldier on horseback. His restless eyes and pallid countenance indicated that he was suffering from great fear. He was dressed in linen trousers, a blue cotton jacket, a cap, and red worsted slippers. The Mexican soldiers, on seeing him, exclaimed, "El Presidente! El General Santa Anna!"

When Santa Anna, in his flight from the battlefield, came to Vince's Bayou and found the bridge destroyed, he plunged in with his horse. The horse was

mired, and was unable to extricate himself. Santa
Anna left him, swam across the stream, climbed the
opposite bank, and continued his flight on foot. He
found some old clothes in an abandoned house, and
exchanged his gilded uniform for them. The next
day he was discovered by James T. Sylvester and a
party of four, who were scouting the country. He
was standing on the edge of a ravine, and when he
saw the party riding toward him he dropped on all
fours in the grass, and was with difficulty compelled
to rise. He claimed to be a private soldier, but his
fine linen and jeweled studs betrayed him to be an
officer. He then said that he was an aid-de-camp to
Santa Anna. As the party started to return to camp
he complained that his feet were so sore that he could
not walk, and he was taken behind one of the men on
horseback.

Santa Anna was brought into the presence of
Houston, who was lying on his pallet in a doze, having been kept awake during the night from the pain
of his wound. Houston was not much more distinguished in dress than his captive. His dandyism had
given way to the exigencies of the campaign, and
he wore an old black coat, a black velvet vest, a
pair of snuff-colored pantaloons, and dilapidated
boots. His only badge of authority during the campaign was a sword with a plated scabbard, which he
tied to his belt with buckskin thongs. Santa Anna
stepped forward, and said, with an impressive bow,
"I am General Antonio Lopez de Santa Anna, Pres-

ident of the Mexican Republic, and I claim to be a
prisoner of war at your disposal." Houston waved
his hand for him to be seated on an ammunition box,
and Colonel Almonte was sent for to act as interpreter. While waiting his arrival, Santa Anna
pressed his hands to his sides as if in pain or fear,
and his restless black eyes glanced around the camp.
When Almonte came up Santa Anna complained of
pain, and asked for a piece of opium. A piece of
about five grains was given him, and he regained
something of his composure. His first words were,
"That man may consider himself born to no common
destiny who has conquered the Napoleon of the West.
It now remains for him to be generous to the van-
quished." Houston replied, "You should have remembered that at the Alamo." Santa Anna endeavored to excuse himself for the slaughter of the
garrison of the Alamo, on the ground that he was
acting under the orders of the government of Mexico
to treat all prisoners taken in arms as pirates, but
was reminded that he was himself the government of
Mexico. He declared that he was not aware that
Fannin had surrendered under terms of capitulation,
and threatened that he would have Urrea executed
for deceiving him, if he ever regained power. Santa
Anna desired to treat with Houston for terms of
peace and his release, but Houston informed him that
he had no authority, and that the matter must be
referred to the government of Texas. Santa Anna
then proposed an armistice, which was agreed to.

He wrote an order to General Filisola for him to
retire to Bexar and to notify General Gaona to do
the same. General Urrea was to be directed to retire
to Guadalupe Victoria, and the prisoners at Goliad,
captured at Copano, were to be released. As soon
as the dispatches were written, they were sent off by
Deaf Smith. Houston then sent for Santa Anna's
tent, which he had erected near him, and delivered
to him his private baggage untouched. There was
considerable excitement among the Texan soldiers
when it was known that Santa Anna was a prisoner.
Some of the more violent wanted to kill him on the
spot, and Houston ordered a guard around his tent
for its protection.

The news of Santa Anna's defeat reached General
Filisola on the afternoon of the 22d, from the mouth
of an officer who had succeeded in crossing Vince's
Bayou on horseback. It was at first disbelieved, but
other fugitives came in and confirmed it. General
Gaona had previously joined Filisola with his col-
umn, and a portion of his troops had crossed the
Brazos on their way to Nacogdoches. They were
recalled, and dispatches were sent to General Urrea at
Matagorda, and to Colonel Salas at Columbia, to join
Filisola as soon as possible. Filisola was informed
that the victorious Texan army numbered 1200 or
1500 men, and decided to fall back to a more secure
position. He retreated to a place on the road to
Victoria, and on the 26th was joined by General
Urrea. The commanders in consultation decided to

retire beyond the Colorado, and await instructions
and reinforcements from the Mexican authorities.
Their troops numbered about 2500 men, but they
were worn out and discouraged, and destitute of supplies. On the 27th, Deaf Smith reached the Mexican
army with Santa Anna's dispatches, and, although
the retreat had already been decided upon, it was
agreed to have it considered as under Santa Anna's
orders. General Woll was sent to Houston's camp
with stipulations on the part of Filisola that he
should be allowed to supply himself with cattle for
provisions on his retreat, and with secret instructions
to inform himself of the condition and strength of the
Texan force. Woll's latter purpose was suspected,
and he was detained as a prisoner. General Cos had
also been captured on the 24th, as he was endeavoring to make his way through the Brazos bottom.
The Mexican troops continued their retreat with great
difficulty, the roads being in a horrible condition, and
the men and animals utterly worn out. They reached
Victoria May 7, where they halted.

The news of the victory of San Jacinto did not
reach the government on Galveston Island until
April 27. It caused great rejoicing, and President
Burnett and his Cabinet, who had been making preparations for a farther flight, if necessary, took passage for Houston's camp. There negotiations were
opened with Santa Anna. He was ready to promise
anything to secure his liberty. Houston addressed a
note to Rusk suggesting the conditions of a treaty to

be made with him. They were the recognition of the independence of Texas by Mexico; the establishment of the Rio Grande as the boundary between the two countries; indemnity for all losses sustained by Texas during the war; Santa Anna and other officers to be retained as hostages until the ratification of the terms of the treaty by the Mexican government; release of the Texan prisoners and Mexican citizens favorable to the cause of Texas who had been arrested, and the restoration of their property; immediate withdrawal of the Mexican troops from the territory of Texas, and the cessation of hostilities by sea and land; a guarantee for the surrender of all Mexican prisoners as soon as the terms of the treaty were complied with. It was also suggested that agents be appointed to the United States to secure the mediation of that country between Texas and Mexico. A minority of the Cabinet, headed by Lamar, who had been appointed Secretary of War, in place of Rusk, who had been made a brigadier-general and given command of the army, opposed any negotiations with Santa Anna. They argued that as a prisoner no agreement that he might make would be binding upon the government of Mexico, and that as he had violated the laws of war of civilized nations by his cruelty, he should be brought to trial and punished with death.

Houston, being incapacitated by his wound from active service, addressed a farewell order to the army : —

COMRADES, — Circumstances connected with the battle of the 21st render our separation for the present unavoidable. I need not express to you the many painful sensations which that separation inflicts upon me. I am solaced, however, by the hope that we shall soon be reunited in the cause of liberty. Brigadier-General Rusk is appointed to command the army for the present. I confide in his valor, his patriotism, his wisdom. His conduct in the battle of San Jacinto was sufficient to secure your confidence and regard.

The enemy, although retreating, are still within the limits of Texas; their situation being known to you, you cannot be taken by surprise. Discipline and subordination will render you invincible. Your valor and heroism have proved you unrivaled. Let not contempt for the enemy throw you off your guard. Vigilance is the first duty of the soldier, and glory the proudest reward of his toils.

You have patiently endured privations, hardships, and difficulties unappalled; you have encountered two to one of the enemy against you, and borne yourselves in the onset and conflict of battle in a manner unknown in the annals of modern warfare. While an enemy to independence remains in Texas your work is incomplete; but when liberty is firmly established by your patience and your valor, it will be fame enough to say, "I was a member of the army of San Jacinto."

In taking leave of my brave comrades in arms, I cannot suppress the expression of that pride which I so justly feel in having had the honor to command them in person, nor will I withhold the tribute of my warmest admiration and gratitude for the promptness with which my orders were executed, and union maintained through the army. At parting my heart embraces you with gratitude and affection.

SAM HOUSTON, *Commander-in-Chief*.

He was taken on his cot on board the steamer Yellowstone May 7, and in company with President Burnett and the Cabinet, Santa Anna and his staff, and the rest of the prisoners, left for Galveston Island. Here Houston was transferred to the little schooner Flora, and sailed for New Orleans for medical treatment. The government and Santa Anna went to Velasco, leaving the Mexican soldiers herded in a camp on the island. At Velasco a treaty was signed, May 14, embodying the conditions suggested by Houston. The portion in relation to the cessation of hostilities, the surrender of prisoners, and the agreement for indemnities was public, but that in regard to the acknowledgment of the independence of Texas by Mexico was made a separate secret treaty, at the suggestion of Santa Anna, lest it should be repudiated by the Mexican government before he arrived home. It was agreed that he should be sent to Vera Cruz as soon as possible in order that he might fulfill the conditions of the treaty.

During the land campaign some operations had been performed by the Texan navy. Two small schooners, the Invincible and the Liberty, had been purchased and put in commission. Two others, the Independence and the Brutus, were afterward obtained. These vessels cruised off the coast for the purpose of interrupting the supplies of the Mexican troops by sea. Early in April the Invincible had an engagement for two hours with the Mexican vessel Montezuma off Brazos Santiago, and drove her ashore. The Invincible also captured the American brig Pocket, bound for Matamoras, with supplies for the Mexican troops. The Texan vessels were manned by volunteer crews, who were as ready to turn their hands to fighting by sea as by land. Some of the sailors had possibly seen service with Lafitte, and the commanders were as handy and brisk in fighting as in meeting the exigencies of navigation in times when the merchant service had all the attributes of adventure. "Mexican" Thompson was by no means the only daring and desperate adventurer upon the Gulf coast in those days, and there was no lack of men ready to take service on either side from sheer love of fighting or the hope of plunder. The American and English governments were obliged to keep cruisers in the Gulf for the protection of their merchant shipping, and on several occasions the belligerents were taken in hand and threatened with prosecution under the laws against piracy. The little Texan vessels inflicted a good deal of annoyance upon Mexi-

can commerce, and the Mexican government sent
agents to Europe to endeavor to secure a more formidable fleet.

A great deal of local controversy has arisen over
Houston's conduct of the San Jacinto campaign, and
some very bitter criticisms have been made upon it.
Some of the leading officers, who were afterward
opposed to him politically, charged him with cowardice, and asserted that he was forced to fight by the
demands of his men, and their threats to depose him
if he did not. Houston's unsparing tongue and re-
criminating charges aggravated their violence, and
the harshest personalities were exchanged. Houston
defended himself at length in his last speech in the
United States Senate, February 28, 1859. In it he
gave a history of the campaign, and accused Colonel
Sidney Sherman and other officers of cowardice and
misconduct. Ex-President Anson Jones, in his volume "Memoranda and Official Correspondence relating to the History of Texas and its Annexation,"
published to exploit himself at the expense of Houston, declared that Houston's plan was not to fight at
all, but to fall back behind the Neches, which at one
time had been claimed by the United States as the
boundary of its territory. It was expected that this
would not be respected by Santa Anna, and that
he would come into collision with the United States
troops which had been advanced beyond the Sabine
under General E. P. Gaines. This would give an
excuse for active hostilities on the part of the United

States, and a war of conquest against Mexico, such as was afterward brought on by the movement of General Taylor's troops to the Rio Grande. Jones asserted that Houston had told him, while the army was encamped in the Brazos bottom, that he intended to retreat, and "win a bloodless victory." He believed that there was an understanding with President Jackson in accordance with this scheme. It is true that on the outbreak of hostilities between Texas and Mexico, General Gaines was ordered to advance to the frontier under instructions from the Secretary of War to prevent any attack by the Indian tribes against the people of either Texas or the United States. But he was ordered to observe a strict neutrality between the contending parties, and to permit neither one of them to cross the boundary in arms. Gaines concentrated several regiments at the Sabine, and applied for permission to cross the boundary in case the Mexicans threatened the frontier with a hostile force. It was given to him in his discretion, but he was advised not to advance beyond Nacogdoches. There is no doubt that President Jackson, like the majority of the people of the United States, earnestly sympathized with the Texan colonists in their struggle for independence. But there is nothing to indicate that it was not his purpose to observe a complete neutrality, and no evidence whatever to show that there was such an understanding between himself and Houston, as intimated by Jones. It was a proper measure of precaution to advance a force to the border to prevent the violation of United States territory by either party, and to prevent the possibility of any disturbance by the fickle and turbulent Indians. The presence of General Gaines's force, undoubtedly, had a quieting effect upon the latter, who might have been persuaded by the Mexican agents to take up arms against the colonists.

Houston's plan of campaign probably was to fall back until he was joined by a sufficient force to give battle to the Mexican army, if it remained concentrated, if he had to retreat beyond the Trinity or even to the Sabine. When the news reached him, at his camp on the Brazos, that Santa Anna had gone south with a small division he moved rapidly after him with the purpose of giving battle, and ending the war at a stroke. He might have attacked and overwhelmed Sesma on the Colorado, but it would only have resulted in a concentration of the Mexican columns under Santa Anna, and a further retreat or a battle at a disadvantage. By not attacking Sesma, the chance was that Santa Anna would scatter his forces to occupy the country, and in his impatience and self-confidence put himself into the power of the Texans. This, indeed, was what happened. |There is no doubt that Houston followed Santa Anna for the purpose of giving battle, and with the assurance of victory.| He addressed a note to Colonel Henry Raguet at Nacogdoches, just before crossing Buffalo Bayou to Harrisburg, in which he said: —

"This morning we are in preparation to meet

Santa Anna. It is the only chance of saving Texas. From time to time I have looked for reinforcements in vain. The Convention adjourning to Harrisburg struck panic throughout the country. Texas could have started at least 4000 men. We will only have about 700 to march with, beside the camp guard. We go to conquer. It is wisdom growing out of necessity to meet the enemy now. Every consideration enforces it. No previous occasion would justify it."

Houston might have attacked Santa Anna on the first day of their meeting, and before the latter was reinforced by General Cos. His reason, as given after the battle, was that he did not want "to make two bites of one cherry." What he did accomplish by waiting was to take the Mexican troops by surprise, although it was hardly to be counted on in the exercise of ordinary intelligence by Santa Anna. His destruction of Vince's bridge showed that he meant to make the battle a decisive one, and that he had the utmost confidence in a victory. There was no opportunity for the display of tactical skill in the battle, but his dash at the works showed the determination for a vigorous and deadly stroke, which was all that was necessary. Houston's plan of campaign was wise and prudent according to the ordinary rules of war. Perhaps he erred in not counting sufficiently on the fighting quality of the Texan as compared with the Mexican soldier, and might have defeated the entire Mexican army with as large odds against him as Taylor had at Buena Vista. But he had no artillery, and his troops were raw and without discipline. It would have been a great risk, which he was not justified in taking, and the event was a vindication of his wisdom.

CHAPTER XII

THE army under General Rusk left the camp at San Jacinto to follow the Mexican forces under Filisola, and see that they continued their retreat. After the victory of San Jacinto, companies which had been on their way joined the army, or gathered at the headquarters of the government at Velasco. Volunteer companies which had been raised in the United States came by sea and land. Felix Huston, a prominent lawyer of Mississippi, enlisted and equipped a force at his own expense. On the protest of the Mexican minister Gorostiza, the district attorney of Mississippi was instructed to arrest him, but reported that he was unable to do so in the condition of popular feeling. Huston brought in his force, which he claimed to be 500 men, but the adjutant-general of the army reported it as much less. On June 1, General Thomas Jefferson Green arrived at Velasco on the steamer Ocean, from New Orleans, with 250 men. The excitement and indignation at the agreement for the release of Santa Anna had been growing. Secretary Lamar had issued a letter, full of impassioned and inflated rhetoric, in which he called for his punishment "by the laws of Draco." When the volunteers from New Orleans arrived the turbulence increased, and it was determined to prevent Santa Anna from sailing for Mexico. He had already gone on board the Texan schooner Invincible with his staff, and had addressed a farewell letter to the Texan soldiers, in which he thanked them for their kindness, and called them his friends. Vice-President Zavala and Bailey Hardiman, the Secretary of the Treasury, were to accompany him to Vera Cruz as commissioners to secure the ratification of the treaty. Captain Brown of the Invincible declared that he would not sail without orders from "the people." President Burnett, making a virtue of necessity, directed General Green to bring Santa Anna on shore, telling him that he would be held responsible for the life of the prisoner. Santa Anna was found in the cabin, and refused to obey. He was frantic from fear. "He lay on his back, and his respiration was difficult." He declared that he had taken opium, and would soon die. On a threat to put him in irons he got up and joined the party. He was put into the boat, and became still more alarmed at the sight of the crowd on shore. He was reassured, and advised to wave the Texan flag. He did so with trembling hands, and was landed at Quintana, on the opposite side of the bay from Velasco, where he was put under guard. Having recovered from his fear of immediate destruction, he addressed a fervent protest to President Burnett, complaining of the violence to which he had been subjected, ⊿

of the breaking of the terms of the treaty agreement. Burnett replied, apologizing for the violation of the agreement, and saying that its fulfillment would have to be postponed for a season on account of "the highly excited popular indignation."

General Rusk was unable to control the turbulent and restless spirits in the army, which Houston had been able to keep in some measure of restraint. They attacked the government for its failure to supply the army with food and clothing, and inflamed the indignation of the soldiers at the proposed release of Santa Anna. On May 29, while the army was at Victoria, a violent and inflammatory address was drawn up, complaining of the necessities of the army, and holding the President responsible for them. It declared that the army would not permit the release of Santa Anna without the sanction of a Texan Congress, and demanded that the President should order an election within two months for the establishment of a new government. The address was simply a declaration of insubordination, and the assumption of supreme authority by the army. President Burnett replied that the Executive was not to blame for the wants of which the soldiers complained, as it was totally without means, and mildly informed them that when the civil government was compelled to receive the dictation of an armed force there was serious danger of its being subverted by military misrule. Subsequently he issued an address to the people and the army, arguing forcibly in favor of the advantages of the treaty with Santa Anna, and the good effect which would be produced on the opinion of the world by sparing the life of the prisoner. President Burnett, however, had no authority beyond his eloquence, and the government of Texas was very nearly in a state of anarchy. The army and the people continued to clamor for the execution of Santa Anna, and there was no means either of enforcing order, or of collecting money.

There was a strong desire for immediate annexation to the United States, which would be an absolute protection against the power of Mexico. On the 20th of May, James Collingsworth and Peter W. Grayson were appointed commissioners to the United States, to ask for the mediation of that country between Texas and Mexico, and for the immediate recognition of Texan independence. They were also instructed to urge the government to accede to the wishes of the Texan people for annexation. The news of the victory of San Jacinto had caused great rejoicing in the United States. Public meetings were held in New York and other cities in favor of the recognition of the independence of Texas. On the 18th of June, Mr. Clay, from the Committee on Foreign Affairs, reported a resolution to recognize the independence of Texas, and supported it in an eloquent speech, but action upon it was postponed. Mr. Henry M. Morfitt was appointed a special commissioner to proceed to Texas and examine and report on its condition.

After a tedious voyage, Houston arrived at New Orleans on the 11th of May. His wound had not received proper attention, and was beginning to show signs of mortification. He was greatly reduced in strength, and lay on his cot on the deck as the vessel ascended the river. News of his approach was forwarded to the city when the Flora reached "English Turn," and the levee was lined with crowds to witness his arrival. He was taken to the house of his old friend, Colonel William Christy, who had served with him as a lieutenant during the Creek war, and who had been very energetic in raising money and volunteers for the assistance of the Texans. Houston was attended by Dr. James Kerr, who had been his physician twenty years before when suffering from the wound received at the battle of To-ho-pe-ka. His recovery was slow and painful. More than twenty pieces of bone were taken from the wound, and he was confined to his bed for several weeks. As soon as he was able to move, he went up the Red River by steamer to Natchitoches. He proceeded by slow stages to San Augustine, which he reached on the 5th of July. The rumor had arrived there that the Mexicans were advancing with another invading army. Houston, leaning on his crutches, delivered an address to the citizens, which resulted in the departure of 160 men for the army within two days. News was also soon afterward received that Colonels Millard and Wheelock had left the army, with an order to the government to deliver up Santa Anna for immediate execution, and for the arrest of President Burnett. Houston at once sent a protest to General Rusk : —

Ayish Bayou, *July 26, 1836.*

To the General commanding the Army of Texas:

Sir, — I have just heard through a citizen of the army that it is the intention to remove General Santa Anna to the army, and place him upon his trial. I cannot credit this statement; it is obviously contrary to the true policy of Texas. The advantages which his capture presented to us will be destroyed. Disregard, if you will, our national character, and place what construction you please upon the rules of civilized warfare, we are compelled by every principle of humanity and morality to abstain from every act of passion or inconsideration that is unproductive of positive good. Execute Santa Anna, and what will be the fate of the Texans who are held prisoners by the Mexicans? What will be the condition of the North Americans residing within the limits of Mexico? Death to them and confiscation of their property is the least that can be expected. Doubtless torture will be added to the catastrophe, when stimulated by ignorance, fanaticism, and the last expiring struggle of the priesthood for power and dominion. Texas, to be respected, must be considerate, politic, and just in her actions. Santa Anna living, and secured beyond all danger of escape, in the eastern section of Texas (as I first suggested), may be of incalculable advantage to Texas in her present situation. In cool blood to offer up the living to the manes of the departed only finds an example in the religion and warfare of the savages. Regard for one's departed friends should stimulate us in the hour of battle, and would excuse us in the moment of victory for partial excesses, at which our calmer feelings of humanity would relent.

The affairs of Texas, as connected with General Santa Anna as President of the Republic of Mexico, have become matter of consideration to which the attention of the United States has been called, and for Texas, at this moment, to proceed to extreme measures, as to the merits or demerits of General Santa Anna, would be treating that government with high disrespect, and I would respectfully add, in my opinion, it would be incurring the most unfortunate responsibility for Texas.

I, therefore, Commander-in-Chief of the army of the Republic, do solemnly protest against the trial, sentence, and execution of General Antonio Lopez de Santa Anna, President of the Republic of Mexico, until the relations in which we are to stand to the United States shall be ascertained.

SAM HOUSTON,
Commander-in-Chief of the Army.

The protest had its effect in calming the vindictive passions of the army, and in preventing the military trial and execution of Santa Anna. The Texan army had been swelled to about 2500 men by volunteers from the colonists and from the United States, and was in a very undisciplined and disorganized condition. The ambitious adventurers all coveted immediate distinction and authority. "There were very few above the rank of captain who did not aspire to be commander-in-chief." The leaders cultivated popularity by the rough and ready methods of frontier politicians, and the camp was a good deal like a prolonged political barbecue. General Felix Huston, known among the soldiers as "Old Long Shanks" and "Old Leather Breeches," assumed authority, and conducted himself like the leader of a popular mob. Meanwhile, the Mexican troops had retreated from the territory of Texas. When the news of the defeat at San Jacinto reached the City of Mexico, Tornel, the Secretary of War, sent a dispatch to General Filisola to hold San Antonio, announcing that fresh preparations would be made for an army of invasion. But Filisola's army was already beyond the Nueces when the order reached him, and he continued his retreat toward Matamoras. He was superseded, and directed to turn the command over to General Urrea, who was already in Matamoras. Urrea commanded the army to halt, but its condition was such that the officers decided that it must reach a place of shelter and supply, or perish. It pushed on and reached Matamoras May 18. No reinforcements were sent by the Mexican government, and the chaos and confusion which resulted from the absence of Santa

Anna prevented any attempt for the renewal of the invasion of Texas. There being no enemy to fight within the limits of the territory schemes were renewed in the Texan army for the invasion of Mexico, and it was proposed to advance upon Matamoras. To add to the confusion and disorganization the government appointed Secretary Lamar to be commander-in-chief, in place of Houston, and he proceeded to the camp to assume the command. This produced great dissatisfaction. The officers protested against his claim. Lamar persisted in his right, and it was agreed to leave it to a vote of the soldiers as to whether they would receive Lamar as commander-in-chief or not. After the usual stump oratory the vote was taken, and, there being an overwhelming majority against Lamar, he retired.

The only thing accomplished by the Texan army during the period was the capture of three vessels in the harbor of Copano by a company of twenty mounted rangers under the command of Captain Isaac W. Burton. The company had been sent by General Rusk to see that no body of the enemy remained below Refugio. In the harbor of Copano they discovered a vessel, the Watchman, laden with supplies for the Mexican army. A portion of the crew were decoyed on shore. Their boat was seized, and the vessel boarded and captured by the rangers. While the Watchman was lying in the harbor, waiting for a favorable wind for Velasco, two other vessels, the Comanche and the Fanny Butler, came in.

The captain of the Watchman was compelled to signal to their commanders to come on board his vessel, where they were seized. The vessels surrendered to boarding parties, and the three were taken to Velasco. Their supplies were valued at $25,000, and were sent to the army. The rangers received the honorary title of the "Horse Marines" for their exploit.

Santa Anna was removed from Quintana to Velasco, and afterward to Columbia. While at Columbia a plot was formed to rescue him by the Mexican consul at New Orleans through the instrumentality of a young Spaniard named Bartholomew Pages. It was asserted that an attempt was made to poison the guard by means of wine. Santa Anna was put in irons, and subjected to other indignities. He was fired at by a drunken soldier through the window of the house where he was confined. Finally, he was removed to Orizamba and kept in close confinement. On the advice of Austin, who had returned from the United States and visited him, he addressed a letter to President Jackson asking him to interfere for his release, and professing a desire for the immediate recognition of the independence of Texas by the United States and Mexico. Meanwhile, the Congress of Mexico had passed a decree that all treaties and agreements executed by Santa Anna while he was a prisoner were null and void.

A proclamation was issued by President Burnett on the 23d of July for a general election, to be held on the 1st of September, for the choice of a President and Congress to take the place of the provisional government. The question of an application for annexation to the United States was also submitted to the popular vote. Politics grew quickly and rankly in Texas. There were two parties, one in favor of Stephen F. Austin, and one, headed by the Whartons, in favor of ex-Governor Henry Smith. Houston was nominated by mass meetings at Columbia, San Augustine, and other places. He professed an unwillingness to be a candidate, but it is not probable that he was very strenuous in resisting the invitations. His prestige as the victor of San Jacinto and his gifts of personal popularity resulted in a triumphant election. He received 4374 votes, to 745 for Smith and 587 for Austin. Mirabeau B. Lamar was elected Vice-President, on the strength, Houston said, of an extra line in the latter's report of the battle of San Jacinto. The application for annexation to the United States was voted for with practical unanimity. The first Congress of Texas assembled at Columbia, October 3. The date for the inauguration of the new President was fixed for December 1, but President Burnett was desirous of escaping from his anomalous position of provisional and inefficient authority, and resigned to allow the permanent government to come into power. Houston was installed on October 22, and delivered an extemporaneous inaugural address. He urged the necessity of maintaining the army in a state of vigilance and discipline to meet any invasion of the enemy. He pointed out the importance of establishing friendly relations with the Indian tribes, which could be secured by a course of even-handed justice. He expressed warm thanks to those who had aided the country in its struggle for independence, and he hoped that the United States would respond favorably to the appeal of a willing people for annexation. In concluding, he indulged in one of the histrionic effects of which he was fond. He disengaged his sword, and, after a pause and apparent struggle with his emotions, he handed it to the presiding officer, saying, "It now, sir, becomes my duty to make a presentation of this sword, the emblem of my past office. I have worn it with some humble pretentions in the defense of my country, and should the danger of my country again call for my services, I expect to resume it, and respond to that call, if needful, with my blood and my life."

Houston addressed himself with great practical sagacity to the duties of his office. He appointed the two competitors for the Presidency to places in his Cabinet. Austin was made Secretary of State, and Smith Secretary of the Treasury. Colonel William H. Wharton was appointed minister to the United States, and General Memucan Hunt was afterward added as a commissioner to urge annexation. Colonel J. Pinkney Henderson was appointed minister to Great Britain and France. The duties of the new government of Texas were heavy. It had to maintain an army to meet a possible invasion, to equip an adequate navy for the defense of the coast, to defend the frontiers against the always turbulent and dangerous Indians, to provide for the administration of justice and all the functions of a civil government, without a dollar in the treasury or any adequate means available for taxation. Congress immediately passed an act authorizing the President to issue bonds to the amount of $5,000,000, payable in thirty years, and commissioners were appointed to go to the United States to attempt to negotiate the loan. Additional bounties were offered for volunteers, and the President was authorized to increase and reorganize the army. An act was passed for the increase of the navy by the purchase of a twenty-four-gun sloop-of-war, two steamers, and two eleven-gun schooners. The rates of duties on imports were fixed. The courts were organized, a land office and mail routes established. The boundaries of the Republic were decided to extend from the Sabine to the Rio Grande, and northward to the forty-second parallel of latitude, which would have included the greater portion of New Mexico. The boundary line of the province had been somewhat indefinite under the authority of Spain and Mexico, but its relative place between Texas and New Mexico was well understood, and there was no foundation for the claim to the forty-second parallel. Among the measures of Congress was one characteristic of the wild-cat schemes invented by adventurers and land speculators. An act was passed to incorporate the Texas Railroad, Navigation, and Banking Company, of which Branch T.

Archer was president. The company was given extraordinary and monopolistic powers. It was allowed to discount $30,000,000 upon a capital of $10,000,-000, to build railroads and canals from the Sabine to the Rio Grande and regulate its own charges, to lay out town sites with extensive land grants, and in general to control the future business and development of Texas. For these enormous privileges, it agreed to pay a bonus of only $25,000 into the treasury. The scheme was a gigantic fraud and confidence game. The capital stock was subscribed, but none of the money was paid in. The fictitious shares were sold and traded as elements of a swindle. An attempt was made to bribe Houston by sending him a share of the stock, but he returned it, and vigorously opposed the bill. The charter, of course, was eventually forfeited by the failure of the subscribers to comply with its conditions. After a session of two months Congress adjourned, to meet May 1 at Houston, the newly founded city at the head of Buffalo Bayou, which was declared the capital.

One of the pressing questions was the disposition to be made of Santa Anna. When Houston arrived at Columbia, previous to his inauguration, Santa Anna sent a request for him to come and see him, and Houston did so. The prisoner was much affected. He embraced Houston, and wept as his head rested on Houston's broad chest. Houston patted him and consoled him as he would a frightened child. He procured Santa Anna some additional comforts, and promised to do his utmost to secure his release. He sent a memorandum to Santa Anna, in which he suggested that he should communicate with President Jackson, expressing his willingness to favor the annexation of Texas to the United States, and to urge Jackson to become responsible for the fulfillment of Santa Anna's stipulations to the people of Texas. He advised him to maintain his authority as President of Mexico, although a prisoner, and to issue his instructions to the Mexican minister at Washington accordingly. After the inauguration, Santa Anna addressed a letter to the President petitioning for his release, which was referred to Congress. The members of Congress shared the prevailing indignation against Santa Anna, and passed a resolution that he should be retained as a prisoner. Houston vetoed the bill, and, after an excited debate, the question was left to the decision of the President. In the mean time, President Jackson had responded in kindly terms to Santa Anna's appeal for his mediation, and invited him to visit Washington on his release. Houston decided to release the prisoner at once, and send him to Washington with an escort. Santa Anna and his party set out for Washington on November 25, by way of New Orleans. He was entertained at dinner by President Jackson, and sent by an American man-of-war to Vera Cruz, where he arrived February 23, 1837. He found that he had fallen into complete disfavor, and retired to his estate at Mango del Clavo. His old rival Bustamente, having been recalled from exile, was triumphantly chosen President at the ensuing election in March, Santa Anna receiving but two votes. It is an evidence of Santa Anna's inherent meanness of character that he borrowed $2000 from Colonel Bernard E. Bee, one of his escort, for which he gave a draft. On his return home he allowed the draft to be protested, and never paid the debt. His more honorable enemies did it for him; the legislature of Texas afterward made an appropriation to indemnify Colonel Bee.

The question of the recognition of the independence of Texas by the United States caused a good deal of political excitement in that country, and was the beginning of the prolonged and violent agitation which accompanied the project of annexation. While the majority of the people of the United States undoubtedly were proud of the courage of their kinsmen in Texas, and enthusiastic over the prospects of their independence, the shadow of the extension of the slave power, foreboded by annexation, alarmed the Northern politicians, and alienated a portion of the people. The stories against the character of the Texan colonists were revived, and the revolt was again attributed to a filibuster conspiracy. There were some prudent suggestions that the recognition of the independence of Texas would bring on a war with Mexico, but as a whole the opposition was generated by political means, and the majority of the people of the United States were really in favor of it. Commissioner Morfitt had returned, and made a fa-

vorable report as to the condition of Texas. He estimated the population of the country at about 58,000,
of whom 30,000 were Americans or Europeans, 3670
Mexicans, 5000 negroes, and 20,000 Indians, exact
figures being, of course, unobtainable in regard to
the Indians. He described the colonists to be in a
condition to maintain their independence, and pointed
out that their character and habits enabled them to
carry on a war with but little cost to themselves. He
estimated the debts and obligations of Texas at about
$1,250,000. President Jackson, notwithstanding his
strong sympathies with the people of Texas, and his
desire and expectation of the ultimate annexation of
the territory, expressed himself in a very conservative
manner in his communication to Congress. In transmitting the report of Commissioner Morfitt he said
in regard to annexation, "Necessarily a work of time,
and uncertain in itself, it is calculated to expose our
conduct to misconstruction in the eyes of the world."
On December 23, he sent a message to Congress in
regard to the recognition of the independence of
Texas, in which he said that "prudence would dictate
that the United States should stand aloof until the
independence of Texas had been recognized by Mexico, or one of the great foreign powers, or until
events should have proved beyond dispute the ability
of the people to maintain their independent sovereignty." He, however, referred the matter to the discretion of Congress, and intimated that he would be
governed by its decision. On the 11th of January,

Hon. Robert J. Walker, Senator from Mississippi, introduced a resolution for the recognition of Texas as an independent nation. The question was postponed until March 1, when the resolution was taken up. After a warm debate, in which speeches in favor of recognition were made by Clay, Calhoun, Benton, Preston, and others, the resolution was adopted by a vote of twenty-four to nineteen. The vote was not on strict sectional or party lines, Senators King, of Georgia, and King, of Alabama, and other Southern members, voting against recognition. An attempt was made to reconsider the vote the next day, and it only failed by a vote of twenty-four to twenty-four. President Jackson approved the resolution as the last act of his official life. Secretary of State Forsyth informed Minister Wharton that the question of annexation could not then be considered by the United States government.

General Henderson, the Texan minister, was favorably received by the British government, although the Anti-Slavery Society promptly protested against the independence of Texas, on the ground that Mexico had declared the abolition of slavery, while the American colonists maintained it. The British ministry agreed to make a special commercial treaty with Texas, although for the time being it refused to recognize her independence from Mexico. A similar arrangement was made with the government of France, and the French minister at Washington was directed to send a commissioner to Texas to examine and report on the condition of the country.

In accordance with his settled policy Houston appointed commissioners to visit the various tribes of Indians, and arrange for treaties of friendship and alliance. No difficulty had occurred, except with the Caddoes, who had recently entered the territory from the United States, and had been committing some depredations upon the outlying settlers. Mexican agents had been busy among the Indian tribes, endeavoring to induce them to commence hostilities against the colonists. A delegation of twenty from the Northern Indians had been persuaded to visit Matamoras to form a treaty with Mexico for that purpose. But Houston's reputation was well established among all the Indians as the friendly white chief, and the efforts of the Mexican authorities to engage them in definite warfare with the colonists were unavailing. No trouble occurred from the Indians during his term as President, except the individual collisions and inevitable depredations and aggressions on both sides which accompany the contact of the two races. Although friendly to the Indians, Houston knew their unstable nature and the perils of the situation, and maintained companies of rangers to punish thefts and attacks, and encouraged the building of block-houses upon the frontier.

Congress reassembled on May 1, and Houston sent them an elaborate and business-like message. He congratulated them on the recognition of the independence of Texas by the United States, and said, "We now occupy the proud attitude of a sovereign and independent Republic, which will force upon us the obligation of evincing to the world that we are worthy to be free." He urged that their legislation should be not only for present emergencies, but for a permanent system adapted to the future growth and development of the country. The finances of the Republic were the most pressing subject of attention. None of the authorized $5,000,000 loan had been raised in the United States, owing to the depressed condition of the money market; and the sales of the land scrip had not been productive, owing, as the President believed, to the mismanagement of the agents in New Orleans and Mobile, who had rendered no account of their transactions, and had allowed drafts upon them to go to protest. Claims upon the treasury had only been met by promises to pay when in funds, and were sold to speculators at a heavy discount. The land law, passed at the last session over the President's veto, had proved impracticable and unsatisfactory, and he recommended measures for ascertaining the location of all the occupied lands in the country to prevent litigation about titles. He spoke strongly in regard to the African slave trade. He declared that there was evidence that thousands of slaves had been imported to the island of Cuba for the purpose of being transferred to Texas. The Texan minister had been instructed to report the facts to the United States government. The navy of Texas was necessary for its immediate defense, and it was the duty of the United States and of England to employ a portion of their force in the Gulf to arrest the accursed traffic. Nothing had occurred in regard to the question of annexation, but it was hoped that the next session of the Congress of the United States would take up the subject in a friendly spirit. England had given indications of friendliness and good-will to the new Republic. No change had taken place in the relations between Texas and Mexico. Texas was confident that she could maintain her rights, and was not willing to invoke the mediation of other powers. Mexico, while apparently determined to protract the war, was torn by internal convulsions, and unable to defend her frontier against the attacks of predatory Indians. The army of Texas was in a good condition, and able to meet any invading force brought against it. Although Mexico had refused to enter into any arrangement for the exchange of prisoners, he recommended the release, upon parole, of the Mexican soldiers still detained in the country.

Although Houston had spoken favorably of the condition of the Texan army, it was still disorganized and turbulent, and he took measures to reduce and practically disband it. General Felix Huston had succeeded to the command on the retirement of General Rusk, who had been appointed Secretary of War in Houston's Cabinet. He had no capacity or training as a soldier, and acted merely as the leader of an armed and turbulent mob. General James Hamilton, who had been governor of South Carolina, and had manifested an active interest in the Texan struggle for independence, was invited to take command of the army, but declined. Albert Sidney Johnston, who had recently resigned from the United States army and come to Texas after the battle of San Jacinto, had joined Rusk's army as a private. His soldierly appearance and manifest ability caused him to be promoted to be adjutant-general, and, after the refusal of General Hamilton to accept the command, he was appointed by President Houston the senior brigadier-general. General Felix Huston had indicated his intention of retaining the command by the summary process of challenging and shooting any one who should be appointed to displace him. When Johnston arrived with his commission on the 4th of February, Huston promptly challenged him, and, in the duel which took place the following day, Johnston was severely wounded in the hip and incapacitated from further service. No one was found to accept the command at the cost of fighting so dangerous a duelist as Huston, and he retained his position at the head of the army. He was full of schemes for the invasion of Mexico, and at the opening of the session of Congress in May he repaired to the capitol to obtain authority for an attack upon Matamoras. Houston determined to put a stop to all such foolish enterprises, and to get rid of an army which was not only a heavy expense, but a peril to the maintenance of the civil government. Under the influence of their commander the volunteers had threatened to "chastise the President, kick Congress out of doors, and give laws to Texas." Among General Huston's ideas of maintaining his popularity with the soldiers was to indulge them occasionally in general sprees, which usually wound up in a free fight in which several would be killed. The President was convinced that the unsettled government and internal troubles of Mexico would prevent any serious attempt at invasion, and that an impromptu levy of the colonists would make a better army, if necessary, than the undisciplined and dangerous force of foreign adventurers collected at San Antonio. While General Huston was urging the Matamoras expedition upon the members of Congress, the President, on May 18, issued orders to the Secretary of War to proceed secretly and swiftly to headquarters, and furlough all the companies except 600 men. There was no leader to resist the order, and the volunteers were apparently wearied of an adventure which promised neither profit nor glory. They were marched to various ports on the coast, and took their departure for the United States under a furlough to return within thirty days if called for. General Huston, deprived of his armed mob, returned soon afterward to the United States. General Johnston was retained in the command, with a furlough to enable him to recover from his wound. There is no doubt that, if the finances of the country had been able to sustain the expense, the maintenance of a well-organized and disciplined army would have been of advantage to

Texas, and prevented the occasional raids by the Mexicans which afterward took place. But the treasury was empty, and the army could only have been paid by the issue of irredeemable paper money, with its certainty of bringing bankruptcy and repudiation. The army was mainly composed of lawless and adventurous volunteers who were ready for any mischievous enterprise that would have driven Mexico into active hostilities. And the temperament of the Congress was neither stable nor judicious enough to make it sure that it would exercise a restraining influence. In the mean time, immigration was coming into the country, strengthening its resources and means of defense, and every day in which fighting could be avoided was an advantage. Already trade was being renewed along the Mexican frontier, in spite of the hostile attitudes of the two governments, and there was a chance that there would be no further war.

The condition of the land grants had made a great deal of trouble. The locations of the leagues and labors under the Mexican system had conflicted with the grants by acres under the new government, and many of the old settlers had resisted the change. The empresario grants, which had been used for speculative purposes, had created a host of fictitious claims, many of them held by innocent persons who had been swindled in buying the scrip. The acts of the last legislature of Coahuila and Texas in disposing of large portions of land in Texas at nominal prices, although repudiated, had produced another batch of claims. The laws giving the preference in locations to volunteers, and the negotiations of public land scrip in the United States, created additional confusion. A large portion of the time of Congress was devoted to struggling with this question. Houston vetoed several unsatisfactory and mischievous bills, and it was not until the close of the last session that the land office was opened under intelligent and practicable regulations.

The total lack of money was the most serious burden upon the new government. The collapse of the banking system in the United States, and the consequent financial distress, had prevented any success in negotiating a general loan. The sales of public land scrip produced little or nothing, owing to the confusion of titles and the doubt as to whether Texas could maintain her independence. It would appear that Houston shared the general delusion in regard to the means to be expected from this source, and blamed the agents for mismanagement when there was really no demand for the lands which was not more than supplied by the sales and trades of individual grants. The treasury remained empty, and the audited claims were used as currency or hawked about at a ruinous discount. On June 6, the President was obliged to send a special message to Congress, calling attention to the condition of the quartermaster's department of the army. He said that the government was unable to obtain any supplies upon its own credit, and the

Executive had been compelled to give his individual obligation, indorsed by some of the members. A part of the army was in an actual state of mutiny for the want of provisions, and Galveston Island would have been deserted but for the relief thus obtained. Since he came into office the President had received only $500 for provisions for the troops. The public officers had received no salary, and had tendered their resignations from time to time on account of being unable to meet their expenses. Congress did the best it could by passing financial acts, but it was like trying to run a mill without water. There were the usual attempts of new and impoverished countries to create money by fiat legislation. In May, Congress passed an act authorizing the issue of promissory notes to the amount of $1,000,000. This was vetoed by the President, on the ground that half that amount was all that was necessary for a circulating medium or could be kept at par. The issue was restricted to $500,000, but a bill was passed authorizing the President to reissue the notes, as they were returned to the treasury, in his discretion, to an amount not to exceed $1,000,000. At the close of Houston's administration the promissory notes, which stood at about sixty-five cents on the dollar, amounted to $739,789. The total indebtedness, including audited claims, amounted to $1,942,000. The customs duties, which were the only source of reliable revenue, amounted to $278,134 for the last year. The record of Texan finance, under the circumstances, was a cred-

itable one, and it was Houston's firm hand and sagacious judgment, restraining extravagance and preventing false financial schemes, which kept down the
indebtedness, and enabled the government to carry
on its operations without collapse.

Among the events of the year was the loss of the
Texan vessel the Independence, which was captured
April 17, about thirty miles off Velasco, by two Mexican vessels, the Libertador and the Vincedor del
Alamo. After a severe fight of two hours, the Independence surrendered, and was taken to Matamoras.
On board was Colonel William H. Wharton, the
Texan minister to the United States, who was returning home. His brother, Colonel John A. Wharton,
was sent with thirty Mexican prisoners, to obtain the
release of the captives by exchange. He was thrown
into prison by the Mexican authorities, but both the
Whartons and the other prisoners eventually effected
their escape by the aid of friends in Matamoras.
The British vessel Ellen Russell was captured in
the Gulf by a Texan vessel, on suspicion of being
laden with contraband of war, but proved to have
only merchandise. She was released by President
Houston, and an indemnity afterward paid by the
government.

Lorenzo de Zavala, who had been elected Vice-
President in the Provisional Government of Texas,
died at his residence near San Jacinto, November 15.
Zavala was a man of strong patriotic impulses, and
more than ordinary capacity and integrity, who, un-

der better circumstances, would have exercised a commanding and wholesome influence on the affairs of Mexico. He would not submit to the tyranny of Santa Anna, and fled to Texas, where he entered heartily into the struggle for independence. Although a Mexican, he was highly esteemed by the Texan leaders for his integrity and sincerity, as well as for his courage and sagacity. Stephen F. Austin died at Columbia, December 27, from an attack of pneumonia. He was but forty-three years of age. Austin was a man of the highest character, of judicial moderation and prudence, as well as energy and perseverance. He appreciated the conditions on which alone a permanent and prosperous colony could be founded, and carried them out with rare tact and sagacity. He encouraged industry, and governed the lawless elements of the population by his weight of character and personal influence. To him more than to any other is due the creation of an American State in Texas. He was forced into political prominence by the demands of the time rather than any desire of his own, and was as modest and self-sacrificing as he was sagacious and practical. Public honors were paid at his funeral by the President and members of Congress, and the remains were taken on the steamer Yellowstone to Peach Point, near the mouth of the Brazos. President Houston issued an address beginning, "The Father of Texas is no more," and ordering all officers, civil and military, to wear crape for thirty days, in honor of his memory.

Houston's manner of life as President of the Republic of Texas was a singular compound of ceremonial dignity and frontier primitiveness, much like that of an aboriginal potentate. He lived in a log cabin in the frank and ready familiarity with all comers which the times compelled, and which suited his genius for popularity. But he put on the airs of state on occasion, and is reported to have worn a sort of velvet robe, which must have been in singular contrast to the furniture and appearance of the audience chamber, when he gave formal audience to the agents of foreign nations. He still kept up his drinking habits, and was king of the riots, as well as of the counsels, of his vigorous and boisterous associates, without losing his sense of dignity or their respect. An interesting glimpse of Houston and his surroundings is given through the keenly observant eyes of Audubon, the naturalist, who visited the town of Houston in May, 1837. He says in his diary: —

"We walked toward the President's house, accompanied by the Secretary of the Navy, and as soon as we rose above the bank we saw before us a level of far-extending prairie, destitute of timber and rather poor soil. Houses, half finished, and most of them without roofs, tents, and a liberty pole, with the capitol, were all exhibited to our view at once. We approached the President's mansion, however, wading in water above our ankles. This abode of President Houston is a small log house, consisting of two rooms and a passage through, after the Southern fashion. The moment we stepped over the threshold, on the right hand of the passage, we found ourselves ushered into what in other countries would be called the ante-chamber; the ground floor, however, was muddy and filthy, a large fire was burning, and a small table, covered with paper and writing materials, was in the centre; camp beds, trunks, and different materials were strewed around the room. We were at once presented to several members of the Cabinet, some of whom bore the stamp of men of intellectual ability, simple, though bold, in their general appearance. Here we were presented to Mr. Crawford, an agent of the British minister to Mexico, who has come here on some secret mission.

"The President was engaged in the opposite room on some national business, and we could not see him for some time. Meanwhile, we amused ourselves by walking in the capitol, which was yet without a roof, and the floors, benches, and tables of both houses of Congress were as well saturated with water as our clothes had been in the morning. Being invited by one of the great men of the place to enter a booth to take a drink of grog with him, we did so; but I was rather surprised that he offered his name instead of the cash to the bar-keeper.

"We first caught sight of President Houston as he walked from one of the grog-shops, where he had been to stop the sale of ardent spirits. He was on his way to his house, and wore a large, gray, coarse hat, and the bulk of his figure reminded me of the appearance of General Hopkins, of Virginia, for, like him, he is upward of six feet high and strong in proportion. But I observed a scowl in the expression of his eyes that was forbidding and disagreeable. We reached his abode before him, but he soon came, and we were presented to his Excellency. He was dressed in a fancy velvet coat and trousers trimmed with broad gold lace, and around his neck was tied a cravat somewhat in the style of '76. He received us kindly, was desirous of retaining us for a while, and offered us every facility in his power. He at once removed us from the ante-room to his private chamber, which, by the way, was not much cleaner than the former. We were severally introduced by him to the different members of his Cabinet and Staff, and at once asked to drink grog with him, which we did, wishing success to the new Republic. Our talk was short, but the impression which was made on our mind at the time by himself, his officers, and the place of his abode can never be forgotten."

Houston was married for the second time in Marion, Alabama, May 9, 1840, to Miss Margaret Moffette Lea. He was then forty-seven years of age, his bride twenty-one. The second Mrs. Houston was a lady of good family, force of character, amiability, and considerable literary talent. She was aware of Houston's weaknesses in habits when she married him, and was confident that she could influence him for the better. She did so, and he reformed his habits of drinking and swearing, until finally they were abandoned altogether.

CHAPTER XIII

THE Constitution of the Republic made the President ineligible for two succeeding terms. There were three candidates in the field for the succession to Houston, Mirabeau B. Lamar, the Vice-President, Peter W. Grayson, and James Collingsworth. The contest was a very bitter one, and virulent personal attacks were made against the candidates. Just before the election Grayson committed suicide by shooting himself at Bean's Station, Tennessee, and Collingsworth by throwing himself from a steamer into Galveston Bay. Lamar was elected President, and David G. Burnett Vice-President. Lamar was a man of extravagant ideas, and regarded Texas as an established empire, with all the possibilities of territorial expansion, unlimited wealth, and military and naval conquest. He was inaugurated December 8, 1838. In his address he declared himself emphatically against annexation to the United States, and drew a glowing picture of the advantages that would accrue to Texas from maintaining her own autonomy. In his first message to Congress he recommended the establishment of a national bank, to be founded on the hypothecation of a specific portion of the public domain, the guarantee of the plighted faith of the nation, and an adequate deposit of specie or its "equivalent." The specie, or its equivalent, was not forthcoming, and the bank was not organized.

Lamar's policy in regard to the Indians was the direct opposite of that of Houston. He declared that they were public enemies or intruders, and had no rights to the soil. If any grants had been made to them by the Mexican government they had been extorted by fear of the tomahawk and the scalping knife, and therefore void. The "solemn declaration" made by the Convention of 1835 had never been ratified, and in any case was void because the Indians had not fulfilled their part of its obligations by keeping quiet. He denounced the Indians as pestilent and merciless enemies to the settlers, and declared in favor of a war against them, which "would admit of no compromise, and have no termination except in their total extinction or total expulsion." There is no doubt that Lamar's policy in regard to the Indians was in accordance with the wishes of the majority of the white settlers. They regarded the aboriginal inhabitants simply as noxious wild beasts, who ought to be cleared from the land like wolves. Constant collisions took place as the restless colonists pushed farther and farther into the interior, and the wild Indians were naturally predatory and barbarous. Those who were partially civilized, like the Cherokees, occupied rich lands which the settlers coveted, and there was little respect for Indian occupancy or agreement as to boundaries. It is one of the most creditable features in Houston's character that he opposed the prevailing animosity of the people against the Indians, and persisted, so far as he had power or influence, in a system of justice and protection of their rights. An occasion for active operations against the Indians was not long wanting. General Canalezo, who had succeeded to Filisola in command of the troops on the Rio Grande, endeavored to stir up the Indians to active hostilities against the colonists. He sent one Manuel Flores as agent to the Cherokees and other tribes, with letters to the chiefs urging them to war. Flores and his party were discovered and attacked near Austin by a number of the colonists. Flores was killed, and his letters fell into the hands of the Texans. Although there was no evidence that the Cherokee chiefs had made, or were likely to make, any agreement with the Mexicans, it was assumed that the danger was pressing, and that the tribe must be expelled from the country. A force was organized by General Albert Sidney Johnston, the Secretary of War, consisting of Colonel Burleson's regiment, which had been fighting the prairie Indians in the West, and volunteer companies under General Rusk and Colonel Landrum, from the eastern settlements, the whole under the command of General K. H. Douglass. The Indians were informed in "a firm but friendly manner," by General Johnston, that they must leave the country and surrender their gunlocks. They refused. They were attacked by the troops on July 14, 1839, near the Cherokee village, and defeated in a sharp engagement. They rallied the following day and were again defeated, Bowles, their war chief, being killed. The troops then advanced against the Shawnees, who surrendered without a battle. The Texans burned the cabins and laid waste the cornfields of both these tribes, and the Indians withdrew across the Red River, or scattered to the northern prairies, where they formed hostile and predatory bands against the settlements. Houston was absent from the country on a visit to the United States when this raid took place. He had protested against the repudiation of the "solemn declaration" in Congress, but without avail. On his return, he addressed the citizens of Nacogdoches, who were unanimous in favor of the expulsion of the Cherokees. The most violent charges were made against him, and he was accused of inciting the Indians to resist the government. Threats were made that he would be shot if he attempted to speak. He came forward and stilled the crowd by his commanding presence. He denounced the administration for its breach of plighted faith, and accused the soldiers of barbarity in mutilating the body of Bowles. The audience listened in silence, and Houston's courage and sincerity triumphed over their tumultuous passions.

Trouble broke out with the Comanches from a more reasonable cause. These haughty and untamable Indians had been accustomed to domineer over the timorous Mexicans, and to conduct their negotiations in a very masterful and contemptuous fashion. A delegation of the chiefs of the tribe came into San Antonio to arrange a treaty of peace with the Texan commissioners on March 11, 1840. They had agreed to bring in their captives, but only surrendered Matilda Lockhart, a little girl. They alleged that the other twelve prisoners whom they were known to possess had been captured by other tribes. The Lockhart girl said that the other captives were detained for ransom in the Indian camp near the town. The chiefs were informed that all the white captives must be brought in, and that they would be detained as prisoners until they were. A company of soldiers was brought into the council room to keep them under guard. The chiefs shouted the war-whoop and drew their knives. A desperate mêlée took place in the room, in which the Indians were all killed. The warriors on the outside took the alarm, and commenced to shoot. There was a running fight in the streets of the town, in which a number of Indians, including squaws, were killed. The Comanches were deeply enraged at the slaughter of their chiefs, and determined to avenge it. On the 4th of August, a raiding party of 600 swept down upon the country, and attacked Victoria. They were repulsed, but gathered a great booty of horses and cattle, and massacred a number of the outlying settlers. They then surprised and burned the little town of Linnville on the coast, most of the inhabitants escaping in boats and lighters off shore into the harbor. As the Indians were returning with their booty, they were followed and attacked by a body of troops raised among the settlers. A battle took place on Plum Creek, in which the Indians were routed and scattered. The government determined to carry the war into the Comanche country. The force under Colonel John H. Moore attacked the principal village of the tribe, on the Red fork of the Colorado, October 23. It was surrounded at daybreak and surprised. Men, women, and children, were indiscriminately slaughtered, and the village burned. The entire Comanche nation was exasperated, and a desolating warfare raged on the frontier during the whole of Lamar's term of office. Companies of rangers were maintained in service during the period at a great expense, and the frontier settlements were kept in continual turmoil and peril as the result of the President's "vigorous Indian policy."

Lamar had no less extensive views in regard to the naval operations of the Republic. In 1838, Mexico had been engaged in a war with France over the claims of French citizens. The French fleet had bombarded and taken Vera Cruz, and in an attempt to drive them out, Santa Anna had lost his leg, and recovered his popularity. Yucatan had also revolted, and was endeavoring to gain its independence. The Texan navy of four vessels had entirely disappeared at the beginning of Lamar's administration. One was captured, one sunk, and the other two condemned as unseaworthy. Appropriations of imaginary funds were made on an extensive scale for the purchase of a new fleet. The steamer Zavala, mounting eight guns, the sloop-of-war Austin, twenty guns, two brigs, the Colorado and Dolphin, and three schooners, the San Bernard, San Antonio, and San Jacinto, were purchased on credit. The fleet was put under the command of Commodore E. W. Moore, and sent to Yucatan to aid the insurgents.

The Federalists in the Northern States of Mexico had taken advantage of the disturbances to organize a revolt. An adventurer by the name of Canales undertook to found a Federal Republic in North Mexico in alliance with Texas, and persuaded a number of Texans, under Colonels Ross and Jordan, to join him in an invasion across the Rio Grande. They were mere filibusters without the authorization of the Texan government. The expedition shared the usual fate of the invasions of Mexico, in arousing the hostility of the inhabitants and experiencing the treachery of their allies. After fighting several battles and occupying several towns, they were deserted on the field of Saltillo by their allies, but fought their way through the enemy, and retreated in safety to Texas.

Lamar's great scheme, however, was the conquest or occupation of New Mexico. An expedition was organized among the adventurers, who had been disappointed in the failures to invade Mexico, and Congress was asked to authorize and make an appropriation for it. Houston, who was a Representative from Nacogdoches, was strongly opposed to it. The debate had gone on apparently in its favor, and the usual fiery and flamboyant speeches had been made about planting the Lone Star flag on the cathedral towers of Santa Fé. When they had been concluded, Houston, who had been sitting on one of the back benches, engaged in his usual habit of whittling, rose, and with his practical sense and humorous illustration demolished the scheme. He pointed out the folly of the expedition across 600 miles of uninhabited country, and the mistake of expecting that the people of New Mexico, who were thoroughly Mexicans in their education and sympathies, would receive the invaders otherwise than as enemies. Such an expedition would inevitably arouse the active hostility of Mexico and provoke an invasion on the western frontier. Houston took up the arguments of the advocates of the expedition, one after another, and answered them. Coming to the speech of Isaac Van Zandt, who had spoken in a very "high-falutin" style, he used one of those familiar illustrations which were a feature of his command over a frontier audience. He said, " A Tennessee neighbor once stationed his negro, Cæsar, with a rifle at a deer drive, and told him to shoot when the animal broke cover. The deer sprang out, but the rifle made no sound. When Cæsar was cursed for not shooting, he replied, 'Lord a mighty, massa, dat buck jump so high, I think he break his own neck.' So with my young friend Van Zandt; he jumps so high in his speech that he breaks his own neck, and it is not necessary to shoot at him." Houston's arguments prevailed, and Congress refused to authorize the expedition.

Lamar, however, persisted, and took the authority which Congress had refused to grant him. He ordered the Secretary of War to issue arms for the troops, and the brass six-pounder was stamped with the conquering name of "Mirabeau B. Lamar." He issued a proclamation to the people of New Mexico inviting them to become citizens of the Republic of Texas, and to acknowledge its laws. He attempted to disguise the warlike purpose of the expedition by announcing that no attempt would be made to subjugate the country, but only to establish friendly commercial relations with the people in case they did not wish to unite with Texas. Its military form was only intended for defense against the Indians. The expedition started from the neighborhood of Austin June 1, 1841. It numbered about 270 soldiers with a number of teamsters and traders, and three commissioners to treat with the people of New Mexico. It was under the command of General Hugh McLeod, and President Lamar bade it farewell with his usual outburst of classical oratory. The expedition started too late. It was oppressively hot, and the grass was poor. The guides lost their way, provisions gave out, and the party was harassed by hostile Indians. As the expedition, after great suffering, approached

the border of New Mexico, a party on the strongest
horses was sent forward to procure relief and provisions from the people whom they had come to conquer. They were made prisoners, and forwarded to
Governor Armigo at Santa Fé. Troops were sent
against the remainder of the expedition, who upon
false promises of safety and return home laid down
their arms and surrendered. The prisoners were
treated with great barbarity. Some of them were
shot for attempting to escape, and the others were
marched on foot to the City of Mexico, where they
were confined in the prisons or made to work with
the criminals on the public roads, until they were
finally released by the interposition of the foreign
ministers. So ended the scheme for the conquest of
New Mexico, which, beside its original loss, had a
very bad effect upon public opinion in the United
States. Jackson wrote to Houston, "The wild-goose
chase to Santa Fé was a very ill-judged affair, and
the surrender without the fire of a gun has lowered
the prowess of the Texans in the minds of the Mexicans."

General James Hamilton had been appointed min-
ister to Great Britain and France. He concluded a
convention with Lord Palmerston for the recognition
of the independence of Texas, on the condition that
Texas would assume $1,000,000 of the debt due by
Mexico to the English bond-holders. The English
Anti-Slavery Society sent its formal protest to Lord
Palmerston, to which he replied with his usual civil

insolence, and the official intimation that they were a set of idiots. Daniel O'Connell announced his purpose to interrogate the ministry on the matter, and proposed a scheme for settling free negroes from the British colonies in Texas under the protection of Mexico. France followed the example of Great Britain, and acknowledged the independence of Texas, as did also Holland and Belgium. General Hamilton had also been appointed a commissioner to negotiate the five million loan, and attempted to obtain the subscriptions of European bankers. He had sanguine hopes of success at one time, and announced that he had made arrangements with the house of Lafitte and Company, of Paris, to open books for the loan. The negotiations fell through, and their failure was charged to the adverse influence of M. Humann, the French Minister of Finance, who had been prejudiced by M. de Saligny, the chargé d'affaires in Texas. M. de Saligny had withdrawn in dudgeon, because of a quarrel with Mr. Bullock, an inn-keeper of Austin, in which he considered that the Texan authorities had not treated him with becoming respect. It appears that Bullock's pigs intruded into the stable and ate up the corn of M. de Saligny's horses. Saligny's servant killed one of the pigs, and Bullock horsewhipped the servant. Saligny entered a complaint against Bullock, and Bullock ordered him out of his hotel. Saligny applied to the Secretary of State for redress, and failing to get it left the country. This was the story to account for the failure of

the French loan, but probably the financial condition
and prospects of Texas were a more sufficient reason.
At any rate, General Hamilton completely failed with
the European capitalists, and Texas was spared the
additional burden of a loan which would probably
have been wasted in extravagance.

The finances of Texas sank to a frightful condition
under Lamar's administration.   There was no revenue except from the customs duties; but as these
were receivable in government money they simply
canceled so much indebtedness without bringing in
any available funds.   The public land sales amounted
to practically nothing, and the sole resource was the
issue of the government promissory notes, called
"red-backs." These were issued of all denomina-
tions down to twelve and a half cents, and fell in
value until they were worth no more than two cents
on the dollar, or would not be received at all.   It is
to the credit of the Texan government, and about
the sole financial folly which it did not commit, that
it did not attempt to make its notes legal tender, and
to compel their circulation under penalties of the law,
as was done later under the Southern Confederacy.
The public debt of Texas during Lamar's administration was increased by $4,855,215, as compared with
$190,000, the expenses during Houston's term, and
the condition of the country was one of financial
chaos.

During the last year of his term Lamar yielded
to the disappointment of his high-flown schemes

and the load of complaint and obloquy, and obtained permission from Congress to abdicate his functions of government. The duties of his office were performed by Vice-President Burnett. At one time, toward the close of his administration, affairs became so desperate, and Congress felt itself so helpless, that the members proposed to abandon their places, and go home. Houston made an eloquent speech recalling them to their duty, and on his motion a resolution was adopted "to adjourn until to-morrow at the usual hour." During Lamar's administration the seat of government was removed to a location on the Colorado River, selected by a commission for that purpose, and a town laid out, which was named Austin. At that time it was far beyond the line of settlements and exposed to Indian attacks, so that the members of the government were sometimes obliged to take their turns at standing guard. The principal redeeming feature to the Lamar régime was the foundation given to a system of public education by a grant of land for a university, and appropriations of the public domain to each county for the establishment of schools.

Houston was the centre of the political opposition to Lamar's administration, and the people were divided into the "Houston" and "anti-Houston" parties, which continued to be the politics of Texas until it became a part of the United States, and, indeed, never entirely lost their power so long as he lived. He was nominated for President, and began those campaigns of stump-speaking which were afterward so marked a feature in the politics of Texas, and such effective means for his retention of power. In the election there were 11,531 votes cast. Houston received 7415, to 3616 for David G. Burnett. Edward Burleson was elected Vice-President. Houston was inaugurated for the second time on the 16th of December, 1841.

' In his message to Congress he said, "It seems that we have arrived at a crisis which is neither cheering for the present, nor flattering for the future." No change had taken place in the attitude of Mexico. Overtures had been made for the amicable adjustment of the difficulties, but they had been rejected, and he would not incur the degradation of further advances. It would be well to encourage Mexican citizens with the kindliest treatment so far as they wished to engage in commerce with the citizens of Texas, but there should be no interference with the revolutions or disturbances in Mexico. It would only exasperate the national enemy, while weakening the resources of Texas. The relations with the Indians were in a very unsatisfactory condition. Immense sums had been spent in fighting them, but without good results. The erection of frontier posts at suitable points, and the establishment of trading stations protected by guards, would insure tranquillity and a lucrative commerce, while just and equitable treaties would maintain a lasting peace. There was not a dollar in the treasury, and the country was involved from ten to fifteen millions. "We are not only without money, but without credit, and for want of punctuality without character." It would be necessary for Congress to totally suspend the redemption of the liabilities. In order to carry on the government it would be necessary to make a new issue of paper money, not exceeding $350,000, to be received at par for the government revenues. One million acres in the newly acquired Cherokee country should' be specially set apart for the redemption of this issue. Finally, retrenchment and the most absolute economy should be established in the expenditure of the government.

Houston's first work was to carry out his recommendations for economy. Upon his suggestion his own salary was reduced from $10,000 to $5000, and those of the other civil officers in the like proportion. Many useless offices were abolished, and the most rigid economy was exercised in every department. All claims, even the most just and pressing, were postponed, and all appropriations by Congress, except those absolutely necessary to carry on the government, were vetoed. Among the claimants was one Colonel Jonathan Bird, who had built a blockhouse at Birdsville at his own expense for the protection of the frontier. He applied to Congress for reimbursement. The members told him that his claim was a just one, but that it would be useless for them to pass a bill for his relief as the President would veto it. They told him, however, that if he would see Houston, and get his approval, they would vote the appropriation. Houston told him that his claim ought to be paid, but that he could not approve any demand on the treasury in its bankrupt condition. Said he, "If it would do you any good, colonel, I would give you half my present fortune; but my only possessions are a stud horse, who is eating his head off in the stable, and a solitary gamecock, without a hen to lay an egg."

The rigidity of Houston's economy is shown by the fact that the payment from the treasury during his three years' term only amounted to $417,175, exclusive of $17,907 paid for the mail service and the collection of taxes.

Houston immediately set to work to pacify the Indians. He sent commissioners to the various tribes with messages of friendship, and to arrange treaties of peace. They were successful in every instance, and although there were occasional troubles, owing to the encroachment of the settlers upon the Indian country and the inevitable conflicts between the hostile races, there was no general war with any Indian tribe during the whole of his administration. Individual hornets were flying about, but the whole nest was not disturbed. Houston addressed the Indians in their own style of language, with which he was familiar, and with a figurative eloquence, which they could appreciate. A number of his Indian "talks," as they were called, have been preserved. This is one of them: —

Executive Department,
Washington, *October* 13, 1842.

To the Red Bear and Chiefs of the Council:

My Brothers, — The path between us is open; it has become white. We wish it to remain open, and that it shall no more be stained with blood. The last Council took brush out of our way. Clouds no longer hang over us, but the sun gives life to our footsteps. Darkness is taken away from us, and we can look at each other as friends. I send councilors with my talk. They will give it to you. Hear it, and remember my words. I have never opened my lips to tell a red brother a lie. My red brethren, who know me, will tell you that my counsel has always been for peace; that I have eaten bread and drank water with the red men. They listened to my words, and were not troubled. A bad chief came in my place, and told them lies, and did them much harm. His counsel was listened to, and the people did evil. His counsel is no more heard, and the people love peace with their red brothers. You, too, love peace; and you wish to kill the buffalo for your women and children. There are many in Texas, and we wish you to enjoy them.

Your Great Father, and ours, of the Uni   f
wishes the red men and the people of ʾ   as to
brothers. He has written to me and t
you wanted peace, and would keep it.   ∶
was good we have listened to him. You, too,

heard his wishes, and you know the wishes of the red
brothers on the Arkansas. Let us be like brothers,
and bury the tomahawk forever.

Bad men make trouble; they cannot be at peace,
but when the water is clear they will disturb it, and
make it muddy. The Mexicans have lately come to
San Antonio and brought war with them; they killed
some of our people, and we killed and wounded many
of them. We drove them out of the country; they
fled in sorrow. If they come back again, they shall
no more leave our country, or it will be after they
have been taken prisoners. Their coming has disturbed us, and for that reason I cannot go to the
Council to meet you, as I had intended. But my
friends that I send to you will tell you all things, and
make a treaty with you that I will look upon, and
rejoice at. You will counsel together. They will
bring me all the words that you speak to them. The
Great Spirit will hear the words that I speak to you,
and He will know the truth of the words that you
send to me. When truth is spoken his countenance
will rejoice, but before him who speaketh lies the
Great Spirit will place darkness, and will not give
light to his going. Let all the red men make peace;
let no man injure his brother; let us meet every year
in council that we may know the hearts of each other.
I wish some of the chiefs of my red brothers to come
and see me at Washington. They shall come in
peace, and none shall make them afraid.

The messenger from the Queen of England and the

messenger from the United States are both in Texas, and will be in Washington, if they are not sick. They will be happy to see my brothers. If the Big Musk is in the Council he has not forgotten my words, and he knows my counsel was always that of a brother; and that I never deceived my red brothers, the Cherokees. They had much trouble and sorrow brought upon them, but it was done by chiefs whose counsel was wicked, and I was far off and could not hinder the mischief that was brought upon his people. Our great Council is to meet again in one moon, and I will send a talk to our agent at the trading house, who will send it to my red brothers.

Let the war-whoop be no more heard in our prairies. Let songs of joy be heard upon our hills. In our valleys let there be laughter, and in our wigwams let the voices of our women and children be heard. Let trouble be taken away far from us; and when our warriors meet together, let them smoke the pipe of peace and be happy.

Your brother,

SAM HOUSTON.

Santa Anna had taken advantage of the popularity which he had gained by his attack upon the French in Vera Cruz to reorganize his party and depose President Bustamente. The great majority of the people of Mexico were bitterly opposed to the surrender of Texas, and Santa Anna felt compelled to at least make a pretense of renewing the invasion. A small body of troops under General Vasquez was sent across the Rio Grande, and advanced upon San Antonio, which they reached on March 6, 1842. The small Texan garrison retreated, and the Mexicans took possession of the town. They hoisted the Mexican flag on the cathedral, but, after some plundering, retreated without attempting to hold the place. Similar raids by small forces were made at the same time upon Refugio and Goliad. These raids caused great excitement among the colonists, and it was apprehended that they were the forerunners of a more formidable invasion. The President issued a proclamation calling out the citizens. A force of 200 or 300 quickly gathered at San Antonio under General Burleson, but found that the enemy had retired. General Alexander Somerville was sent to take command of the levies, which soon amounted to about 3500 men. They were eager to pursue the enemy across the Rio Grande, but Houston was soon convinced that the advance of the Mexicans had been merely a temporary raid, and decided against any offensive war. He issued a proclamation forbidding any advance without authority, and, while professedly encouraging the war spirit, took effectual measures to prevent any expedition into Mexico. After some exhibitions of temper and insubordination the troops were disbanded by General Burleson and returned home.

The war between Houston and Santa Anna was

carried on by paper missiles. Santa Anna issued a public letter in reply to a proposition made by General Hamilton without authority from the Texan government. General Hamilton had proposed that Mexico should acknowledge the independence of Texas for the payment of $5,000,000, and $200,000 in secret, to the agents of the treaty. Santa Anna was justifiably indignant at the proposed attempt at bribery, which he denounced as an insult and an infamy. He declared that Mexico would never surrender her right to Texas, and would never desist from war until she "had planted her eagle standard on the banks of the Sabine." Houston replied with a category of Santa Anna's acts of perfidy and falsehood, and a somewhat disingenuous argument of the peaceful character of the Santa Fé expedition. To Santa Anna's threats of the conquest of Texas he replied with vigorous emphasis: —

"But you declare that you will not relax your exertions until you have subjugated Texas; that you ' have weighed its possible value,' and that you are perfectly aware of the magnitude of the task which you have undertaken; that you 'will not permit Colossus within the limits of Mexico;' t   our ᴵ   ᶦ
is that of 'theft and usurpation;' and t   '᠄   bᵢ   ʀ
of the Mexican nation ' demands of you 'the ᴺ ᴀᴊ
tion of Texas;' that 'if it were an un   ᵈu   ᵛᵉ   ᵎ
sert, useless, sterile, yielding nothing   ᴸᵉ
abounding only in thorns to wound t   feet of t
traveler, you would not permit it to ex   ᶦ   ᵎ

pendent government, in derision of your national
character, your hearths, and your individuality.'
Allow me to assure you that our title to Texas has a
high sanction, — that of purchase, because we have
performed our conditions; that of conquest, because
we have been victorious; it is ours because you cannot subdue us; it has been consecrated ours by the
blood of martyred patriots; it is ours by the claims
of patriotism, superior intelligence, and unsubduable
courage. It is not a sterile waste or a desert. It is
the home of freemen, it is the land of promise, it is
the garden of flowers. Every citizen of Texas was
born a freeman, and he would die a recreant to the
principles imbibed from his ancestry if he would not
freely peril his life in defense of his home, his liberty,
and his country."

He concluded, "Ere the banner of Mexico shall
triumphantly float on the banks of the Sabine, the
Texan standard of the single star, borne by the
Anglo-Saxon race, shall display its bright folds in
Liberty's triumph on the Isthmus of Darien."

The war fever continued to rage, and the demand
for offensive operations against Mexico was so strong
that the President called a special session of Congress, which met at Houston on June 27. In his
message he alluded to the public threats of Santa
Anna, and said that "it was not for us to act on the
supposition that they were merely intended to give
him temporary popularity at home." He did not believe that a formidable invasion would be attempted,

but it was evident that the enemy would continue to
annoy the frontier. He had heretofore been opposed
to offensive measures, but the question was whether
they were not now necessary. He left it for Congress to decide. The war fever prevailed in Congress. It passed an act appointing Houston to the
command of the army with dictatorial powers, and
appropriating ten millions of acres of the public
domain for war purposes. Houston vetoed it in a
message declaring that it was contrary to his principles to accept the powers of a military dictator, and
that the country had no means whatever for carrying
on the war against a powerful nation. It was asserted by the enemies of Houston that his self-deny-
ing declaration was a piece of popular clap-trap, and
his whole conduct in the affair a specimen of his "Indian cunning." They declared that he had consulted
with the members of Congress in regard to the details
of the bill which he vetoed, and that he had created
the demand for the dictatorship in order to refuse it.
During the fortnight which passed before the publication of his veto, great turbulence prevailed, and
there were threats of violence and assassination.
Houston was warned by his friends to have a protecting guard, but his house was open as usual, and the
voice of his young wife could be heard at the piano
in the evening through the open windows, while knots
of desperate men were gathered to curse and threaten
him. Whether Houston played a political trick in
regard to the dictatorship or not, he undoul "

showed great practical sagacity in refusing to allow
the country to undertake the invasion of Mexico
without means, and with only an undisciplined army
of volunteers.

In March, 1842, Houston proclaimed a blockade
of the Mexican coast. The Mexican navy had been
destroyed in the harbor of Vera Cruz by the French
fleet, and the Texan vessels could command the Gulf.
They had been cruising off the coast of Yucatan without accomplishing anything for themselves or the
insurgents. The insurgent government of Yucatan
had agreed to pay their expenses, but nothing was
received from it. The crews were unpaid and the
vessels out of repair when they returned from their
cruise. They were sent to New Orleans to refit, but
there was no money to pay the bills, and the vessels
were given in pawn as security. Houston sent orders
to Commodore Moore to sail for Galveston, but he
refused to do so until the debts, for which he had
given his personal pledge were paid. At a secret
session of Congress in January, 1843, it was decided
to sell the vessels, and commissioners were sent to
take possession of them. The commodore refused to
deliver them up, and sailed for Campeachy on an
appeal for aid, and the promise of a subsidy by the
Yucatan government, which was being besieged in
that place. Houston issued a proclamation declaring
Moore's operations to be piratical, and requesting
foreign navies to seize the vessels and deliver them
up. Moore succeeded in relieving the siege of Cam-

peachy by driving the Mexican vessels from the harbor and cannonading the land batteries. He returned to Galveston, and a paper war ensued between him and the President. The people of Galveston were indignant at the action of Congress in ordering the sale of the navy, and the act was repealed. The vessels were laid up, and remained useless until they were turned over to the United States, after annexation. The whole conduct of the navy, like that of the army, showed the utter want of subordination which existed among the volunteer adventurers, and the difficulty which Houston had in maintaining any regulation or authority.

During the excitement of the apprehended invasion, Houston, who had been opposed to the change of the capitol to Austin, removed the government to Houston, and afterward to the town of Washington on the Brazos. This excited great indignation among the citizens of Austin, and they refused to permit the removal of the archives. Houston sent messengers for them, but the citizens shaved the manes and tails of their horses, and drove them off with contumely. On the 20th of December, 1842, Houston dispatched a company of armed men with wagons to bring off the archives by force. As they were loading the boxes into the wagons at the Land Office, the citizens gathered, and a cannon was trained on the building. It was touched off by a Mrs. Eberly, the Amazonian keeper of a hotel in the town, but, fortunately, no one was injured by the discharge. The company started with their wagons, but were overtaken and surrounded by the citizens at their camp at Brushy Creek, about eighteen miles from Austin. The company was compelled to surrender and haul the boxes back to Austin. Houston complained to Congress of this insubordination, but nothing was done about it, and the boxes remained at Austin.

Disturbances broke out in 1842 on the old "neutral ground" in Eastern Texas among the settlers themselves. A strong element of desperadoes and criminals remained among the people. Forged land titles and squatters' claims furnished the cause of the disturbance. The courts were powerless to enforce claims under the laws, and the citizens formed themselves into a band, calling themselves the "Regulators," to carry out their own ideas of justice by the bullet and the lash. The opposite party organized under the name of the "Moderators," and the whole section was involved in a bitter and vindictive neighborhood war. Appeals were made by the peaceable citizens to Houston to suppress it. He ordered out a force of militia under General Smith, who marched to Shelby County, and found the two parties drawn up in battle array. He persuaded them to disperse without fighting, and the troubles were quieted in a measure. But the private warfare lasted for some years, and the squatters continued to hold their lands by the title of the rifle.

In September, 1843, the Mexicans made a more serious raid across the Rio Grande. General Adrian

Woll entered San Antonio with a force of 1200 men. It was a surprise, and the Mexicans took the members of the district court prisoners. The militia rallied at Gonzales under the command of Captain Matthew Caldwell, known as "Old Paint," and advanced to attack the Mexicans with about eighty men. Captain John C. Hays, the famous Texan Ranger, was sent forward with a small party to draw a sally from the town. General Woll came out with 200 cavalry and 600 infantry, and a battle took place on the Salado Creek. It lasted until sunset, when the Mexicans retreated into the town. A party of fifty Texans, under Captain Nicholas Dawson, in attempting to join Caldwell, were surrounded on the prairie by the Mexicans, who kept out of the range of their rifles, but fired upon them with a cannon, until they were compelled to surrender. The prisoners were all butchered after their surrender, and only one of the party succeeded in making his escape by killing a cavalry man with his own lance, and dashing off on his horse. General Woll retired from San Antonio on the 18th, taking with him his prisoners and plunder. He was pursued by Caldwell, whose force had increased to 400 or 500 men, but the report of a reinforcement to Woll, under General Ampudia, prevented Caldwell from attacking him.

This raid again renewed the excitement and the demand for offensive operations against Mexico. Houston was once more compelled to cater to the war spirit. He issued a proclamation on September 16, announcing that the Texan troops would cross the Rio Grande, and calling upon the levies to muster at San Antonio. General Somerville was again given the command, probably with secret instructions not to attempt any serious invasion. Troops gathered at San Antonio in an ill-supplied and insubordinate condition, and after several weeks of waiting a considerable number of them went home. On November 18, Somerville set out on his march with 750 men, and reached Laredo December 6. He moved down the river, instead of crossing it. His troops were convinced that he had no serious purpose, and became insubordinate. About 200 left him and returned home. Somerville crossed the river with the rest, and took possession of Guerrero. From that place he recrossed the river and informed his army that he intended to return to Gonzales. About 300 men refused to return. They elected Colonel William S. Fisher as their commander, and determined to invade Mexico on their own account. They made an attack on the town of Mier on the night of the 23d, and entered it. During the engagement for the possession of the town the next day the Texans were persuaded to surrender by false representations of the arrival of Mexican reinforcements, and on the promise that they should not be sent into Mexico. The promise was violated, and they were marched as prisoners toward the City of Mexico. They rose on their guards at the Hacienda del Salado, about eighteen miles beyond Saltillo, and made their escape. Unfortunately, they deserted the road and took refuge in the mountains, where they lost their way and were worn out by hardships and want of food. They were tracked down by parties of the soldiery, and all but four recaptured. Every tenth man of the prisoners was shot by order of Santa Anna for their attempt to escape, and Captain Ewan Cameron, the leader of the revolt, who had escaped drawing the black bean in the death lottery, was afterward ordered to be shot. The prisoners were confined in the fortress of Perote near Jalapa. General Thomas Jefferson Green and a few others escaped by tunneling through the wall, and the rest were eventually released at the interposition of the foreign ministers.

A sort of predatory expedition took place the same year. It was an attempt to capture a train loaded with Mexican goods on its way from Independence, Missouri, to Santa Fé. Captain Jacob S. Snively started in the fall of 1843 with about 150 men to capture the train in the region south of the Arkansas, which was claimed to be Texas territory. The train was escorted by a force of United States cavalry, under the command of Colonel Philip St. George Cooke, who obtained information of Snively's design. He informed Snively that he was trespassing on the territory of the United States, and compelled him to surrender. His party was partially disarmed and rendered harmless for mischief. A part accompanied Cooke's cavalry to Independence and a part returned home, having suffered somewhat in skirmishes with

the Indians on the way. It was an error on the part
of Houston to have authorized such an expedition.

On October 13, 1842, President Houston sent a
dignified and forcible appeal to the governments of
the United States, Great Britain, and France to in-
terpose with Mexico, and require that either she
should recognize the independence of Texas, or make
war upon her in a civilized manner. He pointed out
that no serious attempt at invasion had been made
for the past six years, and that the war had only been
carried on by predatory raids and by inciting the Indians to massacre. He said: —

"If Mexico believes herself able to subjugate this
country, her right to make the effort to do so is not
denied, for, on the contrary, if she chooses to invade
our territory for that purpose the President, in the
name of the people of all Texas, will bid her welcome. It is not against a war with Mexico that
Texas would protest. This she deprecates not. She
is willing at any time to stake her existence as a nation upon the issue of a war conducted on Christian
principles. It is alone against the unholy, inhuman,
and fruitless character it has assumed and still main-
tains, which violates every rule of honorable warfare,
every precept of religion, and sets at defiance even
the common sentiments of humanity, against which
she protests, and invokes the interposition of those
powerful nations which have recognized her independence."

This appeal received the approval of Sir Robert

Peel and M. Guizot. Lord Aberdëen, the British Minister of Foreign Affairs, offered to mediate with Mexico for a cessation of hostilities, but declined to act jointly with the United States, on the ground that the latter's relations with Mexico were not sufficiently friendly to justify expectations of any good results from her interference. Under the convention arranged by General Hamilton, the British minister to Mexico had been instructed to proffer a mediation which had been categorically refused by the Mexican government. This offer was now renewed, but with no better apparent success. In the mean time, the efforts for annexation had been revived in the United States. On June 6, 1843, President Houston sent a dispatch to Minister Van Zandt at Washington, directing him to withdraw the application of Texas for annexation to the United States. In further dispatches, which were doubtless intended to be shown to the members of the United States government and to leading men in Congress, he communicated the facts of the friendly proffers made by European governments, and intimated that by an alliance with them Texas would be relieved from the necessity of desiring annexation to the United States. President Tyler was strongly in favor of annexation, and opened negotiations with Houston to induce him to renew the application. The Mexican minister to the United States announced in August that any act of annexation by Congress would be considered a declaration of war. Houston demanded to know if the United

States could be depended upon to protect Texas from invasion while the negotiations were going on. Secretary Upshur did not answer this question, but stated that the Senate had been canvassed, and that there was an assurance of the necessary two thirds who would vote to ratify the treaty. Houston then applied to Colonel William S. Murphy, the United States diplomatic agent in Texas, and was assured that the United States would not permit the interference of Mexico or any other power while the negotiations were pending. Houston accepted this as sufficient, and appointed J. Pinkney Henderson as a special commissioner to Washington to renew the application for the treaty. He also sent a secret message to the Texan Congress, informing it of what he had done, and requesting its approval. During these negotiations Houston wrote several important letters, doubtless intended to affect public sentiment in the United States. On February 16, 1844, he wrote to Jackson, pointing out the advantages in trade and security which Texas would secure by maintaining her independence, but declaring himself in favor of annexation. His desire for peace and a settled order outweighed all other considerations. He said: —

"I have no desire to see war renewed again in Texas. It is not the apprehension of personal danger that would alarm me, but rather the deleterious influence which it has upon our population. The revolution has already introduced into Texas more wicked and ambitious men than could be desired in our present condition. In armies and camps such men have an opportunity of extending their acquaintance, and deriving some prominence from associations which totally disqualifies them from usefulness in a peaceful community. Unwilling to embark in the useful avocations of life, in many instances they become restless demagogues or useless loafers. They are either ready to consume the substance which they have not earned, or to form combinations unfavorable to good order and the administration of the laws. Peace in Texas would relieve us from such people, and in the absence of their baleful influence give to society a vigorous constitution and healthy complexion. All the evils which we have experienced have resulted from such characters, and unless we have peace permanently established among us we cannot tell when a September election might not submerge the country to the misrule of such men for three years.

"Furthermore, I wish to reside in a land where all will be subordinate to law, and where none dare to defy its mandates. I have arrived at that period of life when I desire retirement and assurance that whatever I possess will be secured to me by just laws wisely administered. That privilege I would deem a rich requital for whatever I may have performed useful in life. With it I would be happy to retire from all cares of public station, and live in the enjoyment of the reflection that, if I had been serviceable to any portion of mankind, their prosperity and happiness were ample recompense. I would give no thought to what the world might say of me when I could transmit to posterity the reputation of an honest man."

In conclusion he said: —

"Now, my venerated friend, you will perceive that Texas is presented to the United States as a bride adorned for her espousal. But if, now so confident of the union, she should be rejected, her mortification would be indescribable. She has been sought by the United States, and this is the third time she has consented. Were she now to be spurned it would forever terminate expectation on her part, and it would then not only be left for the United States to expect that she would seek some other friend, but all Christendom would justify her in a choice dictated by necessity and sanctioned by wisdom. However adverse this might be to the wishes or the interest of the United States, in her present situation she could not ponder long. The course of the United States, if it stop short of annexation, will displease France, irritate England, and exasperate Mexico. An effort to postpone it to a more convenient season may be tried in the United States to subserve party purposes and make a President. Let them beware. I take it that it is of too great magnitude for any impediment to be opposed to its execution. That you may live to see your hopes in relation to it crowned with complete success, I sincerely desire. In the event that it speedily takes place, I hope that it will afford me an opportunity of again visiting you at the Hermitage with my family. It is our ardent desire to see the day when you can lay your hand on our little boy's head, and bestow upon him your benediction."

In May, he wrote to Minister Murphy a letter, which shows his enlarged views of the future of Texas as an independent power, and of the possibilities of the creation of a great and rival empire in the West. It was not a wild and extravagant vision, and might have been accomplished but for the annexation of Texas and the subsequent acquisition of California by the United States. He said: —

"If faction or a regard for present party advantages should defeat the measure, you may depend upon one thing, and that is, that the glory of the United States has already culminated. A rival power will soon be built up, and the Pacific, as well as the Atlantic, will be component parts of Texas in thirty years from this date. The Oregon region in geographical affinity will attach to Texas. By this coalition or union the barrier of the Rocky Mountains will be dispensed with or obviated. England and France in such an event would not be so tenacious on the subject of Oregon as if the United States were to be the sole possessor of it. When such an event would take place, or in anticipation of such a result, all the powers which either envy or fear the United States would use all reasonable exertion to build us up as the only rival power which can ever exist on this continent to that of the United

States. Considering our origin, their speculation may seem chimerical and that such things cannot take place. A common origin has its influence so long as common interests exist, but no longer. . . . The union of Oregon and Texas will be much more natural and convenient than for either separately to belong to the United States. This, too, would place Mexico at the mercy of such a power as Oregon and Texas would form; such an event may appear fanciful to many, but I assure you that there are no Rocky Mountains interposing to such a project. But one thing can prevent its accomplishment, and that is annexation. If you, or any statesman, will only regard the map of North America, you will perceive that from the forty-sixth degree of latitude north there is the commencement of a natural boundary. This will embrace Oregon, and from thence south, on the Pacific coast, to the twenty-ninth or thirtieth degree south latitude will be a natural and convenient extent of sea-land. I am free to admit that most of the province of Chihuahua, Sonora, and Upper and Lower California, as well as Santa Fé, which we now claim, will have to be brought into the connection with Texas and Oregon. This, you will see by reference to the map, is no bugbear to those who will reflect upon the achievement of the Anglo-Saxon people. . . . You need not estimate the population which is said or reputed to occupy the vast territory embraced between the twenty-ninth and forty-sixth degrees of latitude on the Pacific. They will, like the Indian race, yield to the advance of the North American population. The amalgamation, under the advisement of statesmen, cannot fail to produce the result in producing a united government formed of and embracing the limits suggested. It may be urged that these matters are remote. Be it so. Statesmen are intended by their forecast to regulate and arrange matters in such sort as will give direction to events by which the future is to be benefited or prejudiced. You may fully rely, my friend, that future ages will profit by these facts, while we will only contemplate them in prospective. They must come. It is impossible to look on the map of North America and not perceive the rationale of the project."

Before Jackson had received Houston's letter he had written on February 13 a letter expressing his strong desire for the annexation of Texas. It was kept secret for political reasons by the Democratic conspirators, headed by Calhoun, who were opposed to the nomination of Van Buren. It was believed that both Van Buren and Clay had come to an understanding by which they hoped to eliminate the Texas question from the coming election, in which they expected to be the candidates of their respective parties. The question had excited a bitter controversy, and each one feared that it would cost him vital votes. Clay wrote a letter, April 11, in which he declared that the annexation of Texas would be certain to bring on a war with Mexico, and endanger the safety of the Union. Van Buren also published a letter expressing his belief that the annexation of Texas would be followed by a war with Mexico, and that in such an event the United States would not be justified in the eyes of the world. The treaty was submitted to the Senate with a message from President Tyler advocating what he termed the re-annexation of Texas. The controversy raged in the country and in Congress, but the influence of these two great leaders upon their respective parties was sufficient to secure rejection. The treaty was rejected on June 5 by a vote of thirty-five to sixteen.

As soon as the treaty was definitely rejected by the United States the British government acted. Lord Aberdeen proposed to Ashbell Smith, the Texan minister to Great Britain and France, a "diplomatic act" in which five powers, Great Britain, France, the United States, Texas, and Mexico should be invited to join. Its purpose was to secure peace between Texas and Mexico and the permanent independence of the former, Texas giving a formal pledge not to unite with any other nation. France agreed to join with Great Britain in the "act," and the three powers were to compel the assent of Mexico. The refusal of the United States was expected. Houston, who had been absent from the seat of government for some time, sent instructions to Anson Jones, Secretary of State, to close with the offer of Great Britain and France. Jones, who was then President-elect, disobeyed the order, and, instead, sent leave of absence to Minister Smith. Why Houston permitted this is an unsolved problem, but it is possible that he was willing that Jones, who was then his friend and a political protégé, should have the distinction of concluding the treaty. At that time Houston and Jones were both regarded as opposed to annexation, and the majority of the people of Texas agreed with them, considering that the action of the United States had rendered it hopeless.

In the mean time independent negotiations had been going on for an armistice and a treaty of peace with Mexico. The ex-provisional Lieutenant-Governor, J. W. Robinson, who had been among the prisoners captured at San Antonio by General Woll, had addressed a communication to Santa Anna from the prison of Perote, proposing, if he was released, to go to Texas, and arrange the terms of a treaty by which Texas would acknowledge the sovereignty of Mexico, on condition that she should have a separate government. The proposition, which was probably made for no other purpose than to secure his own release, was accepted. Santa Anna's communication, which was addressed to "Mr." Houston and claimed Texas to be a province of Mexico, was of course rejected. But in it Mexico had expressed a willingness to suspend hostilities. An armistice was agreed upon through the mediation of the British minister, and commissioners were appointed on the part of President Houston and General Woll, to arrange for an exchange of prisoners, pending negotiations for a permanent peace. They agreed upon the terms of an armistice to last until May 1, and the agreement was signed on February 15. It was rejected by Houston on the ground that it referred to Texas as a province of Mexico. No acts of hostility followed, although General Woll notified Houston that the war was renewed.

Jones was inaugurated President on the 1st of December, 1844. In his last message to Congress Houston had the pleasure of announcing that his measures of economy had resulted in the solvency of the treasury. The expenses of the government had been met. The total cost of his administration during the three years had been only $416,058, and there was a balance in the treasury of $5058. The Exchequer bills, with some fluctuations, had appreciated nearly to par, and the revenues of the country were on a sound and stable basis. Of all Houston's services to Texas none was more important than his firm and judicious economy, and its rescue from the danger of the absolute collapse of the government from the extravagance and wild financial schemes of the preceding administration. In his valedictory address he said in regard to annexation, "The United States have spurned Texas twice already. Let her therefore firmly maintain her position as it is, and work out her own political salvation. Let her legislation proceed upon the principle that we are to be and to remain an independent people. If Texas goes begging again for admission to the United States, she will only degrade herself. . . . If we remain an independent nation our territory will become extensive — unlimited."

The knowledge of the "diplomatic act" and the apprehension that Texas would be bound to Great Britain and France by their guarantee of her independence aroused the alarm and jealousy of the United States. Public sentiment turned decidedly in favor of annexation. Van Buren was defeated in the Democratic Convention, and James K. Polk was nominated as an avowed advocate of annexation. Clay endeavored to satisfy public opinion by declaring that he was in favor of annexation if it could be accomplished without war, but Polk was elected by a small majority in the Electoral College. On February 14, a joint resolution was adopted by both Houses of Congress for the admission of Texas into the Union. President Herrera, of Mexico, who had been elected by the Liberal party, agreed to a treaty by which Mexico consented to acknowledge the independence of Texas, on condition that she would not become annexed to any other power. The United States government became exceedingly anxious. Special agents were sent to make all sorts of promises to the people, and the old war feeling was stirred up by intimations of aggressive movements against Mexico. Lamar, and the other ambitious leaders who had been opposed to annexation, now strongly favored it, and it was even proposed to overthrow the government on the ground of President Jones's supposed opposition to the measure. Houston, who was a friend of Jones, although they afterward quarreled bitterly, lent his strong personal influence to the support of the government. The proposition of President Herrera was made known to the people by proclamation, and a convention was also called to take action on the invitation of the United States. It met in Austin on the 4th of July, 1845, and adopted a resolution for annexation, which was submitted to Congress for ratification. It was accepted with only one dissentient vote, that of Richard Bache, a grandson of Benjamin Franklin. The convention framed a state constitution, which was accepted by the people at a general election. October 14, Texas ceased to be a Republic, and became one of the United States.

Some question has been raised as to the sincerity of Houston's desire for annexation. At the time he was accused of having been bought by British gold, and he was charged with treason with all the bitterness of envenomed political animosity. There is no reasonable doubt that Houston went to Texas for the purpose of bringing about its acquisition by the United States, and with the knowledge and support of Jackson. During the early years of the struggle for independence annexation to the United States would have settled the question in favor of Texas, and was ardently desired by every man in it except those who were blinded by wild schemes of ambition and impossible conquest. Houston was too shrewd and sensible not to recognize its advantages. Nevertheless, he was revolted by the opposition of a considerable portion of the people of the United States, and by the repeated refusals of its government. He came to see the possibilities of a western empire to be founded by and attached to Texas, and recognized that the time had come when the United States must make a definite choice. His patriotism and his pride would not submit to further national humiliation. Ashbell Smith, Secretary of State to President Jones, relates this incident of Houston while the last negotiations were pending, and before Congress had passed the resolution for annexation : —

"He was leaving Washington on the Brazos one morning in February, 1845. He came into my room, booted, spurred, whip in hand. Said he, 'Saxe Weimar [the name of his saddle-horse] is at the door, saddled. I have come to leave Houston's last words with you. If the Congress of the United States shall not by the 4th of March pass some measure of annexation that Texas can with honor accede to, Houston will take the stump against annexation for all time to come.' When he wished to be emphatic he spoke of himself by name, Houston, in the third person. Without another word, embracing after his fashion, he mounted his horse and left."

So far as Houston's personal ambition was concerned, it undoubtedly would have been favored by annexation. He was debarred from being again President of the Republic by the constitutional limitation. He would naturally and inevitably be one

of the Senators of the new State in Congress, with a
fresh career open before him and the possibility of a
still wider ambition in the Presidency of the United
States. He was prepared to sacrifice this rather than
endure another national affront, but he was undoubtedly rejoiced when annexation was accomplished on
honorable terms.

In his private life during his second term Houston
was enabled to establish a home and abandon some
of his manners of a reckless and freebooting frontiersman, as under the influence of his wife he had re-
formed his habits of drinking and swearing. He
still lived, however, in a primitive fashion. One of
the old settlers of Texas thus relates his first interview with him: "I had come to Texas from Alabama,
and was at Washington on the Brazos, then the seat
of government, in 1843. One morning I was approached by Houston's negro boy Tom, who was his
cook and body-servant, with an invitation from the
President for me to dine with him that day. I was
then only about twenty years of age, and was naturally a good deal flustered by the unexpected honor,
which I was unable to account for, as I had never
spoken to the President. The dinner was at one
o'clock. I found the President at the double log-
house which was his residence. He received me with
a kindly and hearty welcome, which put me at once
at my ease. The dinner consisted of wild turkey,
bread, and black coffee. Houston said that but for
the kindness of a neighbor, who had sent in the

bird, the dinner would have consisted of only bread and coffee. He told me all about my family and relatives in Tennessee, and in fact a great many things that I did not know myself. His whole manner and conversation were most gracious and friendly. From that time I was always his devoted friend and political follower." It was Houston's custom to acquaint himself with the antecedents of new-comers to Texas as far as he could, and attach them to himself by friendly interest and hospitality. If, however, they showed signs of rivalry or opposition to him, he was apt to turn his tongue against them, and be as harsh and sarcastic as he had before been friendly.

Mrs. M. H. Houston, a Scotch lady of wealth who made a cruise in the Gulf of Mexico with her husband in a yacht, and wrote a couple of books about her travels in the United States, thus describes a visit to Houston in 1844: —

"The city of Houston is beautifully situated on the banks of the Red River. The houses are built entirely of wood, and the hotels are wretched. Our chief end, however, was answered, for we received a visit from the conqueror of San Jacinto and the friend of the red man. As is invariably the case in the introduction of Americans, either to one another, or to foreigners, much shaking of hands, together with considerable use of the monosyllable 'sir,' took place between us and General Sam Houston, whose costume is a happy mixture of the inevitable black satin waistcoat (donned probably from a sense of con-ventional respect for his British visitors) and a coarse, blanket-like overcoat, which, having much the appearance of green baize, is the ordinary covering of a Texan gentleman. A wan and worn-looking man is the President of the new Republic, and there are, notwithstanding the shrewd and kindly expression of his face, signs thereon that he has (more than his many admirers like to think possible) deserved in his day the sobriquet of 'Drunken Sam,' which was long since bestowed upon him. He has been twice married, having obtained — a thing easily done in America — a divorce from his first wife; his second marriage has, in one respect at least, proved of signal advantage to him, for, thanks to the influence of *Madame la Presidente*, General Houston has eschewed the habits of drinking and using bad language, in which he formerly indulged. He was what I have heard called 'a fine swearer' in days gone by; but he has learned not only to govern men, but to rule his tongue, which he has probably found to be a far more difficult matter. Like most Americans whom I have known, he is very proud of being able to clearly prove his descent from an English, or rather, in his case, from a Scotch family. He told us that his forbears belonged in Lanarkshire, and claimed cousinship with us at once. Never have I seen a man who had 'done,' not alone the 'State,' but the cause of humanity, such 'good service in his day' who was so simple and unobtrusive in his manner, and who seemed to think so little of himself."

Houston endeavored to fulfill his purpose to visit Jackson at the Hermitage with his family, after annexation, but he only arrived a few hours after the death of his "venerated friend," whom he held in such affection and reverence.

CHAPTER XIV.

SAMUEL HOUSTON and Thomas J. Rusk were elected Senators of the United States by the legislature of Texas. Houston arrived in Washington and took his seat as a member of the Twenty-Ninth Congress March 30, 1846. It was the great era of the American Senate. It had among its members a larger number of distinguished and able statesmen than it had before or has had since. There were the great leaders, Webster, Clay, and Calhoun, the scarcely less distinguished Thomas H. Benton, and among the others, who had or were to acquire a national fame, were Lewis Cass, John A. Dix, Daniel S. Dickenson, Reverdy Johnson, Simon Cameron, William Allen, Thomas Corwin, and Jesse D. Bright. Houston's advent, from his romantic career and achievements, attracted much attention, and he was at once a marked, although a rather eccentric figure in the Senate chamber. He continued his habit of peculiarity in dress, wearing his broad-brimmed white hat of soft fur, and draping himself in a cloak with a red lining, or in a bright-colored Mexican blanket. He provided himself with a supply of cypress shingles, and filled his waste-basket during the debates with the shavings that curled from under his sharp knife.

Houston did not manifest any of that false modesty which has created the custom that a new Senator shall be silent during his first session, but at once took his part in the debates. His first speech was delivered just a fortnight after he had taken his seat. It was on the question of the Oregon boundary. He took strong grounds, in agreement with Benton, with whom he allied himself, as the representative of the old Union Democracy of Jackson, and in opposition to Calhoun and the nullifiers and disunionists, in favor of the extreme claims of the United States to the northern boundary. His speech was long, rambling, and discursive, and, if at times forcible in language, indicated that he was not likely to take his place among the leaders of the Senate in logical and legal argument. The Southern members, under the leadership of Calhoun, were not anxious for the extension of free territory at the North, and President Polk, although he had been elected on the platform of "54.40 or fight," was of a much less bellicose temper toward Great Britain than he had been toward Mexico. The motion for which Houston spoke, to give notice of the termination of the joint occupancy of the Columbia River region, was passed by a vote of forty to fourteen, but the question was finally settled, after some not very forcible diplomacy on the part of the United States, by a compromise on the boundary of 49°.

The war with Mexico had been begun before Houston's arrival by the advance of General Taylor's troops upon the Rio Grande. Houston favored the war, at least after it had been commenced, and had always extreme views in regard to the incorporation of Mexican territory into the United States. He was a member of the Committee on Military Affairs, and was, naturally, a good deal consulted in regard to the operations against Mexico. It is charged that he prevented the appointment of General Albert Sidney Johnston to an important command, on account of their old differences in the affairs of Texas, and he doubtless had virtual control of the commissions issued to Texan officers. He reported a resolution for a vote of thanks to the soldiers engaged in the battle of Buena Vista, and for a medal to General Taylor. He was in favor of the vigorous prosecution of the war, and in the Thirtieth Congress supported the bill for the three millions extra credit to carry it on, which was defeated. He made an elaborate speech, in which he defended the character of the settlers in Texas, who had been attacked during the debate, and set forth the claims of Texas to the territory of New Mexico, east of the Rio Grande, under the old Spanish and French treaties. He defended President Polk from the charge of having brought on the war, and argued in favor of giving him a vigorous support. He was strenuous in the advocacy of the claims of Texas, and made a strong speech in favor of incorporating the Texan navy into that of the

United States, about which there had been some difficulty, which was finally settled by an appropriation
for the pay of the Texan officers for four years, on
the condition that they would relinquish their claims
to positions in the navy of the United States. He
offered a resolution for the establishment of a protectorate over Yucatan, as he did at a later period one
for a protectorate over all Mexico. It was in accordance with his views for the extension of the territory of the United States to the Isthmus of Darien,
but it fortunately received little attention. Whatever may be the opinion in regard to "manifest destiny," the adoption of such a scheme at that time
would have involved the United States in difficulties
and responsibilities of the most serious character, and
have been a source of great trouble and weakness.
These views did not accord with the usual practical
sagacity of Houston, but rather with the filibuster
spirit of the earlier adventurers in Texas, whom he
had always opposed.

Houston's most important action and speech, which
fixed the plan in relation to the extension of slavery
that he ever afterward maintained, were on the bill
for the establishment of the territorial government
of Oregon. The bill contained a provision prohibiting the establishment of slavery, in accordance with
the ordinance of 1787 in regard to the Northwest
Territory. This was denounced by Calhoun, who declared that Congress had no right to prohibit slavery
in a Territory, and openly threatened disunion in

case his doctrine was not accepted. Houston followed Benton in a vigorous reply. He said that he had heard the cry of disunion and nullification before. That cry had reached him in the wilderness when an exile from kindred and friends and sections. But it had rung in his ears, and wounded his heart. Now, however, he was in the midst of such a cry, and he was bound to act as a man conscious of the solemn responsibility imposed upon him. He had heard the menaces and threats of dissolution and dis-union until he had become familiar with them, and they had now ceased to produce alarm in his bosom. He had no fear of the dissolution of the Union, when he recollected how it had been established and how it had been defended. Mr. Calhoun and Mr. Butler, of South Carolina, both interrupted Houston's speech. Calhoun denied that the South had threatened to dissolve the Union. Mr. Butler wanted to know if the holding of a Southern convention was treason. Houston replied, "Certainly not." The South could hold all the conventions it pleased, but he would never go into one. He knew neither North nor South. He knew only the Union. Houston's course produced great anger and excitement among the extreme Southerners. He and Benton were denounced by name as traitors at public meetings in South Carolina. But there appears to have been no disapproval of his action at that time among the people of Texas. The large slave-holding element had not become established among the settlers, and they were fresh in their loyalty to the Union. It was not until the social and political conditions had been changed that the fire-eaters and disunionists gained the control.

In the next Congress in 1849, under the administration of President Taylor, Houston declared himself in favor of the admission of California as a free State. The Southern leaders were greatly excited at the prospect of the loss of the territory for which they had caused the Mexican war. An address was issued for a convention at Nashville to consider the threatened rights and interests of the South. Houston refused to sign the address, and ridiculed the convention. He declared that it was a piece of ridiculous flummery, and that ex-Governor Henderson was the sole representative from Texas in it, and "self-constituted at that." The slavery question was continually coming up in every form. On a resolution to invite Father Mathew, the eminent Irish apostle of temperance, to a seat on the floor of the Senate, objection was made that he had signed a petition against slavery with Daniel O'Connell. Houston supported the resolution, and expressed his profound contempt for the attempt to drag slavery into the question of temperance. At that time Houston had wholly conquered his habits of indulgence in liquor. He said, "I am a disciple of the advocates of temperance. I needed the discipline of reformation, and I embraced it. I am proud on this floor to proclaim it, sir. I would enforce the example upon every American heart that influences or is influenced by filial affection, conjugal love, or parental tenderness."

The question of the extent of the boundary of Texas to the north on the Rio Grande, and the claim of the State to a considerable portion of the territory of New Mexico, was renewed by the result of the Mexican war. The United States troops under General Kearney had taken possession of New Mexico, and, after the territory had been ceded to the United States by the treaty of Guadalupe Hidalgo, Texas attempted to exercise jurisdiction over it. The legislature passed an ordinance making it a judicial district, and Judge Beard was sent to hold courts in the territory. By order of President Taylor, Colonel Monroe, the commandant of the United States troops, forbade Judge Beard to exercise his functions, and ordered an election for a territorial delegate to Congress. Houston defended the claim of Texas in an elaborate speech, and attacked Taylor for his uncomplimentary references in his reports to the disorders among the Texan volunteers during the Mexican war. The question at one time assumed a somewhat serious phase, as Governor Wood threatened to call out the militia of Texas to take possession of the country. But he thought better of it when he was informed by President Taylor that they would be repelled by force, and that he would go to the scene of disturbance himself, if necessary. Mr. Clay in his famous compromise measures included a provision for the settlement of the claim of Texas to New Mexico by

the payment of a sum of money for the canceling of
the debts of Texas, for which the customs revenues
had been pledged. In order to avoid a continuance
of the trouble this portion of the compromise measure
was adopted first. Senator Pearce, of Maryland, introduced a bill fixing the boundaries of Texas and
New Mexico, as they now stand, and providing for
the payment of $10,000,000 to Texas. Of this sum
$5,000,000 was to be reserved for the payment of the
debts of Texas upon claims filed and audited in the
United States treasury. There was a strong disposition in the Texas legislature to reject the proposition,
on the ground of the provision compelling the payment of the public debt contracted by the Republic.
In the final disposition a portion of this was repudiated. The public debt, which amounted to $12,-
436,491, was scaled down to $6,827,278, by various
classifications allowing from twenty to seventy-five
cents on the dollar. It was claimed that this was a
just and even a generous adjustment, inasmuch as the
money had been received in some instances at only
two or three cents on the dollar, and there was the
usual talk about speculators and Shylocks, who had
taken advantage of the necessities of the deserving
creditors to obtain possession of the claims. It must
be admitted that the ostensible claims for a reduction
of the debt on account of the actual value received
were very forcible, and the example of Texas will com-
pare favorably with that of the United States after the
Revolutionary war, and of States like Mississippi and

Pennsylvania with much less temptation.   Nevertheless, it was a violation of the bond, which would not
have been permitted on the part of any private debtor,
and not justifiable according to the strict letter of the
law.   Houston defended the action of Texas in scaling
the debt in a speech in the Senate.   In regard to the
relinquishment by Texas to the claim upon New
Mexico, he said in a speech at Galveston that "it
was the best sale ever made of land of a worthless
quality and a disputable title."   At Houston's suggestion the sum of $2,000,000 of the money, remain-
ing after the payment of the debt, was set apart for
a public school fund.

As the controversy raged and the excitement grew
hot over Clay's compromise bill, Houston offered a
resolution that a committee of six Senators be appointed to prepare an address for the purpose of
allaying the agitation, but it was not adopted.   The
various measures embodied in the original bill, for
the admission of California as a free State, for the
creation of a territorial government in New Mexico
without reference to slavery, for the settlement of the
Texan boundary, for a fugitive slave law, and for the
abolition of the slave trade in the District of Columbia, were finally adopted, one after another.   The
fugitive slave law, in a more severe form as regards
the rights of the fugitives before the courts than as
reported by Mr. Clay, and a gross violation of common law, was passed August 26, only twelve Senators
voting against it.   Houston voted for it, as he did

also for the abolition of the slave trade in the District of Columbia. Although ten Senators from Southern States signed a protest against the admission of California as a free State "as a part of a policy which, if persisted in, would lead to a dissolution of the Confederacy," and there were ominous signs of a growing spirit of slave propagandism and resistance to national authority at the South, the country believed that the terrible question had been charmed down for an indefinite period. But the inevitable conflict had hardly been postponed. A new class of statesmen had come upon the scene, more far-seeing in regard to the nature of the controversy, and more determined to bring it to a decisive issue. Seward, Sumner, and Chase represented the more decided resistance of the North against the spread of slavery, and Jefferson Davis, Clemens, Soulé, and others represented the determination of the South to extend the area of slave territory or dissolve the Union. Webster and Clay, the great champions of compromise, passed away. Benton, who had represented Missouri for thirty years in the Senate, was defeated in his own State, leaving Houston as the sole conspicuous representative of the old Union or Jackson Democracy from the South. In January, 1853, he was reëlected Senator by the legislature of Texas without any formidable opposition.

On March 4, 1853, Franklin Pierce was inaugurated President of the United States as the flexible instrument of the aggressive Southern element. In the early part of the session of 1854 Senator Douglas, of Illinois, from the Committee on Territories, reported the Kansas-Nebraska bill, which repealed the Missouri Compromise, to which the country had clung since 1820 as the pledge of peace and security, and opened all the national territory to the chances of slave colonization. Houston rose at once to the height of the occasion. He opposed the bill vehemently and unflinchingly. In a speech, delivered at the night session of March 3, just before the passage of the bill, which marked his commanding power as an orator on a great occasion, and with a prophetic wisdom and prescience, he exposed the follies and dangers of the bill to the country and to the South in particular. He said, in emphatic words, of the peril it would bring to the Union: —

"Mr. President, I cannot believe that the agitation created by this measure will be confined to the Senate chamber. I cannot believe from what we have witnessed here to-night that this will be the exclusive arena for the exercise of human passion and the expression of public opinion. If the Republic be not shaken, I will thank Heaven for its kindness in maintaining its stability."

He pointed out with much sagacity the special perils which it would bring to Texas: —

"I will give you my reasons why I think Texas would be in the most deplorable condition of all the Southern States. It is now the terminus of the slave population. It is a country of vast extent and fertile soil, favorable to the culture and growth of those productions which are most important to the necessities of the world, — cotton, sugar, and tobacco. An immense slave population must eventually go there. The demand for labor is so great, everything is so inviting to the enterprising and industrious, that labor will be transferred there because it will be of a most profitable character, and the disproportion of slaves to the white population must be immense. Then, sir, it must become the gulf of slavery, and there its terrible eddies will whirl if convulsions take place."

He brushed aside the question of the principle of non-intervention, as claimed by the South, and showed that it was as useless in theory as it would be dangerous in practice: —

"I again ask, What benefit is to result to the South from this measure if adopted? . . . Will it secure these territories to the South. No, sir, not at all. But the gentleman tells us, It is the principle we want. I can perceive but one principle involved in the measure, and that principle lies at the root of agitation; and from that all the tumults and excitements of the country must arise. That is the only principle I can perceive. We are told by Southern as well as Northern gentlemen, those who are for it, and those who are against it, that slavery will never be extended to that Territory, that it will never go there; but it is the principle of non-intervention it is desired to establish. Sir, we have done well under the intervention of the Missouri Compromise, if the gentlemen so call it, in other Territories, and I adjure you, when there is so much involved, not to press the matter too far. What is to be the consequence? If it is not in embryo, my suggestion will not make it so. It has been suggested elsewhere, and I may repeat it here, What is to be the effect of this measure if adopted, and you repeal the Missouri Compromise? The South is to gain nothing by it, for honorable gentlemen from the South, and especially the junior Senator from Virginia, characterize it as a miserable, trifling, little measure. Then, sir, is the South to be benefited or propitiated by conferring upon her a miserable, trifling, little measure? Will that compensate the South for her uneasiness? Will it allay the agitation of the North? Will it preserve the union of these States? Will it sustain the Democratic or the Whig party in their organizations? No, sir, they all go to the wall. What is to be the effect on the government? It is to be most fatal and ruinous to the future harmony and well-being of the country. I think that the measure itself would be useless. If you establish non-intervention you make nothing by that. But what will be the consequences in the minds of the people? They have a veneration for that compromise. They have a respect and reverence for it, from its antiquity and the associations connected with it, and repeated references to it that seemed to suggest that it marked the boundaries of free and slave territory. They have no respect for it as a compact, — I do not care what you call it, — but as a line defining certain rights and privileges to different sections of the Union. The abstractions which you indulge in here can never satisfy the people that there is not something in it. Abrogate or disannul it, and you exasperate the public mind. It is not necessary that reason should accompany excitement. Feeling is enough to agitate without much reason, and that will be the great prompter on this occasion. My word for it, we shall realize scenes of agitation, which are rumbling in the distance now."

As to the charge that he was faithless to the South and in alliance with the Abolitionists he replied in manly words: —

"This is an eminently perilous measure, and do you expect me to remain here silent, or to shrink from the discharge of my duty in admonishing the South of what I consider the results will be? I will do it, in spite of all the intimidations, or threats, or discountenances that may be thrown upon me. Sir, the charges that I am going with the Abolitionists or the Free-Soilers affects not me. The discharge of conscious duty prompts me often to confront the united array of the very section of the country in which I reside, in which my associations are, in which my personal interests have always been, and in which my affections rest. Where every look to the setting sun carries me to the bosom of a family dependent upon me, think you I could be alien to them? Never, — never."

IIis apprehensions of the evils which would follow the passage of the bill were no less than a prophecy for the country and himself: —

"I had fondly hoped, Mr. President, that, having attained to my present period of life, I should pass the residue of my days, be they many or few, in peace and tranquillity; that as I found the country growing up rapidly, and have witnessed its immeasurable expansion and development, when I close my eyes on scenes around me, I would at least have the cherished consolation and hope that I left my children to a peaceful, happy, prosperous, and united community. I had hoped this. Fondly had I cherished the desire and the expectation from 1850 until after the introduction of this bill. My hopes are less sanguine now. My anxieties increase, but my expectation lessens. Sir, if this repeal takes place I will have seen the commencement of the agitation; but the youngest child now born, I am apprehensive, will not live to witness its termination."

In conclusion, he made an appeal for the Indians who were to be dispossessed from the territory, and whom none of the other statesmen, who were struggling for or against the extension of slavery, had thought it worth while to consider. His views on the policy of treating the Indians had more than a temporary bearing. IIe said: —

"Mr. President, I have very little hope that any appeal that I may make on behalf of the Indians will do any good. The honorable Senator from Indiana

says in substance that God Almighty has condemned them, and made them an inferior race; that there is no use in doing anything for them. With great deference to that Senator, for whom I have never cherished anything but kind feelings, I must be permitted to dissent from his opinions. He says they are not civilized, and they are not homogeneous, and cannot be so with the white race. They cannot be civilized! No! Sir, it is idle to tell me that. We have Indians on our western borders whose civilization is not inferior to our own. . . . They have well-organized societies; they have their villages and towns; they have their state houses and their capitols; they have females and men who would grace the drawing-rooms ℴ﹍ ⸱alons of Washington; they have a well-
ℴ﹍   . judiciary, a trial by jury, and the writ of
﹍ϩ corpus. These are the people for whom I demand justice in the organization of these territories. . . . But the honorable Senator from Iowa characterizes the remarks which I made in reference to the Indians as arising from a feeling of 'sickly sentimentality.' Sir, it is a sickly sentimentality that was implanted in me when I was young, and it has grown up with me. The Indian has a sense of justice, truth, and honor that should find a responsive chord in every heart. If the Indians on the frontier are barbarous, or if they are cannibals and eat each other, who are to blame for it? They are robbed of the means of sustenance; and with hundreds and thousands of them starving on the frontier,

hunger may prompt to such acts to prevent their perishing. We shall never become cannibals in connection with the Indians, but we do worse than that. We rob them first of their native dignity and character; we rob them next of what the government appropriates for them. If we do not do it in this hall, men are invested with power and authority who, officiating as agents or traders, rob them of everything which is designed for them. Not less than one hundred millions of dollars, I learn from statistics, since the adoption of this government, have been appropriated by Congress for purposes of justice and benevolence toward the Indians; but I am satisfied that they have never received fifteen millions beneficially. They are too remote from the seat of government to have their real condition understood here; and if the government intends liberality or justice toward them, it is often diverted from the intended object, and consumed by speculators. . . . Now I should like to know if it becomes us to violate a treaty made with the Indians when we please, regardless of justice and honor? We should be careful if it were with a power able to war with us; and it argues a degree of infinite meanness and indescribable degradation on our part to act differently with the Indians, who confide in our honor and justice, and who call the President their Great Father, and confide in him. Mr. President, it is in the power of the Congress of the United States to do some justice to the Indians by giving them a government of their own, and encouraging them in their organization and improvement by inviting their delegates to a place on the floor of the Senate and House of Representatives. If you will not do it, the sin will lie at your door, and Providence in his own way, mysterious and incomprehensible to us though it is, will accomplish all his purposes, and may at some day avenge the wrongs of the Indians upon our nation. As a people we can save them; and the sooner the great work is begun, the sooner will humanity have cause to rejoice in its accomplishment."

The bill was passed, Houston and John Bell, of Tennessee, being the only Senators from Southern States who voted against it. Benton was not in his accustomed seat in the Senate, but from his place in the House of Representatives he inveighed against the measure, and protested against the political madness which precipitated it upon the country.

One of the incidents connected with the controversy in the Senate, which showed Houston's courage and manliness, was in relation to the treatment of the petition of three thousand clergymen of New England, which had been presented against the passage of the Nebraska bill. An attempt was made to reject the petition, on the ground that it was insulting to the Senate in pronouncing its action "immoral" and in invoking the vengeance of the Almighty upon the advocates of the bill. Senator Douglas made a violent attack upon it, declaring it an "atrocious falsehood," an "atrocious calumny," and that its signers had "desecrated the pulpit and prostituted the sacred desk." Senators Mason, Butler, Badger, and others denounced it in very severe terms. Edward Everett, who had presented the petition, made a feeble and apologetic defense, which avoided the point at issue in the character of the memorial. While Douglas was speaking, Houston cried out to Sumner, the other Massachusetts Senator, "Sumner, don't speak, don't speak; leave him to me." Sumner replied, "Will you take care of him?" "Yes," said Houston, "if you will leave him to me." His purpose in taking the place of Sumner, he said, was that Douglas should have no opportunity to sustain his charge that the memorial was the work of Abolition confederates. In his remarks he vigorously defended the character of the petitioners and the rights and duty of clergymen to express their opinion on political subjects. He was sharply criticised for making use of the expression of "vice-gerents of God" in regard to them, but he explained it as simply meaning that they were the ministers and aids of the Almighty. As Houston had no sympathy with the Abolition sentiments of the petitioners his course was the more honorable and manly. During the troubles in Kansas which followed the passage of the bill he was silent, and, doubtless, only regarded them as the fulfillment of his prophecies of evil. He was equally silent in regard to the attack upon Sumner in the Senate chamber. He had seen such methods of carrying on political controversy before, and given an example of it in his own person, so that he was hardly in a position to reprimand it severely. But he must have been revolted at the mingled brutality and cowardice of Brooks's attack upon an unarmed and unprepared man within the walls of the Senate chamber.

Houston distinguished himself during his whole senatorial career by his defense of the rights of the Indians. He was indignant at the system of mismanagement, robbery, and oppression which characterized the treatment of them by the government, and in repeated speeches he urged a more humane, intelligent, and practical method of dealing with them. He was almost alone in Congress in defending their rights. The professional philanthropy of the time was almost entirely enlisted in the cause of the negro, and the practical politicians regarded the Indian as a nuisance when he could not be made a prey. A great interest was involved throughout the entire West in getting possession of the Indian lands, and was energetically pushed by its representatives in Congress. Houston's own people were not in sympathy with him, and public opinion was indifferent where it was not hostile. But he spoke out in manly terms on every occasion, and it was to him that the delegations of Indians who visited Washington appealed for advice and assistance. Mr. C. Edwards Lester in his rhetorical pamphlet, "Sam Houston and his Republic," gives a somewhat overstrained, but probably essentially true account of the meeting of a delegation of prairie Indians with Houston in Washington : —

"During the latter part of June, 1846, General Morehead arrived in Washington with forty wild Indians from Texas, belonging to more than a dozen tribes. We saw their meeting with General Houston. One and all ran to him, and clasped him in their brawny arms, and hugged him, like bears, to their naked breasts, and called him 'father.' Beneath the copper skin and thick paint the blood rushed, and their faces changed, and the lips of many a warrior trembled, although the Indian may not weep. These wild men knew him, and revered him as one who was too directly descended from the Great Spirit to be approached with familiarity, and yet they loved him so well they could not help it. These were the men 'he had been,' in the fine language of Acquiquosk, whose words we quote, 'too subtle for on the war-path, too powerful in battle, too magnanimous in victory, too wise in council, and too true in faith.' They had flung away their arms in Texas, and with the Comanche chief, who headed their file, had come to Washington to see their father."

In a speech on the treatment of the Indians, December 31, 1854, Houston said, "I never knew a case when a treaty was made and carried out in good faith which was violated by the Indians," and with one of his vigorous expressions, "I might have hated the Indians if I had a soul no bigger than a shell-bark." In an elaborate speech, January 29, 1855,

against increasing the army he contended that the
military methods were not the best way of dealing
with the Indians, and gave many instances of un-
called-for severity, injustice, and corruption by army
officers. He gave his practical views of how to deal
with the Indians: —

"Withdraw your army. Have five hundred cavalry, if you will, but I would rather have two hundred and fifty Texas rangers (such as I could raise)
than five hundred of the best cavalry now in service.
I would have one thousand infantry so placed as to
guard the United States against Mexico, and five
hundred for scouting purposes. I would have five
trading-houses from the Rio Grande to the Red River
for intercourse with the Indians. I would have a
guard of twenty-five men out of an infantry regiment
at each trading-house, who would be vigilant and
always on the alert. Cultivate intercourse with the
Indians. Show them that you have comforts to exchange for their peltries; bring them around you;
domesticate them; familiarize them with civilization.
Let them see that you are rational beings, and they
will become rational in imitation of you. But take
no whiskey there at all, not even for the officers, for
fear their generosity would let it out. Do this, and
you will have peace with the Indians. Whenever
you convince an Indian that he is dependent on you
for comforts or for what he deems luxuries or ele-
gances of life, you attach him to you. Intercourse
and kindness will win the fiercest animal on earth,

except the hyena, and its spots and nature cannot be
changed. The nature of an Indian can be changed.
He changes under favorable circumstances, and rises
to the dignity of a civilized being. It takes a generation or two to regenerate his race, but it can be
done. I would have fields around the trading-houses.
I would encourage the Indians to cultivate them.
Let them see how much it adds to their comfort; how
it secures to their wives and children abundant sub-
sistence, and then you win the Indian over to civilization; you charm him, and he becomes a civilized
man."

In attending to the confederacy which was said
to have been formed by the tribes of the Sioux nation, he said : —

"Theirs is not a confederacy to assail the whites,
but to protect themselves. I justify them in doing
it. I am sorry there is a necessity for it; but if I
were among them, and they proposed a confederacy
to repel cruelty and butchery, I would join them, and
he would be a dastard who would not !"

These were words in a different and nobler strain
than those which the Senate was accustomed to hear
about the incurable barbarism of the Indians, and the
"sickly sentimentality " of doing anything with them,
except rob them of their lands and butcher them if
they resisted.

In 1856, there was a movement for the nomination
of Houston to the Presidency. The General Committee of the Democracy of New Hampshire issued

an address, urging his nomination as "The People's Candidate," on the ground, mainly, of his opposition to the Nebraska bill and the repeal of the Missouri Compromise. A campaign biography, in the usual style of extravagant eulogy, was published, and Houston made a sort of electioneering tour in some of the principal cities in the North, delivering addresses on the political condition of the country and on the Indian question. This was the period of the brief existence of the Know-Nothing party. Whether Houston ever definitely joined it is not known, but he was in sympathy with its opposition to the easy naturalization of foreigners, and was possibly ready to become its candidate for the Presidency if it exhibited itself in any degree of national strength. He had voted in the Senate for an allotment of lands to the Hungarian refugees, but he was not carried away with the popular admiration for Kossuth. When Kossuth was received by the Senate the following account of his meeting with Houston was given in the newspaper report : —

"Among the incidents of the reception it may be mentioned that when the martial figure of General Houston approached Kossuth there appeared to be a special attraction in the person of the hero of San Jacinto. Mr. Houston said, 'Sir, you are welcome to the Senate of the United States.' Kossuth feelingly replied, 'I can only wish I had been as successful as you, sir.' To which Houston responded, 'God grant you may be, sir.' "

Later, he expressed his opinion of Kossuth in very unflattering terms, accused him of cowardice in retreating from Hungary without striking a blow, and of living in splendor and luxury while his people were "left to bite the dust, or gnaw the file in agony." The very different treatment which he and the people of Texas had received, in comparison with the wild enthusiasm over Kossuth and Hungary, evidently rankled in his thoughts.

He was promptly accused of his affiliation with the Know-Nothings, and of his presidential aspirations, and gave a rather equivocal denial of them both in the course of a running debate in the Senate. As to the Know-Nothings, he said, "I know nothing," but he concurred in many of the principles attributed to them. He would require "every person coming from abroad, before being received here, to bring an indorsement from one of our consuls, and produce evidence of good character from the place whence he emigrates, so that when he comes here we may receive him into full communion, with all the rights guaranteed to him by the laws which may exist at the time of his immigration." He declared that he would not vote for any bill to prohibit Roman Catholics from holding office. In regard to the Presidency, he said, "When the Senator from Iowa supposes that I would cater for the Presidency of the United States he does me great injustice. I would not cater for any office under heaven. But, sir, I know one thing; if it were to be forced upon me I would make a great many changes in some small matters." At the convention of the "American" party in Baltimore, February 22, 1856, which nominated Millard Fillmore for the Presidency, Houston received three votes. Whatever relations he may have had with the Know-Nothing party he afterward abandoned, and denounced it. In a speech at Nacogdoches he declared the party dead, and buried face downward beyond the hope of resurrection.

Houston was undoubtedly aware that his opposition to the extreme Southern element was fatal to his political ambition. As in the case of Benton, he was more bitterly hated and violently attacked on the ground that he was a traitor to Southern interests than if he had been a Northern antagonist of slavery. Henry A. Wise and others made themselves conspicuous by diatribes against him in public meetings in Southern cities, and, although Houston made no public reply in the Senate or elsewhere, it is not likely that he repressed his tongue in private comment on his adversaries, or that they were not made aware of his opinion of them. In the Democratic Convention of 1856, a "Northern man with Southern principles" was nominated, and the Southern conspirators secured four years more in which to make their preparations for disunion. In the mean time, the extreme element had been gaining political power in Texas. The feeling of the danger to slave property and of antagonism to the North had been sedulously cultivated, and the wealthier planters, who had grown up among the original settlers, acquired the political control. They were joined by the old enemies and rivals of Houston, and violent attacks were made not only upon his so-called apostasy to the South, but his past career in Texas. It is probable that Houston realized that his course would cost him his seat in the Senate, and there are some indications that he was willing that it should be so. At least, he made no such determined attempt to retain his place as Benton had done in Missouri. With his strong hold upon the people of Texas, and his wonderful power in a personal campaign of stump-speaking, he might have defeated the combination against him, and rallied the people to his support, as he did later, in 1859, when he swept the State against a still more formidable opposition. But he made no special effort to be reelected, and left the canvass to his opponents. It is possible that Houston did not feel entirely at home in the Senate, where he could not be the undisputed leader, as he could be in a popular assembly, and really had a longing for the ease and tranquillity of private life, such as sometimes comes over the strongest men of action after a life of stress and excitement. At any rate, he was defeated for reelection to the Senate in the Legislature of 1857, and Lewis T. Wigfall, a rampant fire-eater, was chosen in his place. His colleague, Senator Rusk, with whom he had been on the most affectionate and friendly terms, committed suicide by shooting himself at Nacogdoches, July 5, 1857, from grief at the death of his wife. Houston was nominated as an independent candidate for governor, but manifested little interest in the campaign, and was defeated by the regular Democratic candidate, Hardin R. Runnels. The vote stood 32,552 for Runnels, and 23,628 for Houston. It was the only time in which Houston was ever defeated in an election by the people of Texas.

After his defeat Houston continued the performance of his duties in the Senate without sign of discomfiture. On April 20, 1858, he offered a resolution for the appointment of a committee of seven to inquire into the expediency of the assumption by the United States of a protectorate over Mexico, and supported it in an elaborate speech. He described the hopeless condition of Mexico, and urged the measure as a legitimate extension of the Monroe Doctrine. It was an impracticable scheme, which would have eventually compelled the United States to take possession of the country, but it is probable that Houston hoped that it would arouse a spirit of national pride throughout the United States, which would divert attention from the sectional quarrels. He said, speaking of the era of the promulgation of the Monroe Doctrine: —

"At that glorious epoch there was a broad, towering spirit of nationality extant. The States stood in the endearing relation to each other of one for all and all for one. The Constitution was their political textbook, the glory of the Republic their resolute aim. Practically, there was but one party, and that party animated by but one object, — one upward and onward career. As if in atonement for the wrong inflicted upon the country by the angry Missouri Compromise, which was then fresh in every mind, there seemed to be no circumscription which everywhere within our embraces displayed itself. May we not trust, Mr. President, that a similar result will ensue from this still more angry Kansas controversy, and that the benign influence of such results will be as durable as creation?"

The country, however, was too much excited for any such panacea, and its results would only have been mischievous even if it had been adopted.

On January 12, 1859, Houston advocated the southern route for the Pacific Railroad through Texas and asked for the preliminary surveys. In the course of his speech he alluded to the peace and harmony which would exist between the North and South, and he was accused by Senator Iverson, of Georgia, with being a candidate for the Presidency, and with catering for Northern votes. He replied: —

"If every political party of this Union were to tender to me this day the nomination for the Presidency I would respectfully decline it. I have higher, nobler, tenderer duties to perform. I have to create a resting-place for those who are dear to me as the people of this Union, and who form part of them. These are the duties I have to perform. If there is aught of public service that remains to me unfinished I am not apprised of it. My life has been meted out to sixty-five years; and forty-five years of that life devoted to my country's service, almost continuously, should entitle me to an honorable discharge. I claim that discharge from my country. I claim that, having performed every duty which devolved upon me with fidelity, I ought to be permitted to retire from this chamber in accordance with my heart-felt desires, with a constitution, thank God, not much impaired, and with clean hands and a clean conscience, to the retirement where duties are demanded of me as a father. So the defeat which has been spoken of was no disappointment, and by way of explanation that the gentleman may be more perfectly satisfied, I will say that had my lamented and honorable colleague, General Rusk, remained with us, by the providence of God, on the 4th of March last I should have vacated my seat, and retired to the walks of private life."

In conclusion, with that personal self-appreciation which was seldom wanting from his speeches, he accused Senator Iverson of playing the part of the ass in kicking the face of the dead lion. On February 23, 1859, he presented the resolutions of the Texas legislature, impeaching John C. Watrous, United States district judge, and supported them in a long and somewhat vindictive account of the charges against him. On February 26, he delivered his last speech to the Senate. It was a circumstantial review and defense of his conduct as commander-in-chief during the war of independence in Texas, and a retort upon the personal character and conduct of some

of his accusers. In bidding farewell.to the Senators
he said that he had felt it his duty to cultivate
kindly personal relations with every one of them.
His last words were the expression of a prayer that
"the perpetuity of the Union might be secured to the
latest posterity."

It was true that Houston had not carried into the
Senate his habit of personal quarrel on political questions, which he had too often manifested, or readily
responded to, in the turbulent and passionate rivalries
and controversies of Texas. He had grown calmer
since the days when he had struck down Stanberry
in the streets of Washington, and the sober and decorous atmosphere of the Senate doubtless exercised
a restraining influence upon him. There is no instance in which he did not thoroughly maintain the
proprieties of debate, and his tone toward his fellow-
Senators was that of the dignified and impressive
politeness which no one knew better how to exhibit.
He was a solitary as well as a peculiar figure in the
Senate, having no share in the counsels of his party,
and alienated by his political course from the representatives of his own section. He had not the
education, the training, or the capacity for the argu-
mentative debates on questions of law and technical
legislation, which were necessary to command a leading place in the Senate, and, although his shrewd and
practical common sense was often exhibited in matters of detail, it was only from his position and his
fervid utterances against disunion that he attracted

national attention, and manifested his wisdom as well
as his courage. His reverence for the example of
Jackson doubtless gave his mind its original bias,
but he perceived with a clear vision the folly of the
South in precipitating the conflict, in which it was
sure to be overwhelmed, and his love for the Union
was enlightened wisdom as well as patriotic passion.
On the question of slavery he said, "I am not the
enemy of slavery; neither am I its propagandist, nor
will I ever be." He was a slave-holder, and accepted
the institution as a part of the social system in which
he found himself. But his conscience revolted
against its iniquitous principle, and his practical sagacity doubted its continuance. His strength and
friendship lay with the industrious yeomanry, who
cultivated their own lands, and he had no sympathy
or affiliation with the oligarchy of rich planters, who
were leading the South to ruin. In the Senate, he
was the last representative of the hardy frontiersmen
who had built their cabins in the primeval forest, or
turned the soil of the virgin prairie, and he saw with
regret the growth of that class at the South who
were monopolizing the land for great plantations, and
were creating an aristocracy of wealth, based on slave
labor. To him and to Thomas H. Benton is due the
credit of representing the true welfare of the South,
and with courage and wisdom resisting the tendencies
which were leading it to destruction, and to the social
and industrial decadence which would have followed,
even if there had been no civil war.

Mr. Oliver Dyer, in his book of reminiscences of Washington, "Great Senators of the United States," gives an interesting account of Houston's appearance and manners in the Senate in 1848: —

"It was not without apprehension that I first approached General Houston, and looked him over, as he stood in an ante-room of the Senate chamber, talking with his colleague, Senator Rusk. I was not disappointed in his appearance. It was easy to believe in his heroism, and to imagine him leading a heady fight and dealing destruction on his foes. He was then only fifty-five years old, and seemed to be in perfect health and admirable physical condition. He was a magnificent barbarian, somewhat tempered with civilization. He was large of frame, of stately carriage and dignified demeanor, and had a lion-like countenance, capable of expressing the fiercest passions. His dress was peculiar, but it was becoming to his style. The conspicuous features of it were a military cap and a short military cloak of fine blue broadcloth with a blood-red lining. Afterward I occasionally met him, when he wore a vast and picturesque sombrero and a Mexican blanket, — a sort of ornamented bed-quilt, with a slit in the middle, through which the wearer's head is thrust, leaving the blanket to hang in graceful folds around the body.

"Like other men of his class General Houston was a hearty drinker, but he seldom showed the effect of his potations. It seemed to me as though his wild life had unfitted him for civilization. He was not

a man to shine in a deliberative assembly. It was
only at rare intervals that he took any part in the
debates, and when he did speak his remarks were
brief. His principal employment in the Senate was
whittling pine sticks. I used to wonder where he
got his pine lumber, but never fathomed the mystery.
He would sit and whittle away, and at the same time
keep up a muttering of discontent at the long-winded
speakers, whom he would sometimes curse for their
intolerable verbosity. Those who knew him well
said that he was tender-hearted, and had a chivalric
regard for women; that he would make any personal
sacrifice to promote the welfare of a lady friend, — a
reputation that was directly in line with his alleged
conduct toward his wife. It was a matter of common jocose remark that if 'Old Sam Jacinto' (that
was Houston's nickname) should ever become President, he would have a cabinet of women.

"General Houston impressed me as a lonely, melancholy man. And if the story of his early life was
true he might well be lonely and melancholy, in spite
of his success and his fame; for that blow which
smote him to the heart at the zenith of his splendid
young career, and dislocated his life and drove him
into the wilderness, must have inflicted wounds that
no political triumphs or military glory could heal."

Somewhat singularly, considering their marked contrast in education and temperament, Houston appears
to have attracted the regard and approval of Charles
Sumner. In a letter to John Bigelow, February 8,

1851, Sumner wrote: "I am won very much by Houston's conversation. With him the anti-slavery interests would stand better than with any man who now seems among the possibilities. He is really against slavery, and has no prejudices against Free-Soilers. In other respects he is candid, liberal, and honorable. I have been astonished to find myself so much of his inclining."

During his early residence as a Senator in Washington, Houston "experienced religion," as it is termed. In an account of his conversion given by Rev. G. W. Simpson, his pastor in Washington, it is stated that "one Sunday, the tall form of Sam Houston, as he was familiarly called, draped in his Mexican blanket as a shield against the blasts of winter, was seen entering the sanctuary of the Baptist Church near the City Hall. Approaching the pastor after the service he said that respect for his wife, one of the best Christians on earth, had brought him there. He attended regularly thereafter, and kept up his habit of whittling toys for children in his pew. He paid close attention to the sermons, and was in the habit of giving abstracts of them in the weekly letters which he regularly wrote to his wife on Sunday afternoons. After a few months a sermon on the text, "Better is he that ruleth his spirit than he that taketh a city," moved him to a sense of his spiritual needs, and his thoughts and reading became more and more of a religious character. He was much influenced by a book by one Nelson on "The

Cause and Cure of Infidelity," and gave copies of it to his friends. Finally, he made an open profession of religion, and received the ordinance of baptism by immersion at Independence, Texas, in 1854. His reading of the Bible was continuous and earnest, and its phraseology and imagery found frequent places in his speeches. His pastor relates an anecdote in somewhat exaggerated phraseology of his reconciliation with a personal enemy under the influence of an appeal to his religious sentiment: —

"Calling early after his arrival to see him, an hour was spent in conversation on his profession and the grounds which had led to it. On rising to leave, the pastor was followed as usual to the door, and, as often happened, the General asked: 'Brother S., is there anything I can do for you?' — his reference being to claims of humanity sometimes presented to him. The reply was, 'No, General, I have no tax upon you at present.' Immediately, however, the recollection was awakened that the next Sabbath was the season for the Lord's Supper, and that with one of the leading brethren of the church General Houston had formerly a trying and yet unsettled controversy in his official capacity as the head of a Senate committee. At once, prompted by the recollection, the pastor added, still holding his hand, 'General, I recall that statement in part; I have nothing to ask of you as a man, but I have something to ask of you as a Christian pastor.' Fixing his keen eye, as he looked down, upon mine, he meekly but firmly asked,

'What is it, Brother S.?' 'General,' was the reply, 'you know the alienation between you and
Brother W. You will meet at the Lord's Supper
next Sabbath evening; you ought not to meet until
that difficulty is settled. Now I wish you after service on Sunday morning to let me bring you two together, and without a word of attempt at justification
on either side, I wish you to take him by the hand,
and say with all your heart that you will forgive and
forget and bury the past, and that you wish him to
do the same, and hereafter to meet as brothers
in Christ.' The fire began to glow in his eyes, his
brow to knit, his teeth to clench, and his whole frame
shook with the struggle of the old man within him;
but in an instant the man whose passion had been
terrible, indeed ungovernable, on so many a bloody
battle-field, was changed from the lion into the lamb.
He meekly replied, 'Brother S., I will do it.' And
what he promised was done, and in an air of majestic
frankness and nobleness of soul such as moved every
beholder."

At the conclusion of his term in the Senate, Houston returned to his home in Texas, possibly with the
hope that his later years might be spent in peace and
freedom from public care.

CHAPTER XV

WHATEVER hopes Houston may have had of being able to pass his declining years in peace and tranquillity, he found the political condition of Texas more excited and disturbed than at any period since the revolution, and that it was necessary for him to gird up his loins for a tremendous struggle against the conspirators, who were endeavoring to array the State against the Union. The secession element in Texas was more desperate and determined than in any of the Southern States, except South Carolina. It was also more discreditable and criminal. In South Carolina the movement was more general, and in a certain sense more patriotic. It was founded on a definite theory of government, logically held and argued, and it represented the spirit of State pride and independence. In Texas, on the other hand, it was more selfish, and took the darker form of conspiracy. Its leaders were the adventurers who were in sympathy with Walker in his attempts to subjugate Central America, and with Lopez in his descent upon the island of Cuba, and were eager for any scheme that promised them power and plunder. Their avowed purpose was the reopening of the African slave trade, and their unacknowledged, and perhaps unformulated, plans were for the formation of a buccaneer empire, with unlimited designs for aggression and plunder upon their Spanish-American neighbors. They were represented by a secret society, called "The Knights of the Golden Circle," which had a regular military organization, was well supplied with arms, and had a considerable fund of money. The organization was originally formed to set on foot or support filibuster expeditions like those of Walker and Lopez, but the growing antagonism between the North and South offered them a more tempting field in the shape of a Southern empire, which they hoped to control for their purposes. Their lodges, called "castles," were established in all the principal towns, and it was estimated that at the outbreak of the secession difficulty they had a force of 8000 men, formed in regular military organization and to some extent disciplined. They were active in politics, and by their power and energy controlled the official action of the Democratic party. Governor Runnels was in sympathy with this element, as was also the majority of the legislature during his administration. During the excitement of the struggle to force the admission of slavery into Kansas, Governor Runnels issued a special message to the legislature, calling attention to the threatened aggressions upon Southern rights, and distinctly foreshadowing secession. The legislature adopted a resolution denouncing the attempts of the Northern States to exclude slavery from Kansas, and to prevent the slave-holders from carrying their property into the common territory of the Union. It authorized the governor to order an election of seven delegates to a convention of the Southern States, and, in case such a convention was not held, to call a special session of the legislature to consider the question of Texas resuming her independence.

These open attacks upon the permanency of the Union aroused and alarmed the majority of the citizens, who were opposed to secession and the filibuster designs of the conspirators. In the Democratic Convention of 1859, which renominated Runnels, a platform was adopted advocating secession in the contingency of the further invasion of Southern rights, and there was an outspoken expression of opinion in favor of reopening the slave trade. The party in favor of reopening the slave trade did not confine themselves to declarations. Two cargoes of barbarian slaves from Africa were landed in chains, one near Galveston and one near Indianola, and distributed through the country. These events caused great excitement and indignation among the conservative and Unionist classes, and they determined upon political action in opposition to the secession Democracy. Houston was the natural leader from his personal popularity among the people and his vigorous denunciations of disunion. There was no definite organization of the party, but at a public meeting at Brenham, Houston was nominated for governor by acclamation. He accepted in a letter which declared that "the Constitution and the Union embraced all the principles by which he would be governed."

The campaign that followed was one of the most notable and exciting which had ever taken place in Texas. It demonstrated Houston's tremendous hold upon the common people and his extraordinary power as a stump-speaker. All the party machinery, most of the prominent public men, and the influential newspapers were against him. Almost single-handed he defeated them all. He made a thorough canvass of the State, speaking in nearly every town and village. He aroused the enthusiasm of the people by his eloquent appeals for the preservation of the Union, replied to the vindictive personal attacks made upon him by his opponents with a vituperation more scathing than their own, tickled his audiences by his familiar and sometimes coarse humor, and strengthened the attachment of his personal followers by his cordial greetings and intimate conversation. There was no one like Houston for a Texas audience. In joint debates he simply overwhelmed his competitors, and treated them with a contempt partly real and partly affected, as if it was insolence on their part to attempt to speak on the same platform with him. One after another they retired discomfited, and in his closing speech at Galveston he reckoned them up with contemptuous personal epithets. This is a specimen of the manner in which he dealt with them, and manifested his confidence in his hold upon the people. Senator Wigfall had been replying to him in Eastern Texas. At a meeting in the court-house of one of the towns, at which Wigfall was present, Houston concluded his speech by saying: "I am told that there is a little fellow by the name of Wigtail, or some such name, following me about and trying to answer my speeches. What he will tell you will be a pack of lies." So saying he stalked out, followed by a portion of the audience, leaving Wigfall to make his speech to the remainder. Houston, as was his custom, seated himself upon a store-box on the sidewalk among his friends, and commenced whittling and talking familiarly about their families, the crops, and the neighborhood gossip. But all the while he kept his eye on the court-house door. When the audience began to come out after the conclusion of Wigfall's speech, he rose up to his full height, and, waving his big white hat, shouted, "Didn't I say to you that he'd tell you a pack of lies?" His familiar and caustic humor was equally taking, and the anecdotes of his sayings were relished at every cross-roads grocery and by every cabin fire. At the town of Milam a young lawyer, the son of an old friend of Houston, had established his office. Houston visited him, and talked with him in his usual cordial and impressive manner about his family and prospects. Later, while seated among a group of his friends in front of a store, he was informed that the young lawyer was the only man in the town who was going to vote against him. Presently the young man passed the group. Houston asked in a tone loud enough for him to hear, "Who is that long, gangling scarecrow, who is going by?" This was considered a touch of humor, worthy of "Old Sam," and became the current joke of the neighborhood. Houston's triumph was in chief measure that of his personal influence. His course in opposing the Kansas-Nebraska bill had been generally disapproved, and he had been defeated in the previous campaign in which he had not made an active personal canvass. He rallied and invigorated the Union sentiment, and converted a minority into a majority. The actions of the extreme element had undoubtedly alarmed the conservative portion of the community, but it is extremely improbable that the Union sentiment would have preponderated if Houston had not given it force and energy. As it was, the majority of the legislature was in the hands of the disunionists, and his associates in the Executive, except one, were swept away by the tide, when it arose. A considerable portion of his vote was due simply to the fact that he was "Sam Houston," and had a strong personal party, which would have followed and supported him under any circumstances. He received 36,257 votes, to 27,500 for Runnels.

Houston was inaugurated as Governor December 21, 1859. He sent his message to the legislature January 15. Mexican banditti, under the command of Juan de Cortinas, had been preying upon the people on the border of the Rio Grande, and the Indians had been especially troublesome and dangerous on the frontier. Houston promptly applied to the government of the United States for additional troops, and organized three companies of rangers to patrol the frontier. He asked the legislature for an appropriation to pay them. He recommended various changes in the departments, and strongly urged liberal appropriations for the public schools. In regard to the relations of Texas with the United States, he congratulated the legislature on the triumph of conservatism in the nation, and the evident purpose to repress the dangerous agitators on both sides. He said, "Texas will maintain the Constitution and stand by the Union. It is all that can save us as a nation. Destroy it and anarchy awaits us."

The excitement over the coming presidential election was rising to fever heat. Houston took no active part in the campaign. He was opposed to the election of Lincoln as the representative of Northern aggression against slavery. He was equally opposed to the election of Breckenridge and of Douglas, as he had vowed never to vote for any man who had supported the Kansas-Nebraska bill. He saw no chance for the election of Bell, and, besides, did not regard him as a competent man for the Presidency. In a private letter from Austin, dated September 8, 1860, he declared that he stood with folded arms in regard to the candidates, and he could see no way out of the difficulty except by the election of members of the Electoral College who would be pledged to

vote for a Union man, regardless of the official candidates. This was obviously a hopeless and impossible scheme. On the 22d of September there was a
grand Union mass meeting at Austin. Houston addressed it in an eloquent and forcible speech, rising
from a sick-bed to do so. He spoke of the glories
of the common country and its great destiny, and
pointed out the weakness of any State which abandoned the Union. He declared that the possible triumph of the Republican party would not be a sufficient cause for the dissolution of the Union: —

"But if, through division in the ranks of those opposed to Mr. Lincoln, he should be elected, we have
no excuse for dissolving the Union. The Union is
worth more than Mr. Lincoln, and, if the battle is to
be fought for the Constitution, let us fight it in the
Union and for the sake of the Union. With a majority of the people in favor of the Constitution, shall
we desert the government, and leave it in the hands
of the minority? A new obligation will be imposed
upon us, to guard the Constitution and to see that
no infraction of it is attempted or permitted. If Mr.
Lincoln administers the government in accordance
with the Constitution, our rights must be respected.
If he does not, the Constitution provides a remedy."

He denounced the disunion agitators of the South
as merely reckless and mischievous conspirators, who
owned no property and had no interest in slavery.
"I know some of them, who are making the most
fuss, who would not make good negroes if they were

blacked." He paid an affecting tribute to the memo-
ries of Henry Clay and Andrew Jackson, and appealed to the old Whigs and old Democrats to follow
the example of their great leaders in devotion to the
Union. He concluded with words of powerful and
pathetic eloquence: —

"When I look back and remember the names that
are canonized as the tutelar saints of liberty, and the
warnings they have given you against disunion, I
cannot believe that you will be led astray. I cannot
be long among you. My sands of life are fast running out. As the glass becomes exhausted, if I can
feel that I can leave my country prosperous and
united, I shall die content. To leave men with whom
I have mingled in troublous times, and whom I have
learned to love as brothers; to leave the children of
those whom I have seen pass away, after lives of devotion to the Union; to leave the people who have
borne me up and sustained me; to leave my country, and not feel the liberty and happiness I have
enjoyed would still be theirs, would be the worst pang
of death. I am to leave children among you, to
share the fate of your children. Think you I feel
no interest in the future for their sakes? We are
passing away. They must encounter the evils which
are to come. In the far distant future the genera-
tions that spring from our loins are to venture in the
path of glory and honor. If untrammeled, who can
tell the mighty progress they will make? If cut
adrift, if the calamitous curse of disunion is inflicted

upon them, who can picture their misfortune and shame?"

Houston believed in the prevalence of the Union sentiment among the people of the South, and endeavored to give it an opportunity for expressing itself. He addressed letters to the Governors of the Southern States, proposing a convention, and issued a proclamation for an election to be held early in February for the choice of the seven delegates under the resolution of the previous legislature for that purpose. But events anticipated the election, and it was never held. The Governors of the Southern States, who were all disunionists, paid no attention to Houston's letters. He was denounced everywhere as a traitor to the South. Senator Wigfall said in Virginia that he ought to be tarred and feathered and driven from the State. Senator Iverson, of Georgia, his old antagonist in the Senate, went so far as to hint at his assassination. He said, "Some Texan Brutus may arise to rid his country of this old, hoary-headed traitor."

Lincoln was elected. South Carolina seceded, and applied to the other Southern States to unite and form a confederacy. The demand for action on the invitation was so strong that Houston called a special session of the legislature to meet January 21. Already illegal steps had been taken to force the State out of the Union. A proclamation had been issued from Austin, signed by about sixty citizens, clerks in the departments and others, calling for a general election to be held on January 8, for a convention of delegates from the people to meet on January 28. The election was held, but only a comparatively few of the people recognized its validity, the total number of votes cast being less than 10,000. It was to forestall the action of this illegal body that Houston called the legislature together and recommended a properly called and constituted convention. In his message he declared that he believed that the time had come for the people of Texas to take action in accordance with their sovereign will. While deploring the election of Messrs. Lincoln and Hamlin, he could see no reason in it for the immediate and separate secession of Texas. He deprecated any hasty action, and thought that means should be taken for the people to express their will by legal means. "They have stood aloof from revolutionary measures, and now demand an opportunity to express their will through the ballot box." He had not lost faith that their rights could be maintained in the Union, and that it might yet be perpetuated. Between constitutional remedies and anarchy and civil war, he could see no middle course. In his message, January 24, transmitting the resolutions of the legislature of South Carolina, Houston declared his "unqualified protest against and dissent from the principles enunciated in the resolutions." He argued against the right of secession on constitutional grounds, and showed the total lack of any guarantee of permanency in new confederacy. He concluded: —

the dangerous wild tribes of Indians, had called a large portion of the army to be stationed there. It was scattered in various posts along the Rio Grande and on the northern frontier for more than a thousand miles, and numbered about 2500 men. There was an immense amount of arms and military stores collected at the headquarters of the Department at San Antonio. General Twiggs, the commander of the Department, was an old and somewhat distinguished officer of the army. He was in feeble health, and had long been on leave of absence at his residence in Louisiana. He sympathized thoroughly with the secession movement, and was undoubtedly in communication with its leaders. He returned unexpectedly to resume the command on the 5th of December, 1860, superseding Colonel Robert E. Lee, who perhaps could not be relied on to do the necessary work. He immediately began issuing leaves of absence to the officers, and still farther scattering the troops. He expressed himself as convinced that the Union was already dissolved, and declared that he would never order his soldiers to fire on American citizens. He intimated that when a demand was made on him by the State, he would surrender the property of the government. Houston was informed of these assertions on the part of Twiggs, and for the purpose of testing him, or of obtaining the control of the arms in his own hands to thwart the designs of the sec sionists, he sent on January 20, the day ore meeting of the legislature, a special 1 Twiggs with the following letter: —

My dear General, — The present pressure of important events necessarily induces prompt action on the part of all public functionaries. In this view of the matter, I send to you General J. M. Smith of this State on a confidential mission, to know what in the present crisis you consider your duty to do, as to maintaining in behalf of the Federal Government or passing over to the State the possession of the posts, arsenals, and public property within the State; and also, if a demand for the possession of the same is made by the Executive, you are authorized, or it would be conformable to your sense of duty, to place in possession of the authorities of the State the posts, arms, munitions, and property of the Federal Government, on the order of the Executive, to an officer of the State, empowered to receive and receipt for the same.

The course is suggested by the fact that information has reached the Executive that an effort will be made by an unauthorized mob to take forcibly and appropriate the public stores and property to uses of their own, assuming to act on behalf of the State.

Any arrangements made with you by General Smith will be sanctioned and approved by me, and should you require any assistance in resisting the contemplated and unauthorized attack upon the public property, and to place the same in possession of the state authorities, you are authorized to call on the mayor and citizens of San Antonio for such assistance as you may deem necessary.

I will hope to hear from you, General, by my confidential agent, General Smith, as soon as he can have the honor of a conference with you on matters embraced in the present epoch of our national affairs.

I am, General, yours very truly,
SAM HOUSTON.

But Twiggs had no intention of putting the arms into the hands of any such Union man as Houston. He replied curtly that he was without instructions from the government, and that "after secession, in case the Executive of the State makes a demand upon the commander of the Department, he will receive an answer."

Whether Houston believed that by obtaining possession of the arms he could overawe the disunionists and prevent the secession of the State, or whether he merely wished to obtain a definite knowledge of the purposes of Twiggs, is unknown. His whole course showed that he preferred to submit to secession rather than to involve the State in civil war, although, perhaps, if he had been supported by the Federal Government before the movement became so strong he might have resisted it. An account given by Rev. William M. Baker would indicate that he had such a purpose. A Texan merchant, and intimate friend of Houston's, stated that Houston informed him that President Lincoln, although not yet inaugurated, had sent Colonel F. W. Lander to him with a message that he should have all the help he wanted, as soon as Lincoln took office, if he could only hold the State until then. Said Houston, "General Twiggs has agreed to do what he can to help me. I have 800 men waiting to come at a word. Volunteers will come in. I am sure that I can, with the aid of General Twiggs, hold Texas against any force the Confederacy may send." He then made a contract with the merchant for a supply of rations. The following is the account of the interview with Houston after he had received General Twiggs's reply to his message: —

"The instant the Governor had locked me with him in his inner office, he turned to me with rage in his face. 'Sir,' said he to me, in a manner and tone which I can never forget, 'Twiggs is a traitor!' Then he sank down into his chair, the tears trickling down his heroic countenance, and sobbed like a child. He then clenched his fist and smote the table, with what seemed to be a suppressed curse, long and deep. After he had somewhat recovered he repeated to me the message that Captain Smith had brought him from Twiggs. It was in such cautious language as to the General's isolation and want of instructions from Washington that I suggested to Governor Houston that possibly he misunderstood General Twiggs. 'No,' the Governor exclaimed, again smiting the table with his huge fist, 'there can be no mistake. Twiggs is a traitor! We are to have a fearful civil war.' And he appealed to God for wisdom and protection in a manner which touched me to the heart."

There was unquestionably a force in Texas which Houston could have called on, ardent supporters of himself as well as advocates of the Union, and he might perhaps, with the aid of the United States troops, have defeated the secession element. But it would have plunged the State into a civil war, and the action of Twiggs prevented the show of any commanding strength at first to turn the scale in favor of the Unionists.

The commissioners appointed by the Committee of Public Safety acted promptly. On February 11 they made a demand upon General Twiggs for the surrender of all the arms, munitions of war, and public property belonging to the United States in the Department of Texas. There were some negotiations between the commissioners and the board of officers appointed by General Twiggs in regard to terms. Twiggs insisted upon the retention of the arms then in the hands of the soldiers, and of some pieces of light artillery. Colonel Benjamin M'Cullogh had been appointed by the Committee of Public Safety to raise and take command of troops in behalf of the State, and appeared in San Antonio with a force of about 1200 men. The terms of the surrender were agreed upon. The troops were to have transportation to the coast, and to be permitted to return to the United States. The debts due from the quartermaster's department were to be paid out of the funds

delivered to the commissioners. The soldiers were
to retain their arms. The surrender was executed on
February 18, before the people had voted on the
ordinance of secession, and after an order had arrived
from Washington, relieving General Twiggs from
the command of the Department and directing him
to turn it over to Colonel Carlos A. Waite, the
senior officer. Colonel Waite was absent from San
Antonio, but arrived a few hours after the surrender
was made. The number of men surrendered was
about 2500, and the value of the property $1,200,-
000. The sum of $50,000 in money was turned over
to the commissioners, and they afterward seized
$30,000 sent to the State to pay the troops. Bodies
of Texan troops were sent to demand the surrender
of the various detachments in the forts and posts
along the Rio Grande and on the frontier, and, after
some indignant remonstrances on the part of the
officers in command, they were given up. Strong
efforts were made to induce the officers and men to
take service with the Confederacy, but only a few of
the officers of Southern birth did so, almost all of
the enlisted men remaining faithful to their flag.
General Twiggs, having accomplished his purpose,
returned to New Orleans, and on March 1 was dismissed from the army for treachery by order of Secretary Holt. Owing to the lack of transportation,
but few of the troops were removed from Texas
before the outbreak of the war between the United
States and the Confederacy, and the remainder were

made prisoners of war, in violation of the agreement with the commissioners, by order of Colonel Van Dorn, and compelled to give their parole not to bear arms against the Confederacy until exchanged.

Whatever purpose Houston may have entertained at the beginning of the troubles, he abandoned any design of forcible resistance to secession after the surrender of the United States troops. On March 18, after the new administration of Lincoln had determined to maintain the Union by force, General Scott sent orders to Colonel Waite to form an intrenched camp at Indianola, and put himself in communication with Governor Houston, to offer him assistance in defense of the Federal authority. If neither Houston nor any other authority had any considerable number of men in arms in defense of the Federal Government, Colonel Waite was to consider his orders to form an intrenched camp withdrawn. Colonel Waite communicated with Houston, offering his assistance, and received the following reply: —

AUSTIN, *March* 29, 1861.

DEAR SIR, — I have received intelligence that you have, or will soon receive orders to concentrate United States troops under your command at Indianola, in this State, to sustain me in the exercise of my official functions. Allow me most respectfully to decline any such assistance of the United States government, and to most earnestly protest against the concentration of troops in fortifications in Texas, and request that you remove all such troops out of the State at the earliest day practicable, or, at any rate, by all means take no action towards hostile movements till farther ordered by the Government at Washington City, or particularly of Texas.

Thine,   SAM HOUSTON.

Colonel Lander also wrote to Colonel Waite advising him to take no action that would give the secession party the idea that the Federal Government intended to coerce the State. Colonel Waite informed General Scott that it was the feeling of the Unionists that they could effect a peaceable change in the views of the inhabitants of the State by means of the press and the ballot box, and that they believed that a few thousand dollars in the support of newspapers throughout the State would produce a complete revolution in public sentiment. There was evidently at first a considerable Union sentiment among the people of Texas. In San Antonio there was a strong party opposed to secession, and in Austin a large mass meeting was held just before the election on the secession ordinance, at which there was a pole erected and a United States flag displayed.

Houston made a speech at Galveston, which was the hot-bed of secession, a few days before the election. When he arrived his friends gathered about him, and asked him not to speak, as there was imminent danger of mob violence. He replied that he had been threatened before, and should certainly make his speech. It was delivered from the balcony of the Tremont House at eleven o'clock in the forenoon to an excited throng that filled the street. As he had often done before, Houston overawed the crowd, and compelled a respectful attention. Mr. Thomas North, a Northern man who lived in Texas during the war, thus describes Houston's appearance when speaking: —

"There he stood, an old man of seventy years, on the balcony ten feet above the heads of the thousands assembled to hear him, where every eye could scan his magnificent form, six feet and three inches high, straight as an arrow, with deep-set and penetrating eyes, looking out from heavy and thundering eyebrows, a high open forehead, with something of the infinite intellectual shadowed there, crowned with the white locks, partly erect, seeming to give capillary conduction to the electric fluid used by his massive brain, and a voice of the deep basso tone, which shook and commanded the soul of the hearer; adding to all this a powerful manner, made up of deliberation, self-possession, and restrained majesty of action, leaving the hearer impressed with the feeling that more of his power was hidden than revealed. Thus appeared Sam Houston on this grand occasion, equal and superior to it, as he always was to every other. He paralyzed the arm of the mobocrat by his personal presence, and it was morally impossible for him to be mobbed in Texas, and, if not there, then not anywhere."

He spoke with great force and eloquence of the disasters which would surely follow secession, and of the certainty of the defeat of the South. He said:

"Some of you laugh to scorn the idea of bloodshed as the result of secession, and jocularly propose to drink all the blood that will ever flow in consequence of it. But let me tell you what is coming on the heels of secession. The time will come when your fathers and husbands, your sons and brothers, will be herded together like sheep and cattle at the point of the bayonet; and your mothers and wives, and sisters and daughters, will ask, 'Where are they?' and echo will answer, Where? You may, after the sacrifice of countless millions of treasure and hundreds of thousands of precious lives, as a bare possibility, win Southern independence, if God be not against you; but I doubt it. I tell you that, while I believe with you in the doctrine of state rights, the North is determined to preserve this Union. They are not a fiery, impulsive people as you are, for they live in colder climates. But when they begin to move in a given direction, where great interests are involved, such as the present issue before the country, they move with the steady momentum and perseverance of a mighty avalanche; and what I fear is, they will overwhelm the South with ignoble defeat, and I would say Amen to the suffering and defeat I have pictured, if the present difficulties could find no other solution, and that, too, by peaceable means. I believe they can. Otherwise I would say, 'Better die freemen than live slaves.'"

In conclusion he said, however, that he should abide by the action of his State: —

"Whatever course my State shall determine to pursue, my faith in state supremacy and state rights will carry my sympathies with her. And as Henry Clay, my political opponent on annexation, said, when asked why he allowed his son to go into the Mexican war, ' My country, right or wrong,' so I say, My State, right or wrong."

But Houston could not stem the tide. The secessionists were active and violent. Armed bands intimidated the citizens, and mob rule prevailed. In some sections Union men were hung, or compelled to flee for their lives. Houses were burned, and property destroyed. The Union men were still farther discouraged by the news of the surrender of Twiggs, and that the Federal Government made no sign of giving them support. But the prevalence of the Union sentiment was indicated by the fact that at the election out of about 80,000 voters only 52,246 cast their ballots. Of these 34,415 were for secession, and 13,841 against it.

The convention reassembled after the election, and took steps to unite Texas with the Confederacy. It accepted the Confederate Constitution, and elected members of the Confederate Congress. A committee was appointed to inform Houston of its action. He protested against it, declaring that the convention had no farther authority from the people after it had submitted the ordinance of secession for their ratification. In the mean time the Confederate authorities had assumed jurisdiction over Texas. Before the convention had reassembled, L. Pope Walker, the Confederate Secretary of War, sent a circular to Houston announcing that the President of the Confederate States assumed control of all military operations in the State, and over all questions relating to foreign powers. Houston replied that by the act of secession Texas had become independent, and was not yet united with the Confederacy. He denied the authority of the convention to unite Texas with the Confederate States without the sanction of the people. The protest was in mild terms, and at its conclusion he said: —

"The States which have formed the Provisional Government have his ardent wishes for their welfare and prosperity. The people of Texas are now bound to them in feeling and sympathy no less closely than when members of a common Union. Like circumstances induced withdrawal from the Union. Like peril and uncertainty are before them. No matter what the position of Texas may be, she cannot but feel that ties of no common nature bind her to those States. But, however close those ties may be in feeling, there are requirements due the national pride and dignity of a people who have just resumed their nationality which do not sanction the course pursued in annexing them to a new government without their knowledge or consent."

On March 14, the convention adopted an ordinance

requiring the State officers to take the oath of allegiance to the Confederacy. Houston and E. W. Cave, the Secretary of State, declined to obey the order. When the day came to take the oath the presiding officer of the convention called three times, "Sam Houston, Sam Houston, Sam Houston," but the governor remained in his office in the basement of the Capitol, whittling his pine stick, and hearing the echo of the noise and tumult in the hall above his head. Houston and Cave were declared deposed from their offices, and Edward Clark, the lieutenant governor, was installed as governor. Houston protested, and appealed to the legislature, which assembled on the 18th, but it confirmed the action of the convention. Houston issued an address to the people protesting against the illegal acts and usurpations of the convention. But he declared that he should make no attempt to retain his position by force. He said: —

"I love Texas too well to bring civil strife and bloodshed upon her. To avert this calamity I shall make no endeavor to maintain my authority as chief executive of the State, except by the peaceful exercise of my functions. When I can no longer do this I shall calmly withdraw from the scene, leaving the government in the hands of those who have usurped its authority, but still claiming that I am its chief executive. I protest in the name of the people of Texas against all the acts and doings of this convention, and declare them null and void. I solemnly protest against the act of its members, who are bound by no oath themselves, in declaring my office vacant because I refuse to appear before it and take the oath prescribed."

He still continued to go to his office, but on the morning of March 21 he found that Governor Clark had installed himself in the room before him. A hostile newspaper gives this account of their interview: —

"By and by the deposed Governor came hobbling into the office, old Sam's San Jacinto wound having broken out afresh, as it always does on occasions of political trial. Perceiving Governor Clark occupying his chair, old Sam addressed him: —

"'Well, *Governor* Clark,' giving great emphasis to the title, 'you are an early riser.'

"'Yes, *General*,' with a great stress upon the military title of his predecessor, 'I am illustrating the old maxim, the early bird catches the worm.'

"'Well, Governor Clark, I hope you will find it an easier seat than I have found it.'

"'I'll endeavor to make it so, General, by conforming to the clearly expressed wish of the people of Texas.'

"The General, having brought a large lunch basket with him, proceeded to put in numerous little articles of private property, and to stow them away very carefully. Catching his foot in a hole in the carpet, and stumbling, the General suggested to Governor Clark that the new Government ought to afford a new carpet for the Governor's office, whereupon the Governor remarked that the Executive of Texas could get along very well without a carpet.

"Having gathered up his duds, old Sam made a little farewell speech very much in the style of Cardinal Wolsey, declaring his conviction that, as in the past, Texas would call him from his retirement, and he hoped Governor Clark would be able to give as good an account of his stewardship as he could now render. Halting at the door the General made a profound bow, and with an air of elaborate dignity said, 'Good-day, Governor C-l-a-r-k.' 'Good-day, General Houston,' was the Governor's response."

Houston left Austin, and returned to his residence in Huntsville, a small town in Walker County. An enemy wrote, "Houston has sunk out of sight, leaving but a ripple on the surface."

Houston's action in reference to the secession of Texas has been much criticised, and he has been accused of inconsistency and pusillanimity. He certainly did not take the course of Francis P. Blair in Missouri in organizing an armed resistance to secession. He might possibly have done so, if he had been supported by General Twiggs, as Blair was by General Lyon. But it is probable that he would only have hoped to strengthen and give force to the Union sentiment, and overawe the secession element without bloodshed. It is within the bounds of possibility that, if Twiggs had taken a different course, the Union feeling might have prevailed. It is doubtful if the majority of the people of Texas were in favor of secession at the time the vote was taken. But events shaped themselves so that there could not have been a resistance without a bloody civil war within the State. Houston loved his people too much to precipitate this. It is to be remembered, also, that Houston was a Southern man, and, while he ardently loved the Union, and regretted secession as a matter of policy, his feelings were with his section. When the die was cast, his hopes and sympathies were for the success of the South. There is no reason to doubt his sincerity in saying that he yielded up his office rather than subject the people to the horrors of a civil war, and that he was with his State, right or wrong. His courage and firmness were abundantly proved in his resistance to the tumults and violence of secession, and the very serious dangers which accompanied them. The excitement ran tremendously high, and it was by no means impossible that some "Texan Brutus" might have taken Senator Iverson's advice to assassinate him. Events were too strong for Houston. The position of Texas made her naturally a member of the Southern Confederacy. The Union sentiment was rather inert and indefinite, instead of active and passionate like that of the secessionists. It could not have triumphed without a civil war, and it is doubtful if a majority of the Unionists were ready for that, even if Houston had been willing to lead them. The people were mainly Southern, and when the Federal Government proclaimed its purpose

of coercing the seceded States, all but a few, except-
ing the German colonists, threw themselves heart and
soul into the Confederate cause. It is possible that
Houston hoped for a brief time that Texas, having
seceded, would resume her independent sovereignty,
and he was suspected of working for that end. But
he must have soon seen that it was impossible, and
have recognized that the fortunes of Texas were
bound up with those of the rest of the slave-holding
States. He realized the probabilities of the failure
of the Confederacy, but he would not join in over-
throwing the fortunes of his section, and he did not
feel that allegiance to the Union which would compel him to fight against his people. His course was
honorable and consistent from his point of view, and
it was that almost universally taken by the original
Union men of the South. He refused the offer of a
major-general's commission from President Lincoln,
and had no hope or ambition that was not identified
with the welfare of the people of Texas. His eldest
son entered the Confederate service, and he fitted
him out with his arms and equipments. There is a
good-humored jest attributed to him to the effect that
he told his son that the most appropriate place for his
secession rosette would be on the inside of the tail of
his coat, but he subsequently said that if he had more
sons old enough for the service they should go. He
was for the Union, if it could be preserved by peaceful
means, but for the South when the issue was made of
resistance or submission to Federal coercion.

During his administration as governor there was no opportunity for attention to the internal affairs of the State. Everything was swept into the vortex of political strife and excitement. The only measure he could accomplish was the organization of a ranging force for the protection of the frontier, which fell to pieces during the secession excitement, leaving the people defenseless after the United States troops surrendered.

CHAPTER XVI

HOUSTON had not taken the means to secure for himself a life of luxurious ease after his retirement from public life. He had had ample opportunities to acquire wealth by obtaining tracts of rich lands and advantageous holdings in the newly founded towns, by which many of his associates laid the foundations of large fortunes, but he did not take them, nor did he engage in any of the schemes for the profitable development of the resources of a new country. He was indifferent to money, and during his early career in Texas lived in a careless frontier fashion, which often left him in straits for the means to purchase the common necessaries of life. After his second marriage he lived in a more orderly manner, but without much more attention to the accumulation of property. He was always generous after the early Texas fashion, and his horses and belongings were at the service of any one in want or for the needs of his neighbors. The salary of his public office was always expended liberally, and he had no professional income, his practice as a lawyer having only been in the early days, when he addressed frontier juries without much reference to statute and precedent, and took his pay in whatever came handy. He had been almost entirely in public life, and lived by it. In his old age he had only a small piece of property near the town of Huntsville, a house consisting of a double log-cabin, and a limited amount of land around it. To this he retired, after his deposition as governor, without an occupation or an opportunity to earn an income. His later years were undoubtedly passed in poverty, particularly after the commercial and industrial isolation of the Confederacy set in, with its necessary privations upon the whole of the community, but the story that he and his family suffered for the want of the common necessaries of life is exaggerated. They lived like their neighbors, and in the productive soil and genial climate there was no want of the means of living, whatever there may have been of the luxuries.

Shortly after his retirement, Houston passed through the city of Houston on his way to Sour Lake, a bathing place of medicinal waters in Jefferson County, which he visited for the benefit of his health. It was the time of the hottest ebullition of the secession excitement. War had been declared, and the community was in all the furor of military enthusiasm. No one doubted of the success of the South, and any one who should venture to say that it was not sure of victory was regarded as a traitor and a public enemy. Houston was asked to speak by his friends, and there were violent threats from the secession element that he should not be allowed to do so. He treated the threats with his usual contempt, and delivered his speech in the evening from the steps of the Academy. His friends armed themselves to protect him, and surrounded the platform. There was a secession torchlight procession, which paraded up and down the street while he was speaking, and a great deal of noise and disturbance. What was rare with Houston, he sometimes lost the thread of his discourse, and turned to a friend near him to ask him to supply it. But he spoke with his usual force and courage. He told his excited and confident audience that the result of the war would be against them. The South would win victories at first, but the North had the whole of Europe to draw upon to supply its armies, and would work with the relentless force of a machine, while the South was isolated, and had no resources with which to make good its inevitable exhaustion.

There was an uneasiness about what Houston might do, and a dread of his power and influence upon the people among the secession element. Although he had peacefully retired from the governorship, he was suspected of plotting either with the Federal Government or to have Texas set up for herself as an independent Republic. On April 4, 1861, Governor Clark wrote to President Davis, urging the Confederate Government to take more effective measures for the protection of the frontier. He said: "It is more than probable that an effort will soon be made by the submission party of this State, with General Houston at its head, to convert Texas into an independent Republic, and one of the most effective arguments will be that the Confederate States has supplied the place of the 2500 United States troops formerly upon our frontier with only a single regiment;" and there are other references in the correspondence of the time to such a design on the part of Houston. But his enemies took counsel of their fears. There is no evidence that Houston entertained any such purpose, and he certainly took no active steps to bring it about. On the contrary as the war kindled, his sympathies were strongly for the South, and he urged the most strenuous measures of resistance. In a speech at a festival of Baylor University at Independence, May 10, 1861, Houston declared his allegiance to his section, and his readiness to enter the ranks, if necessary, to repel invasion. He said: —

"Now that not only coercion, but a vindictive war is to be inaugurated, I stand ready to redeem my pledge to the people. Whether the Convention was right or wrong is not now the question. Whether I was treated justly or unjustly is not now to be considered. I put all that under my feet and there it shall stay. Let those who stood by me do the same, and let us all show at a time when perils environ our beloved land we know how to be patriots and Texans. Let us have no past but the glorious past, whose glorious deeds shall stimulate us to resistance to tyranny and wrong, and, burying in the grave of oblivion all our past differences, let us go forward determined not to yield until our independence is acknowledged; or, if not acknowledged, wrung from our enemies by the force of our valor. It is no time to turn back now; the people have put their hands to the plough; they must go forward; to recede would be worse than ignominy. Better meet war in its deadliest shape than cringe before an enemy whose wrath we have invoked. I make no pretension as to myself. I have yielded up office, and sought retirement to preserve peace among our people. My services are perhaps not important enough to be desired. Others are perhaps more competent to lead the people through the revolution. I have been with them through the fiery ordeal once, and I know that with prudence and discipline their courage will surmount all obstacles. Should the tocsin of war, calling the people to resist the invader, reach the retirement to which I shall go, I will heed neither the denunciations of my enemies or the clamor of my own friends, but will join the ranks of my countrymen to defend Texas once again."

He did not forget his humorous sarcasm upon his opponents, who had been very vigorous in bringing on the war, but less decided in taking part in it. Mr. North gives an account of a scene at a review in Galveston in which he scored them in his rough and popular fashion: —

"During the first year of the war, Colonel Moore had organized a splendid regiment of 1100 young men, volunteers mostly from Galveston, finely suspended at his side was the same old sword, and on his head was a weather-beaten, light-colored, broad-brimmed planter hat, the left side buttoned up to the crown. There he stood, the very impersonation of the olden times. It was a sight for sensation. All eyes were now upon him, some of them dimmed with tears, and many a throat of soldier and spectator was choking down feeling unutterable, — the writer among the rest. Not a word had yet passed the General's lips, but now the Colonel passed him his own sword and told him to proceed. Then came: —

"'Shoulder arms.

"'Right about face.' The regiment now facing to the rear, the General cried out in stentorian tones of sarcasm: 'Do you see anything of Judge Campbell or Williamson S. Oldham here?'

"'No,' was the emphatic reply.

"'Well,' said the General, 'they are not found at the front nor even at the rear.

"'Right about, front face.

"'Eyes right. Do you see anything of Judge Campbell's son here?'

"'No, he has gone to Paris to school,' responded the regiment.

"'Eyes left. Do you see anything of young Sam Houston here?'

"'Yes,' was the thrilling response.

"'Eyes front. Do you see anything of old Sam Houston here?' By this time the climax of excitement was reached, and the regiment and citizens responded in thunder tones, 'Yes!' and then united in a triple round of three times three and a tiger for the old hero. Thereupon he returned the Colonel his sword with the remark: 'There, Colonel, that will do, I leave you to manage the rest of the manœuvring,' and retired from dress parade."

But Houston's health soon began to fail. His splendid constitution, which had withstood his wounds, his hardships, and his excesses without giving way, began to feel the effects of old age. His old wounds renewed their pains, and he was obliged to walk with a crutch and a cane. He was attacked by painful and wasting illnesses, and at one time in the fall of 1862 he was very near death. His friend, Mr. Hamilton Stewart, gives the following account of the occasion: —

"While he was living at Cedar Point the word came down that he was dying. I took the next boat up, and found Mr. Houston was very sick with the fever. I remained for some days, doing all I could. The house stood in a grove of cedars. The time was the fall of the year. The wind blew and the rain fell. The surroundings were about as desolate as could be. A young doctor, who had n't had much experience, was attending Mr. Houston. One night he came up and called me out. He said he thought the end was near, and asked me to tell Mr. Houston. I did n't much like the duty. After thinking it over I went into the room where Mr. Houston was lying, and told him what the doctor said. He did n't make `any reply for a few minutes. Then he turned to me, and said, 'Call the family.' I went out and aroused Mrs. Houston and the children. After they came in Mr. Houston said, 'Call the servants.' All gathered about the bedside. Mr. Houston proceeded calmly and slowly to give detailed instructions about what he wanted done. He had some advice for each one present. When he had finished he called for the Bible and had a psalm read. Turning to two daughters he asked them to sing a hymn, which he designated. The girls began, but broke down sobbing. Mr. Houston took it up and finished it. After that he sent them all to bed again. He was very low, but he did not die at that time. When he became better I returned to Galveston. As I bade him goodby he sent an expression of his kindest feeling to all of his friends. Then, warming up, he said, 'Tell my enemies I am not dead yet.'"

His mind, afflicted with the calamities of the country, and doubtful of the success of his section, reacted upon his bodily strength. He became melancholy and despondent, and in a measure lost his hold upon life. To his old friends he spoke doubtfully of the success of the South, and looked beyond to the results which would follow the restoration of the Union. To one of them he said that the immense fortunes which were being made in the North during the war would seek an outlet as soon as it was over, and that within less than fifteen years the cars would be running through Texas to the City of Mexico and

to San Francisco. At times the old spirit flashed
out. The military officers of the Confederacy had
established a very stringent system of martial law in
Texas, by which all the male inhabitants over sixteen years of age were required to register themselves, and obtain passes from the provost-marshals.
Houston paid no attention to the order, and at one
time was halted by a superserviceable official, who demanded his pass. The old man waved him aside with
a frowning countenance, and replied, "San Jacinto is
my pass through Texas." He wrote a letter of earnest protest against the proclamation of martial law,
issued May 31, 1861, by General P. D. Hebert,
commanding the Department of Texas, to Governor
Lubbock. He charged General Hebert with the
abrogation of the principles of individual liberty,
and appealed to the governor to maintain the rights
of the people. The decrees of banishment against
Union citizens, and the system of oppression and in-
timidation, were carried out in the most harsh and
vindictive manner, and Houston revolted against the
needless tyranny. His letter to the governor was
not published until six months after it was written,
and made a profound impression upon the people,
discouraged by the reverses to the Confederate armies, and indignant at the military rule of the Confederate officers in Texas. But Houston was still
firm for resistance to the North. After the recapture
of Galveston by the Texan forces on January 1,
1863, he wrote a congratulatory letter to General

Magruder, in which he thanked him for "driving from the soil a ruthless enemy," and said that he would have paid him his respects personally, but that he had just risen from a sick-bed. The Federal soldiers, captured at Galveston, were treated with great harshness, and confined in prison like common criminals. Houston was indignant at this unmanly conduct on the part of the Confederate authorities, and applied in person to the superintendent of the penitentiary to remove the officers and men from convict cells to quarters more appropriate to prisoners of war. The superintendent did so, and took them into his own house, where they remained until they were exchanged.

Houston's last speech was delivered in the city of Houston March 18, 1863. The animosity and bitterness with which he had been regarded for his course in opposing secession had died away, and a feeling of respect for his venerable age, and a consciousness that he had been right in his prediction of the evils which would follow the attempt to dissolve the Union, added to the consideration due to his history and achievements. He was listened to with respectful attention, and spoke with much pathos of his age and the approaching end of his life. He said: —

"Ladies and Fellow - Citizens: With feelings of pleasure and friendly greeting I once again stand before this, an assemblage of my countrymen. As I behold this large assemblage, who, from their homes and daily toil, have come once again to greet the man who has so often known their kindness and affection, I can feel that even yet I hold a place in their high regard. This manifestation is the highest compliment that can be paid to the citizen and patriot. As you have gathered here to listen to the sentiments of my heart, knowing that the days draw nigh unto me when all thoughts of ambition and worldly pride give place to the earnestness of age, I know you will bear with me, while with calmness and without the fervor and eloquence of youth, I express those sentiments which seem natural to my mind in the view of the condition of the country. I have been buffeted by the waves as I have been borne along time's ocean, until, shattered and worn, I approach the narrow isthmus which divides it from the sea of eternity beyond. Ere I step forward to journey through the pilgrimage of death, I would say that all my thoughts and all my hopes are with my country. If one impulse arises above another, it is for the happiness of these people; the welfare and glory of Texas will be the uppermost thought while the spark of life lingers in this breast."

He spoke hopefully of the probabilities of the success of the Confederacy. He pointed out the favorable chances of the interference of France in behalf of the South in the support of its Mexican scheme; spoke of the dissatisfaction caused by the depreciation of the greenback currency in the North, of the dangers of the drafts to the Federal authority, and the weariness of the Northwest with the war. His voice was still for prolonged and desperate resistance. He said : —

"Thus, although I do not look with confidence to these results, nor do I advance them as more than mere probabilities, they certainly indicate that there is discord and discontent at the North, and these always will embarrass its cause, and endanger its success. Yet I do not trust to these things, nor would I have you do so. Let us go forward, nerved to nobler deeds than we have yet given to history. Let us bid defiance to all the hosts that our enemies can bring against us. Can Lincoln expect to subjugate a people thus resolved? No! From every conflict they will arise the stronger and more resolute. Are we deprived of the luxuries which our enemies possess? We have learned how little necessary they are, and it is no privation to do without them."

But his darker forebodings of the fate of the Confederacy were destined to be fulfilled. On the 4th of July, 1863, Vicksburg fell, and Houston must have realized that it was the death stroke to the cause of the South. He was then on his death-bed. His bodily forces had gradually failed him, without any sharp attack of illness. He spent much of his time in reading the Bible, and in prayers for his country and his family. He received the ministrations of a Presbyterian clergyman, with whom he had previously been in antagonism, but with whom he was reconciled by the touch of death. All his family were about him, except his eldest son, Lieutenant Sam Houston, who was wounded and a prisoner in the hands of the enemy. "The day before his death," his daughter writes, "he fell into a comatose state from which we could not rouse him; but during the next forenoon we heard his voice in a tone of entreaty, and, listening to the feeble sound, we caught the words 'Texas! Texas!' Soon afterward my mother was sitting by his bedside with his hand in hers, and his lips moved once again. 'Margaret,' he said, and the voice we loved was silent forever. As the sun sank below the horizon his spirit left this earth for a better land." He died July 26, 1863, aged seventy years, four months, and twenty-four days. He left a widow and eight children, some of whom have since distinguished themselves in the political and professional life of Texas. His will was peculiar and characteristic. After bequeathing his property to his family, he said in regard to the education of his sons: —

"My will is that my sons should receive solid and useful education and that no portion of their time be devoted to the study of abstract science. I greatly desire that they may possess a thorough knowledge of the English language, with a good knowledge of the Latin language. I request that they be instructed in the Holy Scriptures, and next to these that they be rendered thoroughly in a knowledge of geography and history. I wish my sons to be taught an entire contempt for novels and light reading, as well as for the morals and manners with whom they may be associated or instructed."

He bequeathed his sword to his eldest son in these terms: —

"To my eldest son, Sam Houston, I bequeath my sword, worn in the battle of San Jacinto, to be drawn only in defense of the constitution, the laws and liberties of his country. If any attempt be made to assail one of these I wish it to be used in vindication."

The will was dated the 2d of April, 1863. His remains were buried at Huntsville, with a plain slab, bearing the inscription, "General Sam Houston. Born March 2, 1793. Died July 26, 1863;" and he sleeps beneath the tangled vines and grass, after a life of tumult and vicissitude such as falls to the lot of few mortals. At the winter session following his death the legislature adopted resolutions expressing regret at the extinction of so great a light in the dark hours of the nation's existence, and paying tribute to his unblemished patriotism and untiring regard for the people of Texas. It afterward appropriated $1700 to Mrs. Houston to pay the salary for his unfinished term as governor. The mourning of the people of Texas was deep and sincere for one who, with all his faults and all the antagonisms he had aroused, was regarded as the national hero, and detraction was silent in the sense of loss, and the gratitude and reverence for one who embodied the popular pride and typified a heroic history.

CHAPTER XVII

CHARACTERISTICS

HOUSTON, although with such marked and peculiar individual characteristics, was essentially the product of his time and circumstance. He grew out of that condition in which the generation of the descendants of the original settlers of the country were brought into contact with the forces of nature and the savage inhabitants in a way to influence their native character as well as their lives. They were born into the pioneer period, instead of coming to it in mature life, and they had not shared the original education and training of their ancestors. It was a state of barbarism in its outward forms, and they were more essentially a part of it than those who had preceded them. Their education was limited and meagre, and their training and governing influences were in the life of the wilderness, the primeval forest, which enveloped them with its perils and hardships, its temptings to adventure, and the labors necessary to carve out a home in it. This produced a hardy and indomitable spirit, which found its relief in the enthusiasm of perilous adventure and in the pursuit of game, and a vigor and energy of the bodily powers which found their keenest zest in dangerous sports and exhausting trials of strength. It was a race of vikings, drawn by passion and exuberant energy to the life of the forest and the adventures of the wilderness, as their prototypes had been to those of the sea. They retained the restraints of their English descent, and their instinct was to found a settled community with all the germs of civilization, but in their characteristic types they were possessed by an overmastering impulse for adventure, and the hand-to-hand struggle with unsubdued nature. They assimilated to a certain degree the ways and customs of the aboriginal inhabitants with whom they came in contact, with whom they fought, and in the midst of whom they lived. They had the migratory instinct and the fondness for wild life of the Indians, and, if they were governed by the higher traditions and motives of civilization, their lives and natures were also tinctured with savage passions and impulses. Sometimes the resemblance and influence were developed in a remarkable degree.

The kinship of Houston with the Indian character has already been noticed. It led him, when a youth, to desert the restraints of even a frontier civilization, and take up his home among them, and he manifested the characteristic qualities and something of the manners of an Indian chief throughout his whole life. His powers of popular oratory, his perception of character and his influence over men, his courage and bold conceptions of policy, his generosity and indifference to wealth, were the characteristics of a barbarian leader. Then his undisguised personal vanity, his tricky cunning, and his passionate and reckless temperament were alike the attributes of the Indian. He might have figured as one of the leaders of the Greeks at the siege of Troy, with their practical wisdom and their childish simplicity. It has been said that if he had been bound naked upon the back of a wild horse like Mazeppa the first tribe he came to would have elected him a prince; but it would have been a wandering tribe, and not a civilized and settled people. He owed his leadership in Texas to the conditions of tumult and adventure into which the people were thrown, since their lives represented in many ways the features of primitive barbarism. This is not to say that they were barbarians by nature, but in their strife with the wilderness and their hostile contact with the Indians and the Mexicans they were subject to all the conditions of primitive and incessant warfare which colored their lives and governed their actions. Houston's later life manifested distinct traces of his primitive habits and training, and revealed his limitations, in spite of the practical sagacity and broad wisdom which frequently characterized his statesmanship. He was out of place in the Senate, in contact with minds trained to think within the lines of civilized education, and to argue logically upon legal premises. He never adapted himself to its atmosphere or acquired its forms of oratory. He was like an Indian chief in a modern legislature. His strength was when he could appeal to the thoughts and feelings of the common people, sway them by his vigorous and somewhat histrionic eloquence, tickle them by his familiar humor, and influence them by his shrewd common sense. It is doubtful if there has been in modern times any such orator for a crowd, except, perhaps, Daniel O'Connell. Certainly there has been none in American history who could so sway a frontier audience. It used to be said that there were but two things that could draw out the people of Texas, — a circus and Sam Houston. Time and again he awed their turbulent spirits when they were in a state of the highest excitement and passion, and when any other man would have been howled down or subjected to bodily violence. Time and again he converted popular assemblages to his own way of thinking, in spite of the most violent prejudice, and his political power was based on his popular eloquence. Yet he was far from being a demagogue. He did not flatter the passions and prejudices of the multitude, or govern his opinions by theirs. He withstood them with manly courage when there was occasion, and, if he could not convert them, vindicated himself. His power over the people was due to his genuine sympathy with them, as well as to his personal and popular gifts. He felt as they did, and his desires and ambitions were for the welfare and prosperity of those who tilled the soil, and built homes in the wilderness with their own hands. He had no liking for, or affiliation with, that class who were endeavoring to build up a slave oligarchy at the South, and regarded them as the enemies of the section as well as of the nation. The most of his political quarrels were from the rivalries of ambitious schemers, eager for conquest or personal power at the expense of the people. His own personal ambition was predominant, but it was based upon the welfare of the people, and he sacrificed it rather than submit to their erroneous judgment, and lead them in the way to ruin. In the affection and confidence of the people he had no competitor, and when they were swept away from him by the passion and excitement of the outbreak of the civil war, there was no one who could take his place as a popular leader.

As a soldier Houston's career was too brief and limited to entitle him to rank among distinguished military leaders. In his first campaign he was merely the youthful subordinate who had only the opportunity to display his courage and dash, and acquire a reputation for bravery. In the second there were no conditions which involved accomplished military strategy, or tactical skill in battle. The only choice was either to meet the enemy in a mass at the threshold of the country, or allow him to penetrate within it, at the cost of the destruction of the settlements along the line of march, in the expectation that he would either divide his forces, or that they would become weakened by being drawn away from their base, so that they could be attacked with an assurance of victory. The decision simply required the exercise of practical judgment and common sense. There may be doubt whether the fighting quality of the Texans would not have enabled them to defeat Santa Anna's army with even such odds as there were at the beginning, but the chances were uncertain, and a defeat would have meant the destruction of the army and the subjugation of the country. It was a risk which the circumstances would not justify, and Houston was governed by wisdom as well as prudence in the course which he took. The battle of San Jacinto required no tactical mánœuvring. The only thing to be done was to fall on the enemy with all the force of a sudden and crushing attack, and to trust to the *élan* and vigor of the Texan soldiers to overwhelm the feebler physique and fainter spirit of the Mexican. It simply required a leader to head the assault, keep his men in line, and restrain their fire until the deadly moment. This Houston did, and it may be said that the most accomplished soldier could have done no more. What Houston might have done with a larger army and a more extensive field of operations can only be a matter of conjecture. He simply accomplished what the circumstances permitted, and displayed his natural capacity and common sense, but it was not enough to entitle him to a place in the ranks of trained and skillful military leaders. His enemies affected to doubt his physical courage, and ascribed his retreat to personal timidity. But he was wounded in leading assaults in both the battles in which he was engaged, and that may be taken to set-

tle the question of his courage. It was still farther
demonstrated throughout his life by his firmness in
facing turbulent mobs, and in withstanding the
threats of open and secret violence which so often
accompanied his political action. It is true that he
did not have that fighting disposition and that fondness
for personal combat which characterized the fiery
spirits of some of his associates and rivals. He was
not a fire-eater or a desperado. He had too much
common sense to put his life at the call of any individual who desired to provoke him to a duel, and
would not give his enemies the chance of overthrow-
ing his policy by killing him. No one but his antag-
onists blamed him for this wise course, even if there
had been no moral principle involved, and it is
enough to say that he could not have held his place
in such a state of society as that in which he lived
from his youth up without having given abundant
proof of his physical courage.

As a statesman he showed broad wisdom and practical sagacity. His action in the creation of a working government for the Republic of Texas, without
means, and in a turbulent and scattered society, amid
the opposition and intrigue of ambitious rivals, however much he may have been aided by some of his
associates and by the support of the more intelligent
element among the people, was a proof of his great
administrative capacity, and the chief credit is due to
his wisdom and influence. His course in restraining
the eager adventurers who came to the country for

glory and conquest, and the restless spirits among the settlers from undertaking foolish and reckless attempts at the invasion of Mexico, showed his sound and practical judgment, and saved the country from great calamities, if not from destruction. His treatment of Santa Anna manifested his wisdom, as well as his magnanimity, and his dealings with the Indians were those of enlightened statesmanship as well as philanthropy. His prudent and practical economy rescued the Republic from financial collapse, and his negotiations with foreign nations were shrewd and skillful in effect, while dignified in manner and elevated in purpose. They did much to preserve Texas from being attacked by Mexico, and undoubtedly contributed greatly to the annexation of Texas to the United States at the time it was accomplished. Considering the enormous difficulties of creating a government out of such materials, the troubles resulting from the turbulence and lawlessness of the adventurers and the restless and desperate opposition of rivals, the dangers of invasion from Mexico, the constant menace and trouble from the Indians, and the lack of means and credit, it must be admitted that Houston accomplished a task in the highest degree creditable to his wisdom and sagacity, and which it is, perhaps, not too much to say that no other could have done so well.

In the field of national statesmanship Houston exhibited equal qualities of broad wisdom, firmness, and courage. He perceived the dangers which threat-

ened his section from the aggressive designs of the
leading slave-holders, and had the courage to oppose
them at the cost of his political fortunes. To him
and to Benton is due the credit of understanding and
advocating the true interests of the South, as well as
of the nation, and their position was such that it vindicated their courage as well as their statesmanship.
It was easy for Northern statesmen, representing the
predominant sentiment of their constituents, to oppose schemes for the territorial extension of slavery,
but it was quite another matter for representatives of
the South to oppose the apparent interests of their
section, and all the force of active political intrigue
working upon popular feeling. Houston's speeches
on the Kansas-Nebraska bill show a prophetic prescience, as well as a commanding eloquence, and
vindicate his right to a high rank among American
statesmen. Almost alone he advocated wisdom and
justice in the treatment of the Indians, and the plans
which he urged for the improvement of their condition would have saved the nation from the just re-
proach of injustice and neglect towards a feeble and
helpless race. Some of his schemes were less wise,
such as the attempt to induce the United States to
assume a protectorate over Mexico, and the delusive
vision of the presidency led him for a time into affiliation with Know-Nothingism; but as a whole his
action in the legislative councils of the nation was
creditable to his wisdom and sagacity. At the outbreak of the civil war Houston manifested his enlight-

ened devotion to the Union, and his appreciation of
the perils and calamities in which secession would
involve the South. He resisted the folly and madness so long as it could be done by peaceful means,
but events were too strong for him. The condition
and position of Texas were such that he could not
have taken the action that was followed by some of
the Union leaders in the Border States, even if he
wished to do so; and when the rest of the South
seceded, Texas was inevitably taken with it. Houston's sympathies were with his people and with the
South as a section, and when the war began he was
for resistance. His action was by no means governed
by timidity or demagoguery. He showed his personal courage by opposing the tide of violent popular
feeling at imminent risk, and he surrendered his
office in order to vindicate his judgment. His course
was entirely patriotic and consistent, considering his
feelings and circumstances; and the blame which has
been thrown upon him by Northern advocates of the
Union for not plunging Texas into a civil war within
the limits of the State is wholly undeserved. He
believed in and supported the Union so long as it
was possible without bloodshed; but he gave up the
struggle when it involved a civil war among his own
people.

As a politician in the ordinary sense of the word
Houston was extremely skillful. He was a keen and
accurate judge of personal character, and knew at
once those who would become rivals, and those whom

he could attach to himself as supporters. The first
he attacked without stint, and overwhelmed with
opprobrium and abuse, which aroused their fiercest
indignation. The second he flattered, and attached
to his fortunes by kindly familiarity and practical
service. He was always interested in the welfare of
young men, and ready to give them an opportunity to
display their talents, if he did not believe them dangerous to the public welfare, or in the way of his
personal supremacy. It is not true, however, that he
was intolerant to opinion when it was not manifested
in personal opposition, and his friendship for his colleague, Senator Rusk, was by no means the result
of political subservience or lack of independence on
the part of the latter. Many of his friends differed
from him without exciting his animosity, and, if determined and masterful, he was not tyrannical. To
personal enemies he was, however, vindictive, and
never spared them any blow which could contribute
to their discomfiture. His enemies complained of his
"Indian cunning," and he was not always straight-
forward in his political action. He was fond of
tricks and surprises, which he apparently practiced
for the love of them, or to excite the admiration of
the people for his shrewdness, and affected an air of
mystery which sometimes angered his friends as well
as his enemies. A specimen of what he termed a
"ruse," in dealing with a troublesome individual, is
given by Mr. Ashbell Smith in his "Reminiscences
of the Texas Republic:" —

"San Antonio was much the largest, richest, most influential city of Texas of that period. It was remote from the scene of the Texan government. There was no intervening population between it and the Mexican frontier. For its protection and that of the country a considerable squadron of cavalry was stationed in the city. This squadron was indeed the only military force of Texas kept mobilized, that was ready to take the field. Major Western, who commanded this body of cavalry, had by some acts and significant innuendoes intimated that he cared very little for the one-horse government in the city of Houston. President Houston was apprehensive that an order to recall the major or to relieve him might be disobeyed. It was announced publicly that a minister would be appointed to represent Texas at the court of St. James. Colonel William H. Patton was going to San Antonio on his own private business. President Houston, in a long and friendly conversation with Colonel Patton, at length adverted as by accident to the proposed mission to England. He spoke of Major Western, lauded his courtly manners, his polished address, his diplomatic ability; said the major reminded him strongly of Mr. Van Buren; asked Colonel Patton what he thought of the appointment of Major Western to this mission. All this he begged Colonel Patton to hold in strict confidence, — 'nothing was absolutely determined upon,' — 'Colonel Patton need not be surprised at anything.' The President, waiting until he heard of Colonel Patton's arrival at San Antonio, sent through the war department orders to Major Western to report in person at the seat of government. The major presented himself in Houston, radiant and decorous as Titus at the head of the Roman legions organized for the conquest of Jerusalem. Time rolled on. The major became visibly impatient despite the gracious accord with which President Houston greeted him. At length he began to inquire very quietly who was to be appointed to England, — he inquired of your speaker, who was a member of Houston's staff, — but Ashbell Smith 'knew nothing of cabinet matters, he was not a member of the Cabinet.' Finally instructions were being made out in the state department and General Pinkney Henderson was making preparations to leave for London. The rumor leaked out, — the major 'would not believe it.' 'President Houston had better judgment of men.' 'What did Henderson know of diplomacy?' The appointment of General Henderson became an established fact. The major 'was disgusted;' he 'would go back to San Antonio;' and he did, but he found his successor there, well established in the command of the cavalry. Referring to this matter at the time, General Houston said to your speaker that he would have no pronunciamentos of the Mexican fashion in Texas during his presidency. During his second presidency he had to confront and ward off the far more perilous danger of the pronunciamentos which were threatened, and which might have proved disastrous, but for his consummate tact in charming them down. Recurring to the incident just related, General Houston at a subsequent time provided comfortably for his disappointed old friend, the major, by placing him at the head of the Indian bureau."

There are many other anecdotes, perhaps less authentic, of the manner in which Houston tripped up his political adversaries, or led them into skillfully laid traps, and the stories of his cunning added to his stock of admiration among the people.

Specimens of Houston's public speeches have been given. They show in some degree the defects of his education. There is not always a skillful or even a familiar choice of words, and the style is that of the heavy and somewhat stilted oratory of the time, without the massive polish which sometimes distinguished it, as in the case of Webster and Calhoun. But at times it was vivified by the strength of the thought and feeling behind it, and rose to the height of a dignified and forcible eloquence. His style of popular oratory has already been sufficiently characterized. His private speech was vigorous and incisive, and he often characterized his enemies with powerful force and humor. His description of Jefferson Davis was one of those epigrams which may be accepted as the truth of history, "Ambitious as Lucifer, and cold as a lizard." Houston had a personal follower by the name of S——, whom he had obliged with small federal and state offices, and who professed great devotion to him. During the secession difficulties,

however, he turned against Houston, and violently
attacked and abused him. This was mentioned to
Houston with a condemnation of S——'s ingratitude.
"You must n't be hard on S——," said Houston.
"I was always fond of dogs, and S—— has all the
virtues of a dog, except his fidelity."

Houston's most conspicuous weaknesses of temperament were his personal vanity and his tendency to
histrionism. The eccentricity and theatrical display
which characterized his dress have been noticed. It
was almost childish in its manifest purpose to attract
attention, and only his magnificent physique could
have carried off his draping himself in an Indian
blanket or a Mexican poncho, and the other bizarre
eccentricities of his attire, without ridicule, and they
were another evidence of the tendencies of a barbarian chieftain. They passed in the rude and uncon-
ventional society of the frontier which shared in the
same tendencies and irregularities, but they detracted
from the dignity and sobriety which are the customs
of civilization, and gave an air of melodramatic eccentricity to Houston which was an injury to his weight
and influence. Perhaps no other strong and practical-minded man has had this weakness in so marked a
degree as Houston, in spite of the record of the early
velvets and laces of Disraeli. His histrionism was
no less marked. An old associate and friendly observer has remarked that Houston was always acting,
that is, always trying to impress the persons he was
with, whether it was in a room or at a public meet-

ing. Another has said that his air of dignity never
left him, even when drunk, and that he preserved his
native superiority even in the rudest familiarity of
the camp fire or the frontier frolic. This again is
characteristic of the Indian chief. He appreciated
the value of a "scene," like Napoleon, and his out-
bursts of apparently uncontrollable anger were as
artificial as those of his friend and model, Andrew
Jackson. He had the grand air which carried off
the artificiality, as in the case of the elder Pitt, but
there was a sense of the parade in his manner which
alienated practical-minded men, and which only his
real capacity and masterfulness excused. It imposed
upon the people, however, and was one of the sources
of his strength with them. He had a profound sense
of his dignity and importance, and sometimes manifested it in incongruous ways. It was said in jest
that his signature was written so as to read "I am
Houston," instead of "Sam Houston," and, as has
been recorded, he had a habit, when he wished to be
particularly impressive, of speaking of himself in the
third person. He had a good many difficulties about
trifles, and at one time he was sued in the justice
court of Houston by an Irishman who had dug a
well for him. Houston asserted that the man had
left his tools in the well, and that this was an offset
to his claim. Judgment was given against Houston
by default, and he appealed. On the trial of the
appeal he claimed that as a Senator of the United
States he had been called upon by his constituents to

make a speech, and that this was a valid reason for his absence, so that the case should not have been defaulted. He could not understand why his appeal was rejected on this excuse, and the dignity of his office as a Senator disregarded. But his sense of personal dignity had its force under adverse circumstances. He never showed any sign of defeat, and after his deposition as governor he walked the streets of Austin as if he had been the victor in the contest.

Houston was a man of warm affections and kindly nature. His manners to women were remarkably courteous and deferential. His word of address was not "Madam," but "Lady," and no matter what their rank or station his impressive politeness and consideration were always the same. It was not an affectation, but sprang from a genuine impulse of respect and chivalric feeling. His family affection was deep and strong. His second wife, to whom he owed so much for her influence upon his personal conduct, was enshrined in his deepest feelings of love and respect. To borrow Hawthorne's phrase, he had a smile which children loved, and gained their confidence and affection at once. He was fond of playing with children and telling them stories, and was constantly engaged in whittling out toys for them from his supplies of pine sticks. His own children were brought up in kindly freedom and confidence, although with a wise and judicious education and training. His slaves were kindly treated, and were in a measure members of the family. He was generous and helpful to all persons in distress, and his money and property were at the call of all who needed assistance. It is recorded that he once pulled off his coat and gave it to a ragged soldier who had served at San Jacinto, and his acts of charity were numerous and spontaneous.

His excesses in liquor were those of his time and temperament. The mighty men of his era indulged in tremendous exaltations of intoxication, as they did in the excitement of combats, from the craving of their overflowing animal spirits, and fought and drank with equal appetite. Houston in the worst period of his indulgence was not an habitual sot, who drank from a degraded physical appetite, but from the stimulus of his temperament to excitement, and to drown grief and disappointment. There was something Homeric in his debauches, and his freaks of conduct when under their influence were often of wild extravagance. His great physical strength displayed itself in the smashing of furniture, and his wild whoops woke the sleepers with apprehensions of an Indian invasion. But somehow, as has been said, he kept the respect of the people, and no sense of degradation attached itself to his excesses. Drunk or sober Sam Houston was always "Sam Houston."

The limitations of Houston's character will forbid his being reckoned among the world's great men. But no one will deny that he was a strong man, capable of great achievement, practical-minded in spite of his eccentricities and weaknesses, with wise conceptions of statesmanship and policy, determined and courageous, sincerely patriotic, and devoted to the welfare of his people. A type of his time and circumstances, he rose above them by his capacity and energy, and signalized his own individuality, as well as illustrated the tendencies and opportunities which created him. There were others like him, but he surpassed them all except his prototype, Andrew Jackson. There will never be another Sam Houston in American history, for the state of society which produced him has passed away, and there are no longer such opportunities for pioneer adventure, and the creation of a State in the wilderness by aggressive settlements and the expulsion of a weaker race of colonists. He has a marked place in the history of the nation, for what he represented as well as for what he did, and his figure will grow in interest as a type of a peculiar and, with all its faults, a heroic period.

BOOKS RELATING TO HOUSTON AND THE HIS-
TORY OF TEXAS USED IN THE PREPARATION
OF THIS VOLUME.

Almanac, Texas, Galveston, 1856, *et supra*.

Anderson, Charles. Texas Before and on the Eve of the Rebellion. Cin., 1884.

Audubon, J. J. Life and Journals. New York, 1867.

Baker, D. W. C. Texas Scrap Book. New York, 1875.

Bancroft, H. H. History of North Mexican States and Texas.
2 vols. San Francisco, 1889.

Benton, Thomas H. Thirty Years' View. New York. 2 vols.
1854.

Benton, Thomas H. Abridgment of Debates in Congress.
16 vols. New York, 1851.

Bruce, Henry. Makers of America : Sam Houston. New
York, 1891.

Civil and Military History of Andrew Jackson. By an
American Officer. New York, 1825.

Colton, C. The Life and Times of Henry Clay. 2 vols.
New York, 1846.

Compilation of the Official Records of the Union and Confederate Armies. Washington.

Congressional ·Globe. Washington.

Corner, William. San Antonio de Bexar. San Antonio,
1890.

Crane, William Carey. Life and Select Literary Remains of
Sam Houston. Phil., 1884.

Crockett, David. Exploits and Adventures in Texas. New
York, 1845.

De Cordova, J.   Texas, Its Resources and Its Public Men. Phil., 1858.

Dewees.   Letters from Texas.   Louisville, 1858.

Domenech, L'Abbé E.   Journal d'un Missionaire au Texas et au Mexique.   Paris, 1857.

Duval, John C.   Adventures of Big Foot Wallace, the Texas Ranger and Hunter.   Phil., 1873.

Duval, John C.   Early Times in Texas.   Austin, 1892.

Dyer, Oliver.   Great Senators of the United States.   New York, 1881.

Edwards, D. B.   History of Texas.   Cin., 1836.

Featherstonehaugh, G. W.   Excursion through the Slave States.   New York, 1839.

Foote, H. G.   Texas and the Texans.   2 vols.   Phil., 1841.

Gouge, Wm. M.   Fiscal History of Texas.   Phil., 1852.

Graham, Rev. John.   Diary of the Siege of Londonderry. Londonderry, 1823.

Greeley, Horace.   The American Conflict.   2 vols.   Hartford, 1873.

Green, Thomas J.   Journal of the Texas Expedition Against Mier.   New York, 1845.

Holley, Mary Austin.   Texas.   Lexington, Ky., 1856.

Hooton, Charles.   St. Louis Isle, or Texiana.   London, 1847.

Horton, Col. Alexander.   Sketch of the War of '36.   Eastern Texas.   San Augustine, 1857.

Houston, Mrs.   Texas and the Gulf of Mexico.   London, 1848.

Houston, Sam, The Life of.   New York, 1855.

Howard, H. R.   The Life of Virgil A. Stewart.   (The John A. Murrell Conspiracy.)   New York, 1836.

Hutchison, Rev. I. R., D. D.   Reminiscences, Sketches, and Addresses.   Houston, 1879.

Johnston, Wm. Preston.   Life of Gen. Albert Sidney Johnston.   New York, 1878.

Jones, Anson.   Memoranda and Official Correspondence Relating to the Republic of Texas.   New York, 1859.

Kendal, G. W. Texas Santa Fé Expedition. London, 1849.

Kennedy, William. The Rise, Progress, and Prospects of the Republic of Texas. 2 vols. London, 1841.

Lester, C. Edwards. Sam Houston and his Republic. New York, 1846.

Linn, John J. Reminiscences of Fifty Years in Texas. New York, 1883.

Maillard, N. Doran. The History of the Republic of Texas. London, 1842.

Mayo, Robert. Political Sketches of Eight Years in Washington. Washington, 1839.

Miranda. Expedition. In a Series of Letters. Boston, 1809.

Morrell, Rev. Z. N. Flowers and Fruits of the Wilderness. Thirty-six Years in Texas. Boston, 1873.

Newell, Rev. C. History of the Revolution in Texas. New York, 1838.

Niles' Register. Washington.

North, Thomas. Five Years in Texas, from 1861 to 1866. Cin., 1871.

Olmstead, Frederick Law. A Journey through Texas. New York, 1857.

Parker, A. A. Trip to the West and Texas. Concord, N. H., 1836.

Parker, W. G. Unexplored Texas. Phil., 1856.

Parton, James. Life of Andrew Jackson. 3 vols. New York, 1860.

Paxton, Philip. A Stray Yankee in Texas. New York, 1857.

Pierce, Edward L. Memoir and Letters of Charles Sumner. 4 vols. Boston, 1893.

Phelan, James. American Commonwealths. Tennessee. Boston, 1887.

Robinson, Wm. Davis. Narrative of the Expedition of Gen. Xavier Mina. Phil., 1820.

Roche, James Jeffrey. The Story of the Filibusters. London, 1892.

Roosevelt, Theodore. American Statesmen. Thomas H. Benton. Boston, 1887.

Sharp, Wm. Preston. The Prisoners of Perote. Phil., 1845.

Shipman, Daniel. Frontier Life. Houston, Texas, 1879.

Schurz, Carl. American Statesmen. Henry Clay. 2 vols. Boston, 1887.

Schwartz, Stephan. Twenty-Two Months a Prisoner of War in Texas. St. Louis, 1892.

Smith, Ashbell. Reminiscences of the Texas Republic. Galveston, 1876.

Thompson, Waddy. Recollections of Mexico. New York, 1847.

Thrall, Rev. Homer S. A Pictorial History of Texas. St. Louis, 1881.

Thrall, Rev. Homer S. Life of Sam Houston. Round Table Magazine. Dallas, 1892-93.

Truman, Ben. C. The Field of Honor. New York, 1884.

Ward, H. G. Mexico. 2 vols. London, 1829.

Wilburger, J. W. Indian Depredations in Texas. Austin, 1890.

INDEX

ALAMO, description of, 140, 143; capture of, 149 et seq.

Almonte, Col. Juan N., report on condition of Texas, 55–59; protects Mrs. Dickenson, 151; surrenders at San Jacinto, 201.

Alsbury, Mrs., survives massacre at Alamo, 151.

Antonio, San, description of, 102; capture of, 110 et seq.

Archer, Branch T., settles in Texas, 75; President of Consultation, 117; commisioner to United States, 121; President Texas Railroad Co., 231.

Archives, War of, 273, 274.

Audrade, Gen., commands Mexican cavalry, 138.

Audubon, J. J., visits Houston, 246.

Austin, Col. John, captures Velasco, 72.

Austin, Moses, obtains concession in Texas, 61; death, 61.

Austin, Stephen F., birth, 61; goes to Texas, 62; returns from Mexico, 72; delegate to Mexico, 87; arrested, 88; released, 93; given public dinner, 94; elected commander-in-chief, 98; resigns, 106; commissioner to United States, 121; raises money for Texas, 134; Secretary of State, 229; death, 245.

Bache, Richard, votes against annexation, 290.

Baker, Capt. Moseley, attacks provisional government, 122; insubordination of, 192.

Baker, Rev. William M., anecdote by, 248, 249.

Bell, Senator, votes against Kansas-Nebraska bill, 313.

Benton, Thomas H., eulogizes Houston, 21; favors recognition of Texan independence, 235; opposes Kansas-Nebraska bill, 313.

Bercero, Sergt., describes battle of Alamo, 153.

Bernard, Dr. Joseph, report of wounded at Alamo, 152; rescued at Goliad, 178.

Bonham, Col. J. B., joins Alamo garrison, 143; takes message to Fannin, 147; death, 150.

Bowie, James, settles in Texas, 76; commands at battle of Concepcion, 102; character, 143; death, 150.

Bowie, Rezin P., settles in Texas, 76.

Bradburn, Col. John D., commands at Anahuac, 71; deprived of command, 72.

Burleson, Col. Edward, succeeds Austin in command of the army, 106; receives surrender of San Antonio, 114; resigns, 114; commands centre at San Jacinto, 190; Vice-President, 262; commands at San Antonio, 268.

Burnett, David G., settles in Texas, 75; President of the Republic, 159; protests against demands of army, 220; resigns, 228; Vice-President, 249; administers government, 261.

Burton, Capt. Isaac W., captures Mexican vessels, 227.

Caldwell, Capt. Matthew, fights invading force, 275.

Calhoun, John C., rebukes Houston, 20; opposes prohibition of slavery in Oregon, 299.

Cameron, Capt. Ewan, shot by Mexicans, 277.

Carson, Samuel P., Secretary of State, 159; letter of, 159.

Castenada, Capt., defeated at Gonzales, 96.

Castrillon, commands Mexican artillery, 138; pleads for prisoners, 151; death, 201.

Cave, E. W., declines to take oath to Confederacy, 157.

Chambers, Thomas J., settles in Texas, 76.

Clark, Edward, succeeds Houston as governor, 357; interview with Houston, 358; writes to President Davis, 365.

Clay, Henry, favors recognition of Texas, 221; opposes its annexation, 285.

Coleto, battle of, 168, 169.

Collingsworth, Capt. George, captures Goliad, 99.

Collingsworth, James, commissioner to United States, 221; death, 229.

Concepcion, battle of, 104 et seq.

Cook, Col. P. St. G., arrests Texan troops, 277.

Coss, Gen. Martin Perfecto de, takes command in Coahuila, 91; marches to Bexar, 94; surrenders San Antonio, 113; leads attack on Alamo, 149; reinforces Santa Anna, 197; made prisoner, 208.

Crockett, David, character, 143; joins Alamo garrison, 143; death, 150.

Dawson, Capt. N., defeated by Mexicans, 275.

Dickenson, Mrs. A. M., survives Alamo massacre, 151.

Douglas, Senator, introduces bill to repeal Missouri Compromise, 306; attacks New England clergymen, 314.

Duque, Col., wounded at Alamo, 149.

Dyer, Oliver, description of Houston, 327–329.

Edwards, Hayden, incites Fredonian war, 60.

Edwards, Munroe, singular career of, 71, 72.

Ellis, Richard, President of Convention, 155.

Evans, Major T. C., attempts to blow up Alamo, 150.

Fannin, Col. James W., commands at battle of Concepcion, 103; appointed "agent" by Council, 128; elected colonel of volunteers, 131; attempts to relieve Alamo, 148; retreats from Goliad, 167; surrenders, 171; death, 179.

Farias, Gomez, President of Mexico, 87; arrests Austin, 88; banished, 89.

Filisola, Gen. Vincente, second in command of Mexican army, 138; retreats, 207; suspended, 225.

Fisher, Col. William S., invades Mexico, 276.

Flores, Manuel, agent to Indians, 251; killed, 251.

Gaines, Gen. E. P., moves troops into Texas, 214.

Gaona, Gen., commands brigade in Mexican army, 138.

Garay, Col., rescues prisoners at Goliad, 178.

Goliad, Massacre of, 175 et seq.

Golladay, Frederic, letter of, 24.

Golladay, Isaac, befriends Houston, 23.

Grant, Dr. James, organizes expedition to invade Mexico, 125; death, 164.

Grayson, Peter, commissioner to United States, 221; death, 249.

Green, Gen. Duff, protests against award of contract to Houston, 42.

Green, Gen. T. F., arrests Santa Anna, 219; escapes from Perote, 277.

Hamilton, Gen. James, minister to Great Britain and France, 258; attempts to negotiate loan, 259; proposes treaty with Mexico, 269.

Hardiman, Baily, Secretary of the Treasury, 159.

Hays, Col. John C., draws out Mexican troops, 275.

Hebert, Geo. P. D., commands department of Texas, 372.

Henderson, Geo. J. Pinkney, minister to Great Britain, 229.

Herrera, President, agrees to treaty with Texas, 289.

Hockley, George W., chief-of-staff to Houston, 159; commands artillery at San Jacinto, 199.

Holzinger, Lieut.-Col., receives surrender of Fannin's troops, 173.

Horton, Capt., driven off from Fannin, 178.

Houston, Mrs. Eliza, marriage, 34; separation from Houston, 36.

Houston, Mrs. Elizabeth, removes to Tennessee, 3; sends her son to the war, 13.

Houston, John, emigrates to America, 2.

Houston, Mrs. M. H., description of Houston, 242–244.

Houston, Mrs. Margaret M., marriage, 248.

Houston, Robert, settles in Virginia, 2.

Houston, Samuel, Sr., career, 2, 3.

Houston, Sam, birth, 1; ancestry, 1, 2; education, 3, 4; runs away to the Cherokees, 5, 6; keeps school, 8; enlists, 10; appointed ensign, 11; wounded at To-ho-pe-ka, 14; carried home, 17; appointed lieutenant, 18; sub-agent of Cherokees, 18; attacked by slave-traders, 20; resigns from the army, 20; studies law, 22; prosecuting attorney, 26; major-general of militia, 26; Representative in Congress, 26; writes against Clay, 27; fights duel with Gen. White, 29, 30; anecdotes of controversies, 31, 32; reminiscences of, by Col. D. D. Claiborne, 33; resigns the governorship, 34; separation from his wife, 34–36; goes to Indian Territory, 37; Indian life, 38 et seq.; assaults Hon. William Stanberry, 45; tried for breach of privilege of the House, 46-49; takes up with Indian wife, 50; duel with employee, 51; goes to Texas, 74, 75; anecdote of journey, 78; holds council with Indians at San Antonio, 79; reports to Jackson, 79–81; life at Washington, 82; makes arrangement with Indians, 93; elected commander of troops in eastern Texas, 97; declines to supersede Austin, 110; approves absolute independence, 120; elected commander-in-chief, 121; issues proclamation, 123; complains to Governor Smith, 129; discourages expedition to Matamoras, 133; elected delegate to Convention, 133; prepares "solemn declaration" in behalf of Indians, 134; makes treaty with Indians, 134; reëlected commander-in-chief, 157; leaves for Gonzales, 159; orders Fannin to abandon Goliad, 161; retreats from Gonzales, 163; falls back to the Brazos, 186; moves up the river, 189; moves in pursuit of Santa Anna, 192; orders Vince's bridge cut down, 199; commands battle of San Jacinto, 200; wounded, 202; suggests terms of treaty with Santa Anna, 209; issues farewell address to soldiers, 210; removed to New Orleans, 211; letter to Col. Raguet, 215; reception at New Orleans, 222; returns to Texas, 222; protests against execution of Santa Anna, 223; elected President, 228; inaugural address, 229; interview with Santa Anna, 231; releases Santa Anna, 232; message to Congress, 237; disbands army, 240; manages finances, 243, 244; manner of life, 246; marriage to Miss Lea, 248; defends Indians, 252; opposes Santa Fé expedition, 256; reëlected President, 262; measures of economy, 263; Indian talk, 265–267; letter to Santa Anna, 269, 270; vetoes army bill, 271; declares blockade of Mexican ports, 272; appeals to European governments, 276; letter to Jackson, 280; letter to Minister Murphy, 282; last message to Congress, 288; elected Senator, 296; first speech, 297; opposes extension of slavery to Oregon, 300; defends Father Matthew, 303; reëlected Senator, 305; opposes Kansas-Nebraska bill, 306 et seq.; defends Indians, 310 et seq.; defends New England clergymen, 313; movement to nominate for presidency, 318; criticises Kossuth, 319; voted for in Know-Nothing Convention, 320; defeated for Senator, 323; defeated for governor, 323; advocates protectorate over Mexico, 323; farewell speech in Senate, 325; "conversion," 329–331; nominated for governor, 335; canvass, 336–338; election, 338; attitude toward secession, 339 et seq.; letter to Gen. Twiggs, 346, 347; letter to Col. Waite, 351, 352; speech at Galveston, 354; letter to Secretary Walker, 356; deposition, 357; speech at Houston, 365; speech at Baylor University, 366; letter to Governor Lubbock, 372; congratulates Gen. Magruder, 373; relieves officers of Harriet Lane, 373; last speech, 373,374; death, 376; will, 377, 378; character, 378 et seq.

Hunt, Gen. Memucan, commissioner to United States, 229.

Huston, Gen. Felix, recruits volunteers in Mississippi, 218; duel with Gen. A. S. Johnston, 239.

Huston, James, signs address to King William III., 2.

Iverson, Senator, controversy with Houston, 325; denounces Houston, 342.

Jackson, Andrew, commands at To-ho-pe-ka, 12, 13; Senator from Tennessee, 27; sympathetic letter to Houston, 41; entertains Santa Anna in Washington, 272; message relating to Texas, 234; approves resolution for recognition of independence, 235; favors annexation, 255; death, 295.

Johnson, Cave, acts as friend to Houston, 44.

Johnson, Col. F. W., second in command in attack on San Antonio, 109; empowered by Council to take command of expedition against Matamoras, 127; escape from San Patricio, 164.

Johnston, Albert Sidney, joins Texan army, 239; appointed brigadier-general, 239; duel with Gen. Felix Huston, 239; commands expedition against Indians, 251.

Jones, Anson, criticises Houston's conduct at battle of San Jacinto, 213; recalls Minister Smith, 287; President of Texas, 288.

Key, Francis Scott, counsel for Houston, 46.

King, Capt., sent to relief of Refugio, 165; death, 166.

Kossuth, Louis, interview with Houston, 319.

Lamar, Mirabeau B., commands cavalry at San Jacinto, 200; protests against release of Santa Anna, 218; appointed to command army, 226; Vice-President, 228; President, 249; policy of, 259 et seq.; sends expedition to Santa Fé, 257; abdicates, 260; opposes annexation, 289.

Lander, Col. F. W., sent to Texas, 248; advice to Col. Waite, 352.

Lee, Col. R. E., superseded by Gen. Twiggs, 245.

Lester, C. Edwards, describes meeting of Houston with Indians, 315, 316.

Lincoln, President, sends messenger to Texas, 348; offers major-general's commission to Houston, 361.

Lockhart, Matilda, released by Indians, 253.

McLeod, Gen., commands Santa Fé expedition, 257.

M'Culloch, Benjamin, commands troops at San Antonio, 349.

Meigs, Gen. Return J., agent to Cherokees, 19.

Mexia, Gen., disgraceful conduct in expedition to Tampico, 115.

Milam, Col. Benjamin F., arrested in Coahuila, 91; joins attack on Goliad, 92; calls for volunteers to attack San Antonio, 104; death, 111.

Millard, Lieut.-Col., commands infantry at San Jacinto, 199.

Miller, Capt., captured at Copano, 175.

Moore, Com. E. W., commands Texan navy, 255; sails for Yucatan, 272.

Moore, Col. John H., commands at Gonzales, 96; defeats Comanches, 254.

Morfitt, Henry, commissioner to Texas, 221; report of, 234.

Murphy, Col. William S., minister to Texas, 280.

North, Thomas, anecdote by, 353; description of Houston at review, 368, 369.

O'Connell, Daniel, opposes recognition of Texas, 259.

Palmerston, Lord, recognizes independence of Texas, 258.

Parmer, Col. Martin, anecdotes of, 59, 60.

Pierce, Franklin, President, 305.

Polk, James K., favors annexation, 289.

Portilla, Col., ordered to execute prisoners at Goliad, 175.

Potter, Robert, Secretary of the Navy, 159.

Ripley, Henry, wounded at Coleto, 171.

Robertson, John C., President Committee of Public Safety, 344.

Robinson, James W., Lieut.-Gov., 124; proposes treaty with Mexico, 257.

Runnels, Hamilton R., defeats Houston for governorship, 322; secession message, 334; defeated by Houston, 338.

Rusk, Thomas J., settles in Texas, 76; Secretary of War, 139; joins army, 190; opposes attack at San Jacinto, 198; at battle of San Jacinto, 200; disbands army, 241; Senator of the United States, 296; death, 322.

Saligny, M. de, minister from France, 259.

Santa Anna, Antonio Lopez de, character and career, 83, 85; wins battle of Zacatecas, 90; takes command of army of invasion, 138; besieges Alamo, 145; orders massacre of prisoners at Goliad, 175; starts to join Gen. Sesma, 183; captures Harrisburg, 191; alarm at New Washington, 195; flight from San Jacinto, 201; capture of, 204; orders troops to withdraw from Texas, 207; signs treaty, 211; arrested, 218; plots to release, 227; interview with Houston, 231; release of, 232; repudiates debt to Col. Bee, 233; deposes Bustamente, 267; letter to Houston, 269.

Santa Fé, expedition to, 257, 258.

Sesma, Gen., sent to relief of Gen. Cos, 137; crosses Colorado River, 190.

Scott, Gen. W., orders Col. Waite to offer assistance to Houston, 351.

Shackleford, Dr., rescued at Goliad, 177.

Sherman, Col. Sidney, commands left wing at San Jacinto, 199.

Simpson, Rev. J. W., account of Houston's conversion, 324 et seq.

Smith, Ashbell, minister to England, 286; anecdote by, 291, 384.

Smith, Erasmus, character, 106; cuts down Vince's bridge, 199; at battle of San Jacinto, 202.

Smith, Capt. J. W., enters Alamo, 147; escapes with message, 152.

Smith, Henry, settles in Texas, 76; governor, 121; quarrels with Council, 124 et seq.; deposed, 130; Secretary of the Treasury, 239.

Snively, Capt. Jacob S., commands expedition to New Mexico, 277.

Somerville, Gen. Alexander, commands Texan troops, 268; leads expedition to Rio Grande, 276.

Stewart, Hamilton, anecdote by, 371, 372.

Sumner, Charles, assault on, by Brooks, 314; opinion of Houston, 329.

Sylvester, James T., captures Santa Anna, 205.

Taylor, Zachary, President, 301; asserts authority in New Mexico, 302.

Texas, early settlement of, 53 et seq.; character of settlers of, 64 et seq.; convention to ask separation from Coahuila, 86; general council of citizens, 98; General Consultation, 117; declaration of provisional independence, 118, 120; provisional government, 121; bounty for volunteers, 123; General Convention, 155; declaration of independence, 156; constitution, 160; operations of the navy, 212; first Congress, 228; army disbanded, 240; land grants, 241; finances, 242; under Lamar's administration, 260 et seq.; navy of, 272; disturbances in neutral ground, 274; annexation, 280 et seq.; boundary, 302; public debt, 303; secession, 333 et seq.; union with the Confederacy, 356.

Thomas, David, attorney-general, 159.

Thompson, T. M., depredations on the coast, 96.

To-ho-pe-ka, battle of, 13 et seq.

Tolsa, Gen., commands brigade in Mexican army, 138.

Travis, Col. William B., takes command at Alamo, 132; character, 143; appeals for assistance, 144; death, 150.

Twiggs, Gen. David E., commands department of Texas, 345; reply to Houston, 347; surrenders troops, 350.

Tyler, President John, favors annexation, 279.

Ugartchea, Col., captured at Velasco, 72; demands surrender of cannon, at Gonsales, 95; relieves San Antonio, 112.

Urrea, Gen., sent to Matamoras, 138; captures San Patricio, 164; attacks Fannin's troops, 269; supersedes Filisola, 225.

Van Buren, Martin, opposes annexation, 286.

Van Dorn, Col., compels surrender of U.-S. troops, 351.

Van Zandt, Isaac, minister to Washington, 279.

Viesca, Augustin, governor of Coahuila, 90; arrested, 91.

Waite, Col. Carlos A., succeeds Gen.

Twiggs, 350; reports to Gen. Scott, 350.

Ward, Col. William, defends Refugio, 166; death, 179.

Walker, Hon. R. J., introduces resolution for recognition of the independence of Texas, 235.

Wharton, John A., settles in Texas, 76; escapes from Mexico, 244.

Wharton, William H., settles in Texas, 76; commissioner to United States, 121; minister to United States, 229; captured, 244.

Wigfall, Louis T., Senator of the United States, 322; denounces Houston, 342.

Wise, Henry A., attacks Houston, 321.

Woll, Gen. Adrian, sent to Texan camp, 208; invades Texas, 275.

Zavala, Lorenzo de, flees to Texas, 91; Vice-President, 159; joins army, 190; death, 244.

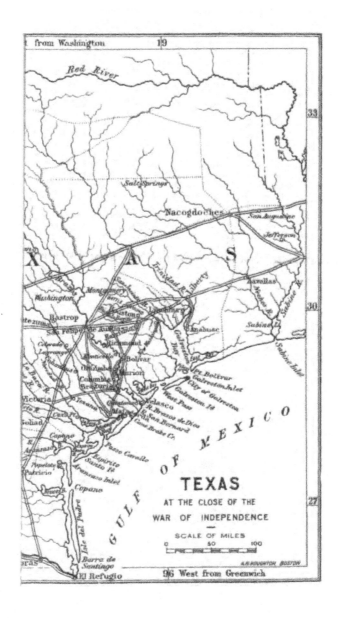

TEXAS

AT THE CLOSE OF THE

WAR OF INDEPENDENCE

SCALE OF MILES

0   50   100

John T. Morse, Jr.

John Quincy Adams. In American Statesmen Series. 16mo, gilt top, $1.25 ; half morocco, $2.50.

Thomas Jefferson. In American Statesmen Series. 16mo, gilt top, $1.25; half morocco, $2.50.

John Adams. In American Statesmen Series. 16mo, gilt top, $1.25; half morocco, $2.50.

Benjamin Franklin. In American Statesmen Series. 16mo, gilt top, $1.25 ; half morocco, $2.50.

Abraham Lincoln. In American Statesmen Series. With Portrait and Map. 2 vols. 16mo, $2.50; half morocco, $5.00.

Theodore Roosevelt.

Thomas H. Benton. In American Statesmen Series. 16mo, gilt top, $1.25; half morocco, $2.50.

Gouverneur Morris. In American Statesmen Series. 16mo, gilt top, $1.25 ; half morocco, $2.50.

Carl Schurz.

Henry Clay. In American Statesmen Series. 2 vols. 16mo, gilt top, $2.50; half morocco, $5.00.

Abraham Lincoln. An Essay. With Portrait. 16mo, gilt top, $1.00.

Horace E. Scudder.

Noah Webster. In American Men of Letters Series. With Portrait. 16mo, gilt top, $1.25 ; half morocco, $2.50.

George Washington. An Historical Biography. In Riverside Library for Young People. With Portrait and Illustrations. 16mo, 75 cents.

William P. Trent.

William Gilmore Simms. In American Men of Letters Series. With Portrait. 16mo, gilt top, $1.25.

HOUGHTON, MIFFLIN & CO., Publishers.

James Elliot Cabot.

A Memoir of Ralph Waldo Emerson. With
new Portrait. 2 vols. crown 8vo, gilt top, $3.50; half calf,
$6.00.

Large-Paper Edition, uniform with the Large-
Paper *Riverside Edition* of Emerson's Works formerly
published. Limited to 500 copies. With Portrait. 2 vols.
8vo, boards, uncut, $10.00, *net*.

Thomas Carlyle and R. W. Emerson.

Correspondence of Carlyle and Emerson, 1834–
1872. Edited by Charles Eliot Norton. Including newly-
found Letters and with new Portraits. 2 vols. crown 8vo,
gilt top, $4.00; half calf, or half morocco, $8.00.

New *Library Edition*. 12mo, $3.00; half calf,
$6.00.

George Willis Cooke.

George Eliot: A Critical Study of her Life,
Writings, and Philosophy. With Portrait. 12mo, $2.00;
half calf, $4.00.

Ralph Waldo Emerson: His Life, Writings, and
Philosophy. With Portrait. In one volume, 12mo, $2.00;
half calf, $4.00.

Thomas De Quincey.

Autobiographic Sketches. *Riverside Edition.*
12mo, $1.50.

Autobiographic Sketches. *Popular Edition.*
16mo, $1.00.

Literary Reminiscences. *Popular Edition.*
16mo, $1.00.

Biographical and Historical Essays. *Popular
Edition.* 16mo, $1.00.

Edward Waldo Emerson.

Emerson in Concord. A Memoir. Written for
the "Social Circle" in Concord, Massachusetts. With
new Portrait. Crown 8vo, gilt top, $1.75.

HOUGHTON, MIFFLIN & CO., Publishers.

Made in the USA
Coppell, TX
21 October 2023

23163435R00233